YO-BST-183

780

CASS LIBRARY OF AFRICAN STUDIES

AFRICANA MODERN LIBRARY

No. 2

General Editor : E. U. ESSIEM-UDOM

PLATE I

GYE NYAME ("Except God").

THE AKAN DOCTRINE OF GOD

A FRAGMENT OF
GOLD COAST ETHICS AND RELIGION

J. B. DANQUAH

SECOND EDITION

With a New Introduction by
KWESI A. DICKSON

With Nine Illustrations by
KOFI ANTUBAM OF ACHIMOTA

"If your peer is scorned, you are scorned." (No. 1118)

"The Lizard says: 'If ever man attains complete satisfaction, he will go crazy.'" (No. 509)

"The tall and the short Teeth have but one Grind
between them." (No. 2832)

"When all the world makes God its burden no one
becomes humpbacked." (No. 2434)

—*Akan Proverbs*, see Appendix I.

FRANK CASS & CO. LTD.
1968

Published by
FRANK CASS AND COMPANY LIMITED
67 Great Russell Street, London WC1
by arrangement with Lutterworth Press

First edition	1944
Second edition	1968

Printed in Great Britain by
Thomas Nelson (Printers) Ltd., London and Edinburgh

To
THE FOUNDERS
OF
UNIVERSITY COLLEGE, LONDON
WHO
FACILITATED THE ENDEAVOUR OF A
RAW AFRICAN TO DRINK DEEP OF THE
PIERIAN SPRING

INTRODUCTION
TO THE
SECOND EDITION

Joseph Buakye Danquah was born at Bepong in Kwahu on 21st December 1895. Having worked as a law clerk, then as Secretary to the Omanhene of Akim Abuakwa, he proceeded to the University College of London in 1921, after obtaining the London Matriculation certificate through private study. He obtained the B.A. and LL.B. degrees and was elected John Stuart Mill Scholar in the Philosophy of Mind and Logic. He entered the Inner Temple, and was called to the Bar in 1926. In the following year he obtained his doctorate degree in Philosophy for which he offered the thesis *The Moral End as Moral Excellence.*

On his return home he established legal practice, and, busy as he was with his practice, he nevertheless found time to write a number of books and pamphlets; he also undertook considerable research in Akan religion and culture. Another consuming interest of his was politics. He served in the legislature during the colonial period, and together with others, founded the United Gold Coast Convention in 1947. He was one of the six arrested during the 1948 disturbances which preceded the attainment of independence by the Gold Coast.

With independence and the formation of a government under Kwame Nkrumah, the founder of the Convention People's Party, J.B., as he was popularly known, featured prominently in the Opposition; he never could hide his conviction that Ghana could be governed differently. On two occasions he was detained under the unpopular preventive detention law.

He died in detention on the 14th of February, 1965.

* * *

To appreciate *The Akan Doctrine of God*, it is important for the reader to recognise that there are two assumptions which form the basis of Danquah's exposition of Akan theology.

The first is that the Akan, by their own wisdom, have been able to perceive God in a way that gives the west no basis for a feeling of superiority. In Danquah's own words, " Enquiry into the nature of the Akan God has been going on for upwards of a century, but the doctrine was never stated in a form recognisable by students, theologians and moralists as akin to previous discoveries of scientific or speculative thought and of a nature to fit in with, but without disturbing, the *organon* of accepted truth." [1]

Danquah's desire, therefore, is to expound Akan thought in such a way as to make it comprehensible to western thinkers and to demonstrate that it is comparable to their system; [2] in pursuance of this objective, he calls forth his philosophical training and indulges in metaphysical and ethical speculation. The effects of this are evident in the whole book, whether in his discussion of the nature of the Supreme Being or in his exposition of Akan ethical thought; indeed, he never permits the reader to lose sight of his philosophical approach. This is not to suggest that his study is worthless merely because it is couched in such terms. Christian theologians there have been who have legitimately expressed Christian theology in the mode of prevailing philosophical systems; however, not all such philosophical theologians have completely succeeded in avoiding the obvious pitfall of substituting philosophy for *theo*logy. Likewise, though Danquah was learned in the ways and thought of the Akan, yet it is impossible not to reject his presentation at some points for the very reason that he falls a victim to his desire for speculation, much of which is, as far as the available evidence goes, groundless.

The second assumption, which is inseparably linked up with the first, is this: ". . . among Europeans, the popular idea of Akan ' religion ' is as part of West Africa's ' fetish ' cult. Actually, Akan religious doctrine knows only one God. Everything else found in the land, in the form of religion, is nothing else but superstition, . . . in justice to the Akan, the cults of the private man desirous for short cuts to satisfy the natural craving for some religion, should not be ascribed to the Akan as their racial or national conception of God." [3] Fifteen years before the publication of *The Akan Doctrine of God*, Danquah had written thus: " There seems to be evidence for believing that the present form of Akan fetish worship is a foreign acquisition which historical research may prove to have entered into their way of life at the time they were driven from the plains of central Africa to the mountainous and rocky West African littoral." [4]

Danquah would therefore readily apply to the Akan Voltaire's view that " men began by knowing a single God, and that later,

[1] *The Akan Doctrine of God, p.* 2.
[2] See pp. 104–107, ibid., where he contests the ascription by anthropologists of Akan ideas which are not ' primitive ' to borrowing.
[3] Danquah, ibid. p. 39.
[4] *Akim- Abuakwa Handbook* (1929), p. 84.

human weakness adopted a number of deities ", [1] and reject as inapplicable the one expressed by David Hume, presumably on the basis of the ethnographical material available in his time, that " polytheism or idolatry was, and necessarily must have been, the first and most ancient religion of mankind." Indeed, Danquah would take particular exception to Rousseau's endorsement of Hume in the words, ". . . Negro *fétiches*, all the works of nature and man, were the first deities of mortals." [2]

It is not easy to see how Danquah's conviction that the Akan know only one God can be justified in view of the evidence to the contrary. That he was aware of the writings of such scholars as Christaller and Rattray is clear from his references to these scholars with whose researches students of Akan life and thought are familiar; however, his theory of the nature of Akan religion, in line as it is with Schmidt's ' devolutionary ' theory of *Urmonotheismus* or ' primitive monotheism ', [3] leads him to set aside completely the evidence that has been brought to light through the hard work of such men. Hence his statement that " altars and shrines to ancestral and divine gods are unknown things to the Akan."![4]

In the absence of any evidence adduced by Danquah to enforce his approach to Akan religion, one is led to explain his approach in terms of a reaction to another type of approach. Not infrequently, writers on African religion have shown a decided preference for sensationalism rather than objectivity, and have drawn greater attention to the gods as the essence of African thought and belief; either the Supreme Being has been pictured as playing a very nebulous role in the complex of beliefs, or any ideas of God have been attributed to borrowing, as when Ellis suggested that the Akan *Nyankopɔn* [5] was borrowed from Christian missions. [6] Danquah's line of approach may very well be a reaction—howbeit an extreme

[1] *Dictionnaire philosophique*

[2] For these quotations see Raffaele Pettazzoni, *Essays on the History of Religions*, trans. by H. J. Rose, pp. 1–2.

[3] Father Wilhelm Schmidt, *The Origin and Growth of Religion, Facts and Theories* (1935), trans. by H. J. Rose. In a lecture delivered at the University College of Ibadan, Nigeria in the Extra Mural Studies Course (June-July 1957) on " Four African Kingdoms " (Ashanti, Dahomey, Yoruba and Benin), Danquah said: " There is a growing opinion among anthropologists that the first type of religion ever to be practised by mankind was monotheism, and I am myself inclined to that view."

[4] Danquah, ibid., p. 53.

[5] The orthography and spelling of Akan words in this Introduction will be in accordance with present usage. However, when such words appear in quotations, or in connection with other writers' expositions, the spelling adopted by the authors cited will stand. For example, *Nyankopɔn* is written here with the vowel ɔ instead of of o as in *The Akan Doctrine of God* and others.

[6] See his *Tshi-speaking Peoples of the Gold Coast*. Ellis did revise his opinion in a subsequent publication, *Ewe-speaking Peoples of the Slave Coast*.

one—to this misrepresentation of African—certainly of Akan—religious beliefs. He does valuable service to scholarship in drawing attention to the importance of the Supreme Being in Akan religious thought.

Naturally, however, in pursuing this line of approach so strictly certain aspects of belief that are of importance for the understanding of the Akan doctrine of God are ignored.

It seems to us that any objective statement of the Akan doctrine of God should include some reference to the Akan conception of the place of the gods in the Akan religious system. *Onyame* (or *Nyame*) or *Onyankopɔn* (or *Nyankopɔn*) is such because other gods or *abosom* exist. The *abosom* are in fact held to be God's children and spokesmen. Further, the *asuman* or charms which are considered to be repositories of power and which are worn on the body for protection, are supposed to derive their power from the *abosom*. Any examination of Akan doctrine should, therefore, involve an attempt to discover the nature of the links that hold together the various strands of belief. Very little study has been made of this aspect of Akan, and for that matter, of African religion. Meanwhile, the matter of the place of the Supreme Being in a spirit world of other beings and agencies is put more acceptably by Busia when he writes: " The gods are treated with respect if they deliver the goods, and with contempt if they fail; it is the Supreme Being and the ancestors that are always treated with reverence and awe . . . The Ashanti, like the other tribes, esteem the Supreme Being and the ancestors far above gods and amulets. Attitudes to the latter depend upon their success, and vary from healthy respect to sneering contempt."[1]

Danquah wades into the field of philology, demolishing as he proceeds some of the views that have been advanced with regard to the origin of the God-names *Nyame* and *Nyankopɔn*, and God's praise-names. When Edwin Smith notes that this " philological region is the happy hunting-ground of fantastic etymologists ", [2] he has ample justification, considering the colourful array of etymologisings, for sounding as unconvinced as he does. Danquah, for example, seems particularly anxious to establish the Babylonian or Palestinian origin of certain Akan ideas and concepts. On the basis of verbal similarities he concludes that " the language of Akkad or Akana was the same as the language of the Akan to-day." [3] He

---

[1] *African Worlds*, ed. Daryll Forde, p. 205.
[2] Smith, ed. *African Ideas of God*, p. 3.
[3] Ibid., p. 51. The present writer was shown by Danquah a four-volume manuscript entitled *The Ghana Doctrine of Man* in which Danquah had adopted J. J. Williams' (*Hebrewisms of West Africa*) equation of the Hebrew *torah* and *ntorɔ* in Akan.

equates the name Twi with Cush (or Kush), the latter form being a corruption, he contends; by this equation he identifies the ancient Akan with the Cush tribes of north-east Africa. Hence, the honorific *Twerampɔn*, which is written as *Twi-Adu-ampon* by Danquah, [1] is considered by him to have been given to *Onyankopɔn* " by a neighbouring race of the Twi who, comparing Nyankopon to Anu ("clearly a variant of Adu "), the high one of Sumer and Akkad, must have said of him that he was ' the High One of the Twii.' "!

Various other honorifics and God-names are examined in detail by Danquah with a view to establishing their origin. Though his solutions are sometimes questionable, and his equations with extra-Akan languages fruitless and misleading, [2] yet he is right in stressing the importance of the study of the meaning of these names and honorifics for the understanding of the nature of God. " In Africa," Edwin Smith notes, " names are not mere labels, but often express qualities for which the owners are conspicuous." [3] This is not to imply that a religious system, in its entirety, can be derived from this exercise and this alone; the results of such an exercise would complement what is to be derived from other sources. While Smith is right in asserting that " up to now no satisfactory derivation has been found for such names as Nyame. . . ", [4] yet enough has been written to enable us to see some grain, no matter how small, when all the chaff has been blown away. The chaff, however, is considerable.

When Beecham published his *Ashantee and the Gold Coast* in 1841, his material on the religion practised by the people of the Gold Coast (now Ghana) may have been based, at least in part, on information supplied him by Joseph Smith, a Fanti who was put in charge of Cape Coast Castle School established in the 1820's by Governor Charles McCarthy. [5] Beecham's interpretation of *Nyame*, like that of others, was based upon a mis-spelling of the God-name. He wrote the God-name *Nyame* as *Yehmi* and derived it from *ye*, meaning ' make ', and *emi*, ' me '; so that *Yehmi* meant ' He made me ', being a reference to God the Creator. [6] God, to the Akan is

[1] Ibid., p. 51.
[2] Ibid., p. 58. He relates the Akan name *Bɔrebɔre* to the Hebrew *bara'* which he considers to derive from *berith*. As Edwin Smith correctly notes, *bara'* is not the root of *berith*, and it does not mean ' to hew '—see Edwin Smith, *Africa*, Vol. XV, No. 1. article, ' Religious Beliefs of the Akan ', pp. 23 ff.
[3] *African Ideas of God*, p. 4.
[4] *African Ideas of God*, p. 3.
[5] Dr. Beecham, one of the Secretaries of the Wesleyan-Methodist Missionary Society, sent off a questionnaire in 1839 to Joseph Smith, a class leader in the Methodist Church of the Gold Coast from its inception, about the " customs and beliefs of the inhabitants of Cape Coast."
[6] Op. cit., p. 172.

Creator, as the honorific *Bɔadeɛ* [1] indicates; however, as an etymolo-
gical exercise, Beecham's effort was valueless, as was Cruickshank's
when he arrived at the same conclusion as Beecham by spelling
Nyame as *Yaamie*.[2] Casely Hayford wrote the God-name
Nyankopɔn as *Nyiakropon* and broke it up into *nyi-nuku-ara-oye-pon*,
He who alone is great [3].

With regard to the etymology of these two God-names, the most
common solutions have been to derive *Nyankopɔn* from *nyanko*,
' friend ', and *pɔn*, ' great ', and *Nyame* from *nya*, ' to receive '
and *mee*, ' satisfaction.' The Great Friend derivation has found
favour with Casely Hayford, [4] Beecham, [5] and Cruickshank [6] among
others. Riis, on the other hand, considered that this derivation was
not in accord with " the notions of the people." [7] The derivation of
Nyame from He-who-gives-satisfaction has recently been revived by
Abraham who explains that he was " led to believe " that this was
the " correct and proper derivation " by a consideration of " the
proliferation of minor deities which the Akans claimed to be an
avenue to God's munificence and bountiful protection." [8] This
derivation, which was considered by Rattray to be the true one, is
classed by Danquah with " ignorant popular etymologies ", [9] and is
considered by St. John Evans to be unacceptable " on etymological
and other grounds."[10] We believe Danquah and St. John Evans are
right in rejecting this derivation.

Danquah flirts with the notion that the letters NYNM (*Nyame*)
probably correspond to the Hebrew tetragrammaton—YHWH.[11]
By deriving *Nyame* from *nyi-oye-emi*, He-who-is-I-am, Casely
Hayford accepts this view that Nyame recalls the Hebrew I AM.[12]

---

[1] Danquah, *Boadee;* op. cit., p. 58.

[2] See *Eighteen Years on the Gold Coast of Africa*, Vol. II, p. 126.

[3] See his *Ethiopia Unbound*, p. 7. This work followed his *Gold Coast Native Institutions* in which he interpreted this God-name as ' Great Friend.'

[4] *Gold Coast Native Institutions*, referred to by Danquah, ibid., pp. 44–45.

[5] Op. cit.

[6] Op. cit., p. 126.

[7] H. N. Riis, *Grammatical Outline and Vocabulary of the Oji (Twi)-Language, with special reference to the Akwapim-Dialect* (Basel, 1854), p. 220.

[8] *The Mind of Africa*, p. 54.

[9] Ibid., p. 36.

[10] *African Ideas of God*, p. 246.

[11] Danquah considers NYNM to be the basic consonants of *Nyɔnmɔ*, *Nyame* and other variants of the God-name; ibid., pp. 33, 37.

[12] See *Ethiopia Unbound, Studies in Race Emancipation*, p. 8. Also, J. J. Williams' *Hebrewisms of West Africa* in which the author equates *'asa 'obh* (to practice necromancy) with the Akan *obayi* = witch. Such parallels may lead to confusion over the real significance of the things considered to be parallel. On the subject of parallels see P.E.S. Thompson, art. ' An Approach to the Old Testament in an African Setting ', in *Ghana Bulletin of Theology*, Vol. 2, No. 3, December, 1962.

This view is more fanciful than enlightening.

The various etymologisings often strike one as unhelpful because their authors approach this task from a particular theological or other bias. Casely Hayford's *Nyiakropon* or *nyi-nuku-ara-oye-pon* is theologically rather than etymologically sound. Abraham's etymologising appears to be based on grounds whose significance is not immediately apparent. He writes, " The method of teaching, that of oral instruction, would seem to make the occurrence of *Onyame-nko-pon* significant. It suggests this as the original form from which Onyankopon was contracted." [1] He goes on to reject the derivation of *Nyankopɔn* from one-who-bears-the-weight-of-others-without-crooking since this idea of dependability is already present in *Twerampɔn*; " it would not be reasonable to hold it too as expressing the same dependability." [2] No explanation is given of how oral teaching suggests *Onyame-nko-pɔn* as the derivation of *Nyankopɔn*; moreover is there any reason why only one name, and not more than one should express dependability? Indeed the honorifics *Brɛk-yirhunnade*, *Abommubuwafrɛ*, *Nyaamanekɔse*, *Tetekwaframoa*—all these, in various ways, express the dependability of God. [3]

Riis, to whom reference has been made, derived *Nyankopɔn* from *nyanku* and *pon*, the latter meaning " high or great." He considered the derivation of *nyanku* as uncertain, though it was his opinion that it came from the same root as *nyame*, " two different forms of the same word." [4] Their root, he pointed out, might be *nyan*, ' to awake ', ' to raise ', so that *nyanku* and *nyame* " in their primary signification, would be synonyms of *sorro*, the high, that which is above, *pon* being added to *nyanku* for the sake of greater emphasis to it, so that the meaning of *Nyankopon* would be ' the very high, the most high.' " [5] Further, Riis noted, this explained the use of *nyame* and *nyankopɔn* for sky and heaven.

There is reason to believe that Riis was not completely satisfied with this derivation, especially with regard to *nyanko* which, as he pointed out, seems to occur in compounds: *nyankuensu*, ' rain-water', *nyankunton*, ' rain-bow ' (from *nyanku* and *enton*; the latter, notes Riis, seems to mean arch, hence *entonka*—eyebrow). [6]

[1] Op. cit., p. 55. Actually, Abraham slightly misquotes Rattray when he understands him to be saying that *Onyame-nko-pon* was the form of the God-name in the Akim dialect. Rattray writes, " The derivation of this word as Onyame-nko-pon (Onyame, alone, great one) seems borne out by noting the word in the Akyem dialect where it is Onyan-koro-pon (Onyame, one, great) "—see his *Ashanti Proverbs*, p. 19.

[2] Ibid.

[3] Danquah, ibid., p. 55.

[4] Ibid., p. 220.

[5] Ibid.

[6] Ibid., p. 178.

The importance of Riis' attempt lies in the attention he draws to the fact that part of *Nyankopɔn* is found in various combinations, but while he identified this part as *nyanku*, it is more probable that this component is *nyankom*. Three Basel missionaries identified the word *nyankom* as a Fanti word meaning 'rain', [1] and Casely Hayford, writing of the Fanti, makes the point that "the god of rain . . . was, and is, known as *Nana Nyankum*." [2]

It is instructive to look at some of those words of which *nyankom* forms part. Reference has already been made to *nyankoensu* (rain water) and *nyankontɔn* (rain-bow). The list below is based on Christaller [3] and Denteh: [4]

(*nyankom*	=rain)
nyankommiremire	=noise produced by rain in the air before falling on the earth. The second part of the word (*miremire* in Akyem-Asante; Christaller, *meremere*) seems to be onomatopoeic.
nyankompasakyie	=the vulture, "the great flier of the sky" (Denteh).
nyankonneɛ	=things ordained by God; synonymous with *nkrabea* and *hyɛbea*, which words mean fate, destiny, appointed lot, allotted life, final lot, etc. The *nkrabea* is given by God, according to Akan belief.
nyankonsoro	=the highest heaven; 'space'. This word is of special interest because the word *nyankom* is coupled with *soro* which properly means 'sky'.
nyankonsoromma	=stars. *Nsoroma* means 'children of the sky'.
nyankommedurui (*nyankon-duru*)	=a parasitic plant supposed to have perched on the host-plant from the sky (Denteh).

[1] Christaller, Locher and Zimmerman, *A Dictionary, English, Tshi* (*Asante*), *Akra* (Basel, 1874), p. 198.

[2] *Ethiopia Unbound*, p. 213.

[3] *Dictionary of the Asante and Fante Language*, Second Edition, Revised and Enlarged.

[4] Mr. A. C. Denteh is a language specialist in the Institute of African Studies, University of Ghana.

Other words featuring *nyanko(m)* could be cited, but those listed above are enough to indicate that any etymological exercise should proceed on the basis that *nyankom* is a word the elucidation of whose meaning would throw light on the origin of the God-name *Nyankopɔn*. That *nyankom* could not mean ' friend ' is clear; it has been suggested that " the real reason for rejecting this (Great Friend) interpretation is theological. The idea of God as the Great Friend, or Neighbour or Fellow, might occur in Christianity but it is totally foreign to Akan sentiment on this point suggesting, as it does, impudent disrespect." [1] As a matter of fact, God as *Nyaamanekɔse* (He in whom you confide troubles which come upon you) and *Abommubuwafrɛ* (He upon whom you call in your experience of distress) [2] is indeed a Great Friend! It seems to us that one cannot but reject the Great Friend derivation, not because it suggests " impudent disrespect " but because it is a derivation that cannot be supported by any available evidence.

Now, the various examples of combinations with *nyankom* given above indicate that *nyankom* has to do with the sky. *Nyankom* is in fact ' rain ' in Akyem-Asante, as it is in Fanti. Christaller also translates it as ' rain ', making it a synonym of *osu*, the more usual word for ' rain ', and we have already noticed Casely Hayford's reference to *Nana Nyankum* as the god of rain as known among the Fanti. Moreover, Christaller gives the word *Onyankome* as the name for God in Fanti; apparently, this information was obtained from a book written in 1670 by one W. T. Müller. [3]

It would appear, then, that *nyankom* was not only the word for rain (it still is), but also, by itself, it was a God-name; in that sense it is equivalent to *Nyankopɔn*, which is also used to mean ' rain '. The phrase *Nyankopɔn aba* or *atɔ* means ' rain has fallen '; [4] likewise *Nyankopɔn bɔm'* means ' it thunders '. [5] Hence *nyankom* and *Nyankopɔn* were interchangeable, the *-pɔn* of the latter signifying ' great '. As rain was seen to come from above, *Nyankopɔn* was therefore used also to mean " the apparent arch or vault of heaven." [6] This is not to say that God was identified with the sky. [7]

The connection that exists between *Nyankopɔn* or *nyankom* and

---

[1] C. G. Baëta ' The Akan High God ', paper presented at a Conference on *High Gods in Africa* organised in January 1965 by the Department of Anthropology, University of Ife, Nigeria.

[2] See Danquah, ibid., p. 55.

[3] We have not had the opportunity of reading Müller's book. See Christaller, op. cit., p. 358.

[4] See Riis, *Dictionary*, p. 220.

[5] Christaller, ibid., p. 358.

[6] Christaller, ibid., p. 358.

[7] See below p. xvii.

Nyame must now be considered. It was Riis' opinion, it will be
recalled, that *Nyame* and *nyanku* were two different forms of the
same word. *Nyame* is used in more or less the same senses as
Nyankopɔn. It does not only stand for the Supreme Being; it also
means ' heaven ', and 'sky ', despite Danquah's reluctance over
accepting this. It is also used to mean ' rain ', so that *Onyame
bɛba* means ' it is about to rain.' [1]

Granted that *Nyame* and *Nyankopɔn* are used in practically
identical senses, what is the origin of *Nyame* and *nyankom*? On the
basis that the two are interchangeable, they might, with some
plausibility, be related to a common source. Riis considered that
Nyame derived from *nyan*, ' to awake ', ' to raise '; [2] so did Ellis
who thought it " probable that Onyam, ' the awakener ', was an
old name for the sky. There is, it appears, no such name for it now
in existence." [3] *Nyan* does preserve Nyame's connection with the
elements, but in this respect it would be more appropriate to derive
the God-name *Nyame* from *nyam*, as does Danquah who translates
this root as " shining, glory or bright." [4] Perhaps, even more
basically, it means to move quickly or rapidly; hence its use of
witches to describe " their rapid and phosphorescent movements
this way and that when performing." [5] Thus Nyame is so called
because of a certain connection between his nature and the bright
sky, more especially the sky as lightened by lightning.

That *nyam* would likewise underlie *Nyankom* is not a matter for
doubt; *nyankom*, then, is made up of *nyam* and *kom*, the latter most
probably meaning ' to bend '.[6] One imagines that *nyankom* is
used in the sense of ' rain ' because it pictorially describes the
darkening sky which goes with rain; the sky's brightness is ' bent '
or dulled by dark clouds which presage rain.

[1] See W. Ringwald, *Die Religion de Akanstaeme und das Problem ihre
Bekehrung*, p. 17. Danquah's reluctance to accept the use of *Nyame* for
' heaven ' or ' sky ' arises from the fact that Christaller never gives *Onyame*
that sense, whether in his Dictionary or in his edition of the Twi Bible—see
Danquah, ibid., p. 34. Perhaps the terms *Nyameso-yere* and *Nyameso-kunu*,
used among the Kwahus of the Volta Basin of Ghana to mean the wife (*yere*)
or husband (*kunu*) who stays with God above are worth mentioning here.
The use of *-so* (' on ') with *Nyame* would be incomprehensible if *Nyame* were
not also capable of being used to mean ' sky '. But not enough is known
about the Kwahu belief; the two terms *Nyameso-yere* and *Nyameso-kunu* are
paralleled in Krakye usage—see art. ' Notes·on the Kenekra, Boasekye and
Boasekuri and *kra* Traditions among the Guans of the Volta Basin ', by
J. C. S. Steemers, in *Ghana Bulletin of Theology*, Vol. 2 No. 8.
[2] Ibid., p. 220.
[3] *The Tshi-speaking Peoples of the Gold Coast.* pp. 24–25.
[4] Ibid., p. 40.
[5] Abraham, ibid., p. 53.
[6] Used in such phrases as *n'ani kom*, his eyes bend, i.e. he is sleepy.

Thus, *Nyame* or *Nyankopɔn* was known as such because of a certain connection between his nature and the elements, but especially in his capacity as the one who gives copiousness through his rain which he makes to fall on the earth. This is not to say that *Nyame* or *Nyankopɔn* is a sky-God; God's dwelling is not identified with the sky, though the Deity and the sky are connected in an undefined, perhaps indefinable, way, as the well-known story of how God left for the sky away from the level of men shows. [1] These God-names " may refer to certain natural processes associated with the sky, as raining and thundering; but it may also have merely the sense of ' on high ' or ' above ' . . . God is Spirit, which, like wind and air, is invisible and ubiquitous. But though God is not these things he is in them in the sense that he reveals himself through them. In this sense . . . he is in the sky, falls in the rain, shines in the sun and moon, and blows in the wind." [2]

It has been necessary to go through the question of etymology in some detail in order partly to indicate the uncertainty that has surrounded this, and partly to point out the ways of approach which are erroneous, and which are most likely—on the basis of the known evidence—to yield results. The idea of *Nyame*- the-great (*Nyankopɔn*) arises from the importance attached to the giving of rain by the Deity—rain brings growth, harvest and sustenance; the -*pɔn* witnesses to the regard in which Nyame is held in his character as the giver of sustenance. It is not accidental that in Akan thought there is a close connection between *Nyankopɔn* and *Asase Yaa*, earth whose day is Thursday. [3] St. John Evans quotes the invocation, *Onyankopon Kwame . . . ne wo yere Asase Yaa*, that is ' *Onyankopɔn Kwame* . . . and your wife Asase Yaa.' [4]

To deduce a fertility cult from this is to make the wrong deduction. *Nyankopɔn* is not a fertility God; the use of ' wife ' is probably figurative, expressing as it does, man's dependence on both God and the earth. Certainly, Akan religion does not exhibit traits commonly associated with fertility cults. [5] Indeed, it is doubtful

[1] S. G. Williamson, *Akan Religion and the Christian Faith*, p. 88.

[2] E. E. Evans-Pritchard, *Nuer Religion*, pp. 1–2.

[3] Among the Fanti the earth is *Asaase Efua* or *Afua*—earth whose day is Friday. Meyerowitz believes that *Asase Yaa* and *Asase Afua* are two separate earth ' goddesses ', the former representing the barren soil of the earth, and the latter the fertile earth. She further affirms that in some Akan states the two are combined in *Asase Yaa*. We have found no evidence to support her theory of two ' goddesses '. The Fanti consider the earth's day to be Friday, while other Akan peoples consider it to be Thursday.

[4] *African Ideas of God*, p. 253.

[5] Cyril Eastwood writes thus on fertility rites among farming peoples: " For the most part the Goddess was a small image which was the result of their own crude workmanship. On special occasions the image was adorned

whether the earth can with accuracy be described as a goddess, as is usually done; the earth has " no priests or priestesses, nor do the Ashanti consult her for divination in case of illness or need as they do other gods (*abosom*). The Ashanti say '*Asase nyɛ bosom*; *ɔnkyerɛ mmusuo*' (The Earth is not a goddess; she does not divine). The conception is rather that of a power or principle possessed by the Earth." [1] Man's means of sustenance comes from the earth which receives its fruitfulness from God. Hence *Nyankopɔn*, the Great *Nyame*, the Giver of Life.

In the foregoing we have used the God-names *Nyame* and *Nyankopɔn* interchangeably. Danquah, however, draws a distinction between *Nyame*, the general term for Deity, and *Nyankopɔn*, the knowable and worshipful God, so that *Nyankopɔn* is the " Greater Nyame ". [2] While admitting that *nyam* underlies both God-names, [3] he nevertheless sees *Nyankopɔn* as the really knowable God. He suggests that " originally, Nyame must have been in competition with some other concepts of gods . . . *Onyankopon* would appear to have risen triumphant over all other competitive gods as the Great Shining One." [4] Moreover, argues Danquah, the fact that *Nyankopɔn* is called *Kwame*, he of Saturday, that is, that he has a personal name, makes him " a personality not an abstraction ", in contrast to *Nyame*.

There is no valid basis known to us for this distinction. That *Nyankopɔn* must have " risen triumphant over all competitive gods " remains a conjecture. Moreover, it is doubtful whether the use of the day-name *Kwame* to back up this supposed distinction is valid.

The use of *Kwame* for *Nyankopɔn* has been explained in various ways. It is believed by some that it was on a Saturday that *Nyankopɔn* was born, hence *Kwame*. Others explain that " God completed his work of creation on a Saturday, and used to appear to men on that day to receive their worship." [5] This explanation was given to

with flowers and offerings of food were placed before it. The Goddess's male partner was usually in the form of a bull, hence the prominence of the bull in the art of the farming peoples. Various phallic rites and ritual nuptials were associated with it, for it was believed that in some way human fertility would be reflected in the fertility of their land."—see *Life and Thought in the Ancient World* (University of London Press), p. 7.

[1] K. A. Busia, *The Position of the Chief in the Modern Political System of Ashanti*, p. 40.
[2] See ibid., Section Two, chapter 2. The use of the comparative is meant to underline the distinction.
[3] Ibid., p. 45.
[4] Ibid., p. 45.
[5] *African Ideas of God*, p. 247. Williamson finds this explanation suspect on the grounds that it is reminiscent of the Jewish Creation myth—see his Ph.D. thesis (London University), *Akan Religion and the Christian Faith*, p.361.

St. John Evans, the author of the words just quoted, by certain Ashanti whom he consulted; it appears to be borne out by what Amon d'Aby reports in connection with the Agni of the Ivory Coast whose belief it is that after the work of creation God visited the earth on a Saturday. [1] Whatever the explanation, it is doubtful whether Danquah is justified in considering the day-name as indicating that *Nyankopɔn* is the " Greater *Nyame.*" The uncertainty surrounding the significance of the day-name as used for Deity is not removed by St. John Evans' attempt to postulate " another Being ", *Nyankopɔn Kweku* (the male born on Wednesday) who is said to be cruel and malevolent. [2] One wonders whether the use of *Kweku* with *Nyankopɔn* is not capable of being interpreted differently and with greater plausibility. Does *Kweku* refer to God in his punitive aspect?

It would appear that the day-name commonly attached to the God-name among the Agni is that of the Monday-born; the Sanwi, the Ndénié and the Morofóè call Deity *Alluko-Nyamiã-Kadyo*, [3] as do the related people the Nzimas (*Nyamenle Kodwo*), the *Kadyo* or *Kodwo* being the day-name of the male born on Monday. One would imagine that the Agni would call God by the name of the Saturday-born in accordance with their belief that God visited the earth on Saturday. From the point of view of Agni usage, therefore, the significance of the day-name given to *Nyamiã* (clearly related to *Nyame*) must lie concealed in the folds of their. group history. It may very well be, in the absence of more certain information, that the day-names are to be traced to particular historical events, so that *Kwame* may recall a particular Saturday not to be forgotten, *Kweku* a Wednesday, and *Kodwo* a Monday, not to be forgotten (a day of special blessing, or one of special evil, etc.)

If among the Akan *Kwame* is used with *Nyankopɔn* and not with Nyame, there is probably no deeper significance in this than that *Nyankopɔn Kwame* is more sonorous and more poetic than *Nyame Kwame*. There certainly is no cult of *Nyankopɔn* as a deity separate from *Nyame*; indeed, one known means of approaching the Akan Deity is to be seen in some Ashanti homes in the three-forked branch known as *Nyamedua.*

Danquah was not one to hesitate about pursuing new ideas. Such an idea, intriguing it may be but incapable of being satisfactorily substantiated, at least not on the basis of the evidence

---

[1] F. J. Amon d'Aby, *Croyances Religieuses et Coutumes Juridiques des Agni de la Côte d'Ivoire* (1960), p. 41. There is strong evidence (linguistic, etc.) for linking the Agni or Anyi and the Akan of Ghana.

[2] *African Ideas of God.*, p. 254. St. John Evans' idea is taken up by Ernst Dammann in his *Die Religionen Afrikas*, p. 233.

[3] Amon d'Aby, op. cit., p. 41.

adduced by Danquah himself, is that "Akan knowledge of God teaches that he is the Great Ancestor. He is a true high God and manlike ancestor of the first man." [1] Indeed, it is his view that all gods are glorified ancestors. [2] This view has the approval of Smith who considers it as enabling us "to perceive more clearly than before the nexus between man and God." [3] We believe that this claim that in Akan thought God is the first ancestor and all gods are glorified ancestors is a very debatable one.

Two observations may be made. Firstly, Danquah's contention that God is the First Ancestor and that the gods were ancestors once might be considered as his way of resolving the tension between a hierarchical presentation of Akan religion, which sets out the various strands of belief in such a way as to suggest an order of importance, beginning with God, and a functional view, which is backed by strong sociological evidence. [4] Danquah conceives the Supreme Being as the beginning and end of Akan religion; yet his awareness of the vital role played by the ancestors leads him to quote with approval Rattray's words, "The predominant influences in the Ashanti religion . . . are the Asamanfo, the spirits of the departed forebears of the clan." [5] Whatever intentions he may have had, the evidence in support of the view that God is the Great Ancestor is unconvincing; certainly, the use of the term *Nana* with *Nyame* or *Nyankopɔn* does not lend probability to this theory. If this were really so, one would expect *Nyame* to be spoken of as a deified ancestor; this is never done. Secondly, this theory seems to suggest a possible overemphasis of the anthropo-centric nature of Akan religion, an impression which is strengthened when one considers the statement made towards the end of the book that "Akan religion, in its highest expression, is the worship of the race." [6] As a matter of fact, *Nyame* or *Nyankopɔn* is con-sidered to be wholly other by the Akan; on him "a man leans and does not fall, the final hope and refuge of those who find no redress in this life, the one who can do what no other spiritual agency can do, particularly in granting requests in connection with a man's destiny." [7] He is the creator of all things. [8]

[1] Ibid., p. 27.

[2] p. 28. To Danquah the myth of the removal of *Nyame* to the sky away from the level of men symbolises the apotheosis of the ancestors.

[3] See Edwin Smith's article, 'Religious Beliefs of the Akan', in *Africa* Vol. XV. No. 1.

[4] On this see Clarke, *Africa* Vol. III, pp. 431–430, and S. G. Williamson *Akan Religion and the Christian Faith*, pp. 94 ff.

[5] Danquah, ibid., p. 21.

[6] Ibid., p. 169.

[7] Williamson, ibid., p. 97.

[8] i.e. ɔbɔadeɛ, which Danquah translates as "He created the Thing",

The purpose of this introduction is not to undertake a complete review of Danquah's *The Akan Doctrine of God*—the reader has the book at his disposal; moreover, some thoughtful reviews have been written, notably Edwin Smith's ' Religious Beliefs of the Akan.' Our purpose is to underscore the complex nature of the task undertaken by Danquah when he set out " to elucidate the nature and significance of the divinity whom the Akan call *Nyankopon Kwaame*, the ' Greater ' God of Saturday." [1] A great deal has been written on Akan religion, by Busia and Rattray, among others. Danquah's work, however, is of a different order. Unlike Busia's or Rattray's writings, Danquah's is in part a polemic. [2] Inevitably, the reader begins to question various aspects of the presentation, wondering how much of what he writes is his own and how much is Akan. When in translating *Onyankopon, onye Domankoma Sunsum* as " God is the Infinite God's Personality " he comments, " This is one of the most difficult notions in the Akan Doctrine of God, of psychology and epistemology ", [3] the reader is tempted to ask whether Danquah is not seeing more in those words than there actually is. There are what appear to be contradictions, as Edwin Smith has pointed out. *Onyame, Onyankopɔn* and *Ɔdomankoma* are considered a triad, [4] yet *Onyame* is referred to elsewhere as " the physical basis of Ultimate Reality." [5] *Nkara* or *nkra*, equated with the Greek *nous*, is at one point distinguished from *ɔkra* or *ɔkara*; [6] yet, Danquah seems to identify the two at another point. [7]

Matters which he might logically have discussed are not dealt with. What might be considered by students of Akan ethics to be of interest, such as the extent to which ethical and psychical ideas are derived from the body or parts of the body, is left undiscussed. This particular omission is not surprising since, as Edwin Smith notes, the *nipadua* or material body is never referred to in Danquah's examination of the meaning of *ɔkra*.

The matter of the value of *The Akan Doctrine of God* as an exposition of Akan theology is made somewhat more complex by a consideration of the intriguing possibility that if in his later days

---

reserving " He created all things " for *ɔbɔ ade nyinaa*. It is indisputable that *ɔdɔadeɛ = ɔbɔ ade nyinaa =* He is Creator or He created all things. Elsewhere Danquah translates *ɔbɔadeɛ* as " He created the universe "—see lecture cit. footnote 3, p. ix.

[1] Danquah, ibid., p. xii.
[2] See pages 104–106, ibid.
[3] p. 66.
[4] p. 42.
[5] p. 130.
[6] p. 28.
[7] p. 114.

Danquah had attempted another systematic exposition of Akan religion the result might have been a step closer to the views that have been expressed on the subject by scholars like Busia and Rattray.

In an unpublished collection of papers and letters written by Danquah, the author, in one or two places, takes positions which he had earlier considered untenable, and simplifies concepts whose significance had been obscured through excessive speculation. The papers in question do not constitute a systematic treatise on Akan religion; among them are a few addresses given before church groups. To be sure, Danquah's interest in seeking the sources of certain Akan ideas and practices from the East remains undiminished; in one address he affirms the Sumerian origin of Akan culture, a theory which he apparently explores further in another manuscript entitled *Revelation of Culture in Ghana*. [1]

However, there are indications in some of these papers of a modified approach—certainly a less rigid one than is evident in the *The Akan Doctrine of God*. In an address to " the Ghana Seminar held in Aburi on 29th July to 18th August, 1961 " Danquah said the following:

" At the lowest, the sacred object, either a tree or rock, or a river, was conceived of as ' animate ', as containing a spirit, and the worship of that spirit fell into the category of what is described in Sir E. B. Tylor's minimum definition of religion as ' the belief in spiritual beings.'

But we did have, and, I believe, we still have ' fetishes '. We do have fetishes of the type named by Captain R. S. Rattray somewhat euphemistically as ' lesser gods ', but whose true name is abosom or ' animate powers '. Included in this category are Tanoh, Buruku, Anokye, Katawere and many others." [2]

He goes on to refer to other spiritual agencies: "natural spirits, disembodied or otherwise ", such as *Sasabonsam* and *mmoatia* or gnomes (the little men of the forest), ancestors, and the Supreme Being. He then poses the question, " Which of these various religious objects is the highest purpose of Akan or Ghanaian religion?" Among other things, he explains, " the relationship of ancestors to the gods, or to God, is usually that of inferior to superior." The ' fetish ' or lesser god is inferior to the ancestor, as the latter is inferior to God.

[1] We have not read this manuscript; it is referred to in a letter to an American professor.

[2] In a lecture given in 1956 at the Kumasi Cultural Centre entitled 'Akan Culture Through the Ages ' Danquah referred to Rattray's writings as among the " oldest reliable " books.

In this, Danquah seems to move away from the rigid view
expressed in *The Akan Doctrine of God* that Akan religion knows
basically nothing but God, and that such aspects as the *abosom*
entered in from outside the Akan. Of course, he still maintains,
quite rightly, that it is inappropriate to describe Akan religion as
fetishism, which term suggests that certain material objects are
themselves feared because supernatural powers are inherent in them.
" It can be said without fear of any contradiction," he writes, " that
pure fetishism, in the sense of the cult of the purely material,
' recognised as such ', cannot be found in Ghana." [1] Nevertheless
the *abosom* now seem to find a place in the Akan system as set out
by Danquah in the address in question.

Again, he appears to play down the rather philosophical concept
of a divine triad. He refers to " the Supreme Being, *Nyame,*
Nyankopon and *Odomankoma* . . . who must be worshipped
' comprehensively, attaching no conditions.' " It is true that the
distinction drawn in *The Akan Doctrine of God* between *Nyame* and
Nyankopɔn on the basis of the day-name *Kwame* is re-iterated;
however, he notes that after *Onyame,* " the next name the Akan
have for God is *Nyankopon* "; *Odomankoma* is " the conception of
God as the Creator." He also refers to " the Ghanaian or Akan
name for God, *Nyame, Nyankopon* or *Odomankoma.*"

" . . . to understand the cultus of Akan or Ghanaian religion,"
Danquah further writes, " we should take account of the following
postulates . . . all of which are sacred to the Akan, or, at least, are
considered as essential elements in the practice of religion in the
Ghanaian society." As given in *The Akan Doctrine of God* these
postulates number eight; in the address under discussion there is an
additional postulate—*Obosom* or *ntoro.* The nine postulates are
grouped in three classes—" Individual Postulates ", concerned
with the life process of the individual; these are *Esu, Sunsum* and
Honhom. Next, " Social Postulates "—*Okra, Obosom,* and *Nana*—
these are concerned with the ethical or moral aspect of life. Lastly,
" Theological " or " Universal Postulates ", *Onyame, Onyankopon,*
and *Odomankoma.* In the brief explanations provided of these terms
Danquah, unconfined by the need to express Akan ideas in philosophical terms, sounds more in line with the accepted understanding
of these concepts. Thus, he refers to *honhom* as a term " used in the
sense of pure spirit of a living or active being, be he a man or God." [2]

The tenuity of the evidence for believing that Danquah's views
had undergone some change over the years is evident, the address

[1] Address cited.
[2] Cp. Christaller, ibid.

under discussion being a very short one; nevertheless, there is some evidence of a mellowing. This might suggest that *The Akan Doctrine of God* is an untrustworthy account of Akan theology, a suggestion that is not completely defensible. Danquah was a restless inquirer who did not hesitate to examine afresh the possibilities of a subject, challenging accepted positions and formulations, thereby presenting a challenge to uninquiring minds. In *The Akan Doctrine of God* there is much that is valuable, there is much that is authentic Akan wisdom; points of light blink through the clouds of speculation and etymologisings. In view of the fact that the role of God in African religion is generally underestimated, Danquah's insistence on the supreme reality of God is a valuable corrective; he seeks to convey something of the Akan understanding of the *majestas dei*. Moreover, he recognises that the polar notions of distance and nearness are an integral part of Akan religion. In the Greek religion, as Webb informs us, " the very fullness with which the personality of the Olympian God is imagined tends to make personal sympathy, and still more, personal intimacy out of the question between the worshipper and such a different kind of person from himself as the God he worships." [1] In contrast to this, Danquah would undoubtedly insist that there is the possibility of personal relationship between the worshipped and the worshipper; the individual, who is related *directly* to God through the *ɔkra* which is given him by God, has the right of a direct approach to God. Further, Danquah, recognises that the experience of the ultimate reality is inseparably related to ethics and morality. Hence, the fact of each individual being unique through the *ɔkra* underscores one of the two main foci of ethical action: " the freedom of the man's will and his consequential responsibility for his own use of this freedom." [2] And yet, religious experience expresses itself in some form of " togetherness "; [3] man must exercise his freedom within the bounds of society. In Danquah's own words, " It is inaccurate . . . to speak of the Akan conception of freedom as grossly undetermined, and it is also inaccurate to speak of it as absolutely decreed, beyond the man's own powers. Each individual has an eye in which he sees the world of being reflected in himself, he only errs when he believes that his being is the eye of the world." [4]

Finally, a true understanding of the nature of Akan religion calls for a new evaluation of traditional Christian attitudes. In recent

---

[1] Webb, *God and Personality*, p. 79.

[2] Danquah, ibid., p. 114.

[3] See Joachim Wach, ' General Revelation and Religions of the World ', *Journal of Bible and Religion*, Vol. XXII, No. 2 (1954), p. 86

[4] Ibid., p. 114.

years, thanks to a more objective study of man's religions and an intensive ecumenical striving, traditional exclusivist attitudes to non-Christian religions have been called in question. Danquah's own attitude, gleaned from his references to Westermann and from scattered statements, in a sense anticipates the liberal attitudes of today. Cantwell Smith asks, " Is God . . . not Creator? If so, then is He not to be known—however impartially, distortedly, inadequately—in creation? Is He not active in history? If so, is His spirit totally absent from any history, including even the history of other men's faith? " [1] To this Wach would say that non-Christians past and present, have had the " grace of God." [2] Danquah does not write from as wide an experience as Wach or Cantwell Smith; he does not approach the subject of the Christian attitude to other religions as a seasoned sociologist or historian of religions, but he was a thinker of considerable ability. In the address to " The Ghana Seminar " he said, " I have said somewhere that Christianity is a fulfilment of the religious conceptions of our own people. But long before Christianity came, we can be certain that God had himself been his own witness, he had given evidence of his existence and his goodness, to lead to the development of a high religion in the Ghanaian Society." [3] In *The Akan Doctrine of God*, written about twenty years earlier, he makes the same declaration more succinctly and more dramatically: "The Spirit of God is abroad, even in the Akan of the Gold Coast." [4]

University of Ghana, Legon.   KWESI A. DICKSON
7th January, 1966

---

[1] *The Faith of Other Men*, p. 125.
[2] Joachim Wach, art. cit., pp. 88–91.
[3] See supra p. xxii.
[4] p. 187.

FOREWORD

THE co-operation of a mysterious power of which I am little conscious has rendered it possible for the MS. of this work to be extant. The story may here be told.

Two or three years of self-devoted labour had produced in three volumes an original effort of 640 pages, the present work being its third and crowning portion. In part for my faith in those younger than myself in years, and, in part for the willing co-operation which the learned among the younger generation of Gold Coast men gladly accord me, my MSS. were submitted to Mr. C. A. Ackah, of the Accountant General's Department, who had recently obtained the London M.A. Degree with Honours in Philosophy. The work had reached its final stages, with only the index and the bibliography to be arranged, and Mr. Ackah had returned the first two volumes to me with his comments and criticisms. The third was to follow soon with his final appreciation. That was in December, 1940.

On the night of January 29th, 1941, within a twinkling of the eye, the first two volumes were reduced to a heap of ashes. A fire which completely consumed the house in which I lived and everything therein, consumed also in its devouring flames the two volumes. I had that night been working on the bibliography, and, even now, I can see a picture of my ancient note-books and old rare books and the two MSS. volumes on the table of my study as I went out to the adjoining verandah for a dose of fresh air. Obviously, as it now appears, after reading for some part of the night, I was overcome by the fumes of a slowly smouldering fire which had been brewing in the ceiling, caused by what the Government electrician disclosed at the subsequent enquiry, by a spark induced by the " arching " of an electric wire.

" Gold Coast Ethics and Religion " (A Theory of Morals and Religion in the Akan Tradition) was the title of the original work. It set forth the Akan idea of the good, or the supreme good, and examined for the purpose, all the anthropological evidence available : the Akan gods, the " fetishes," the customs, the maxims or proverbs (3,680 of them), the festivals, the religious observances, the calendars, folklore, the family system, the social and moral codes, racial history, racial fears and hopes (*i.e.*, the philosophy of their life) ; and it arrived at a conclusion confirming the thesis expressed in the first line of the first Chapter :

" *What the Akan take to be the good is the family* . . ."

The text went on to show why the Akan, above all else, held the family (*i.e.*, the interest of the community) to be the supreme good, and that, to them, the worst vice in life was to bring dishonour or indignity or disgrace to the family name, or to the community (of whatever size).

The ideal, to give it a name, was not benevolence, or passive impersonal love, as commonly understood, but beneficence—doing good, active love and prosperity (*yiyeyo*) of which the New Testament writer seemed to speak to the Hebrews when he said to them : " And do not forget beneficence and neighbourliness, for by such sacrifices God's favour is obtained " (Heb. xiii. 16, Douay (R.C.) version) ; or St. Paul to the Romans, when he said : " For as we have many members in one body, and all members have not the same office, so we, being many, are one body in Christ and every one member of one another. . . . Let love be without dissimulation . . . distributing to the necessity of the saints. . . ." (Rom. xii. 4–13).

In a word, the Akan ideal of beneficence (*yiyeyo*) was discovered to be both of the earth and of heaven. In the language of Christaller [1] *yiyeyo* or *yiyeye* is " well-doing ; doing good ; performance of duties ; prosperity," at once connoting and denoting all the motives and ends and purposes and goods which true love can pursue and ensure : goodness and prosperity, not of one only but of the " saints " or " neighbours " of the entire community of one family.

This granted, the rest was a matter of evidence, or as they say in the Courts, a question of fact, the truth of which was not to be decided by the learned Judge (theory) but by the Jury (experience of the common man).

This question of fact is : " Who are the family ? "   " Who are the saints or neighbours among whom goodness and prosperity are to be distributed in beneficence ? "

Many Akan proverbs, scores of them, pointed to one truth, that the family, the neighbours, were those of the blood, the group held together by community of origin and obligation to a common ancestor, the Nana, and held together also by the high standard of attainment in goodness and prosperity enshrined in the Nana's memory. It was for this group that morality was of value and, for it, beneficence was truly beneficial and profitable —in both senses ; in worth and in increment.

Says Maxim 3560 [2] : " *He treats you like a beast who does not reciprocate your goodness.* " Which is to say, where the reciprocity

---

[1] Rev. J. G. Christaller: *Dictionary of the Asante and Fante Language*, 2nd Ed., p. 595.

[2] See Appendix I.

of beneficence is denied you, the humanity in you is denied, placing you a little lower than man—on the lower plane of a beast. Or again in Maxim 1985 the Akan version of the golden rule points to one fact, that beneficence for you must be beneficence for your neighbour or you are less than a saint, with your consequent share of the distributed prosperity smaller than your proper portion : Says the maxim : " *They will not accord you ten if you will not accord your neighbour nine.*"

Again, who is my neighbour ? He whose goodness makes me good and who, rather than place me a little lower than man, would accord me the beneficence of the good Samaritan. He is my neighbour, because neither is he a disgrace to nor does he dishonour my family or race, the race called Akan (*Animguase mfata Okanniba*).

The Akan is a small race in the greater race of mankind. The Akan family of the Gold Coast and West Africa probably does not number more than 4,000,000. It contains all kinds of families, or community groups : the agnatic family of male ancestor and descendants ; the cognatic family with the mother's brother, your uncle, as head, and traced through their mother—your maternal grandmother ; then the clan or enlarged family ; then the tribe or larger admixture of cognates and agnates and clans, possessing one speech or dialect and common customs ; then the state or nation-group with one family upraised or acknowledged by their moral or physical efficiency above the rest, and from among whom the successor to the Nana is chosen and accorded the honour of the religious *sacra* because held to be the exemplar of the Great Ancestor, creative source of the great family ; and so on and so forth in an expanding crescendo of all-embracing forms. For, it would appear, bounds cannot be set to the meaning of " family " until every trace of the quality which is other than beastly is exhausted ; to embrace, that is, not only the Akan, but the entire race of that quality, the manlike family of humanity. " *To the spirit of man there are no bounds,*" says Maxim 1420 (*Ohonam mu nni nhanoa*).

So came the solution in Maxim 2436 : " *All men are the offspring of God . . .*" The saints, the neighbours, the family, are sons of God, who created all men as His offspring. All men are issue of the first progenitor, the ultimate ancestor and creative Nana whose day is Saturday : *Nana Nyankopon Kwaame.* Those of Him are " the neighbours," and to treat any who are of Him as entitled to less than their share of beneficence is to exclude them from the manlike family—to treat them as beasts.

That, in brief, was the question of fact which had to be discovered, and one had to go to the Stoic poets, Aratus and

Cleanthes, referred to by St. Paul or his apt disciple St. Luke,[1] for the ancient and Christian confirmation of that question of fact. The Unknown God of the Greeks is the God that made the world and all things therein . . . " and hath made of one blood all nations of men for to dwell on all the face of the earth . . . For we are also his offspring."

This is the universal community of the great family which Akan theory postulates as that for which the good is divinely willed. " . . . . What the Akan take to be the good is the family . . . of whatever size."

Volumes I and II brought a wealth of evidence in support of that thesis ; and Volume III, which providentially has been preserved, aims to elucidate the nature and significance of the divinity whom the Akan call *Nyankopon Kwaame*, the " Greater " God of Saturday.

As it is, not on the banks of the Nile, nor of the Niger, nor of the Volta, would there be much weeping and lamentation for the death of Cæsarion and Antyllus. They were but " European " issue of Cleopatra, and Cleopatra herself survives to tell the tale.

In matter of fact terms, if we know truly what the Akan doctrine is concerning God, it should be no difficult matter to deduce who His community of saints ought to be and what their saintliness or supreme neighbourliness should be accounted to embrace.

*　　*　　*　　*　　*

The title of this book, " The Akan Doctrine of God," was chosen in place of the original title, " Gold Coast Ethics and Religion," which had covered a wider field. Here and there in the text the reader will come across a reference to the earlier books or chapters now lost. It is thought better to retain such references than to delete them, lest unaccountable gaps confront the reader and upset the flow of thought. Parts of the chapters have been rewritten, however. It is enough to say that what now appears in " The Akan Doctrine of God " as Chapter I was originally Chapter XXI, Book V, of " Gold Coast Ethics and Religion."

*　　*　　*　　*　　*

In making acknowledgments, I go first to the young : in addition to C. A. Ackah aforesaid, to William E. Ofori Atta, B.A., of Achimota College, who, having read the three original volumes, expressed genuine sorrow on learning that the middle volume which dealt with Akan ethnology and the various Akan religious

---

[1] Acts xvii. 22–31.

sacra, ritual calendars and myths, had perished in the fire ; and to my clerk, K. A. Adufo, whose informed interest in the work made lighter the burden of copying and typing.

I go next to various Gold Coast teachers and students of anthropology, in particular to my great friends K. Brakatu Ateko, formerly of Achimota ; J. C. de Graft Johnson, O.B.E., formerly Assistant Secretary for Native Affairs, and his brother Dr. J. W. de Graft Johnson, M.A., D.C.L., Barrister-at-Law, who inspired and encouraged me with their discussions and works.

Lastly I go to Græco-Roman Europe, ancient and modern, to express my unbounded gratitude to Vladimir Sergevich Solov'ev, the great Russian philosopher, whose very Christian doctrine of the good [1] made me what I am in philosophy, and after whom therefore I named my first son Vladimir ; to Plato, without whose " Republic " I should have lived in vain ; to Baruch Spinoza, who compels all souls to think ; to John Stuart Mill and F. H. Bradley for making logic possible for English students ; to my three teachers, Professor G. Dawes Hicks, of University College, London, who made it easier for me to understand Kant and a little of Hegel and Aristotle, Professor A. Wolf, whose scientific method makes research a pleasure, and Professor Leonard Trelawny Hobhouse, of the School of Economics, London, without whose work on sociology I could never have understood the true significance of the Akan doctrine of God.

As an African I believe it is not meaningless to acknowledge also my debt to Milton and Macaulay and the King James Bible for helping me to understand the rich and balanced English language which, with its many " s's," is so very different from Akan with its many " m's," but is so very much like Akan in enabling a writer to sing in prose if we wants to.

J. B. D.

ODOR, ADABRAKA, ACCRA,
June 10th, 1942.

[1] *The Justification of the Good*, 1898. English translation in Constable's Russian Library, 1915.

TABLE OF CONTENTS

SECTION ONE
THE QUEST OF THE DOCTRINE

SECTION TWO
THE AKAN MEANING OF GOD

LIST OF ADINKRA ILLUSTRATIONS

NOTE ON THE ADINKRA ILLUSTRATIONS

THE Adinkra symbols are stamped in Adinkra mourning cloths worn only on the occasion of a funeral ceremony, and then only during the day.

The name Adinkra is spelt variously. In " Religion and Art in Ashanti " (p. 264), Rattray uses the intensive Ashanti form, Adinkira, but Christaller in his Dictionary (p. 85), uses the correct forms Adinkara and Adinkra. The word is clearly made up of *di*, to make use of, to employ, and *nkra*, message, the substantive being derived from the combination of these two by the subjunctive of the Akan prefix for an abstract noun or the infinitive, " A." *Di nkra* means to part, be separated, to leave one another, to say goodbye.

The word *"nkra"* or " *nkara* " as shown in the text (Section IV) means message, intelligence, and where human destiny or the life span is concerned, it refers particularly to the intelligence or message which each soul takes with him from God upon his obtaining leave to depart to earth. The " soul " itself is called *okra* or *okara*, that is to say, the *nous*, of a person. According to the Akan belief, only human beings have the opportunity of saying goodbye to God upon their departure to earth, and only human beings therefore have souls on this earth.

Clearly, use of the Adinkra cloth and symbols is intended to mark the link forged between the living and the dead, the present and the future, the affairs of the now and the affairs of the hereafter, and may therefore be called the " present-and-future " cloth, or simply the " future " or " futurist " cloth, using the English word " futurist " as near as possible to its original theological sense of one believing that the prophecies of the Apocalypse are still to be fulfilled, that is to say, in the sense that there is a future beyond the grave which continues with the present in the living, and waiting to be made good. In modern art, "futurist" or "futurism" refers to a movement marked by violent departure from traditional methods and by the use of arbitrary symbols in the expression of emotion. The Akan Adinkra symbols may be said to express a certain measure of emotion upon reflection on the here and the hereafter, but one must go warily in insisting that they represent a "departure" from "traditional" methods, or that they are merely "arbitrary." We know as yet very little of the motif of Akan art to be able to say much on that score.

Rattray tries to say that the Akan "merely borrowed these patterns . . . amulet signs or symbols introduced by the Mohammedans from the North." This may be so, and there will be no point in disputing the assertion as to its truth. All art is imitation and borrowing, either from Nature, or from our fellow-men. It is the motive for borrowing a particular type and not another, as well as the meaning put into it and the use made of it when so borrowed, which matters, for it indicates for us, and helps us to understand and appreciate a nation's or race's "side" in nature. It may be curious that the Mohammedans themselves do not seem to know many of these symbols, and the names and uses for them among the Akan are entirely un-Mohammedan. At any rate no cloths stamped with the Adinkra symbols are met with among the Mohommedans, and the Adinkra system of mourning is unknown to them. We may safely conclude that there is something intensely native in these symbols interpretative of the Akan faith and tradition.

I am grateful to Spio Garbrah, Teacher in the Achimota School of Art, and to Kofi Antubam, a student in the same School, for providing the illustrations. The index figures (e.g., R. 148/12) refer to Figs. 148, 149 and 150 in Rattray's "Religion and Art in Ashanti" (pp. 264–267), and the descriptions are mostly based upon Rattray.

THE QUEST OF THE DOCTRINE

CHAPTER I

IN SEARCH OF THE AKAN GOD

1. THE ''NATIVE'' QUALITY OF GOD

THE Akan doctrine of God is the doctrine of an Akan type of God. The true God is not of several kinds, but he can be known under several degrees or colours, for each people has a name for God, and in the name is to be found that quality or colour in God which most appeals to their racial mind.

To discover the meaning of this name or quality is to discover the doctrine, the teaching and impression of, *e.g.*, the Akan race concerning God. What a race takes God to be, or believes he ought to be, hangs upon the meaning of the name. If a people, for instance, call God by their own vernacular name for " rainfall," it must be because the copious nature of God as provider of the fructifying rain is the seed of their impression, teaching and knowledge of God. If they call him king, or God of war (" Jahveh "), or of light, or of goodness, then the seed of their doctrine hangs upon the meaning or quality in the particular name.

Obviously, no nation, ancient or modern, can claim to possess an original doctrine of God, unless there is a certain amount of " seed "-quality about their native ideas of God, unless, that is, their conception was the result of an original impression of " godliness " in their racial spirit.

When, therefore, this book speaks of the Akan as possessing a doctrine of God, it does so in the knowledge that there is a " native " or seed-quality about their name for God which is evidence that they had, of themselves, found God. And the value of this independent awareness or discovery of God is measured by the depth and warmth of the meaning in that " colour " or godliness in God which had made most appeal to them.

2. THE RACIAL IN ETHICAL THOUGHT

With the possible exception of Sir A. B. Ellis, in his " Tshi-Speaking Peoples of the Gold Coast," no one who seriously studied the products of Akan thought ever doubted that they have had a definite conception of the true nature of God or what it ought to be. Chief among such thinkers have been one English and two

German scholars—Rattray, Westermann and Christaller, the last a German-Swiss of the erstwhile Basel Mission Society of the Gold Coast.

Enquiry into the nature of the Akan God has been going on for upwards of a century, but the doctrine was never stated in a form recognizable by students, theologians and moralists as akin to previous discoveries of scientific or speculative thought and of a nature to fit in with, but without disturbing, the *organon* of accepted truth.

The greatest advances towards that objective were made by the earliest of the three writers above mentioned—Christaller— but the results of his enquiry were scattered under different headings or titles in his great dictionary of the Twi (Tshi) language, and thus lacked the value which an uninterrupted story naturally possesses.

The present enquiry is rendered possible by the lead which Christaller gave. Actually, the motive that spurred me to embark upon the study was not any special interest in the theological development of Akan thought. My own speculative interest in thought has always been ethical. That bent may have prejudiced me in favour of the view that the sum and substance of a people's thought about the nature of things in general could be deduced almost with a Kantian apodeictic certainty if once their way of interpreting what is right and what is wrong in the social community could be ascertained with adequate precision.

The following at least can be granted by a good many : that, if a people centre the good around the family, or community, they are bound to conceive of God (" the ideal of the Chief Good ") as beneficent, respectable, paternal, patriarchal, and catholic. If a people centre the good around the individual, they, of necessity, conceive of God as king and ruler, and, like the egoistic individual, master of all he surveys and omnipotent. He will be, by choice more than necessity, benevolent, and can be merciful and kind. Thirdly, if a people build up their ideas of God around heroes and demigods and mystic elemental powers and mythological potentates, they are apt to arrive at a conception of God which involves a sharp duality between heroism and treachery, Ormuzd and Ahriman, Light and Darkness, Heaven and Hell, a world of Exalted Angels and their opposites of the Fallen among Angels and men. In such a society abnormal sympathy or charity, and abnormal cruelty, or oppression, joust for places in the established order.

Each of these conceptions has its peculiar system of ethics, of philosophy and theology. Each has its peculiar system of politics, economics and art. Each has the tendency to dominate men's lives as it dominates their thought and spirit. It moulds their environment and bends them to be what they are or become.

Equally, the virtues get classified under these peculiar national and racial ways of thought and action. When the family is the chief ideal, things that are dishonourable and undignified, actions that in disgracing you disgrace the family, are held to be vices, and the highest virtue is found in honour and dignity. Tradition is the determinant of what is right and just, what is good and done.

Where the isolated individual is the chief ideal, personal excellence, as among the Hebrews, and high Majesty, are, above all, the greatest virtues, and goodness is measured in terms of material prosperity in a life of each against all, a free community in which unbridled competition has the freest possible scope.

Thirdly, where the heroic is the chief ideal, as among the Greeks and the Wiro races of Europe, beauty and strength of body, the ponderous power of the thunderbolt, a Zeus above all, a conqueror of life over death, are the ideal virtues. Opportunity is here created for the advent of the superman, blazing the way, eventually, for the total dictator, with all that the dominance of this type of man implies for high contrasts of excessive good with excessive evil in politics, economics, and even art.

3. ''TOOLS'' OF THE CHIEF GOOD

Withal, the political ideology of communism, democracy or dictatorship is each a product of what a people take to be their chief good in ethics. It determines their culture, tones their habits, and manufactures the implements and tools of their civilization.

These tools have often been mistaken for culture itself, the truth being that true culture is ethical, not material. The tools of a people are merely indicative of their reach in civilization, not necessarily of their culture. Thus, among the first-mentioned, family class of ethics, the " tool " of their civilization is almost indiscoverable : it is, with them, a matter of spirit, as among the Japanese the ancestor is taken to be. Every single activity of the Japanese is centred around the Goddess of Heaven and her successor the Emperor. Everything else has value only in its relation to the ideal of the great ancestor as the " tool " of their culture. Here, all are for each ; for all are of the ancestor of the family, be he a Chief or Emperor, or merely a patriarch.

Among the second, the tool or determinant is the individual king and ruler or sultan, the temple, the throne, every man master of his own home, his own castle, thrashing all else in the freedom of individual competition, to make of each a democrat or king in his private domain.

Among the third, obedience, with the implement of the iron rod to compel that obedience—wars and rumours of wars, power politics and imperialism, dominant, intolerant, assertive in the mass, the individual lost and unable to find himself except in the picture and reflection of the Hegelian State—that is the determinant of their God's spirit on earth. Here, the opposite of the democratic extreme is reached : All are against each.

Naturally, not all will pronounce for the truth of the above propositions. But in the main, and in so far as one man's cogitation can sum up the trend of man's history throughout the ages, there is justification for saying that if, upon the basis of the above analysis, the Akan people, too, are to set out on a quest for what is peculiar in their products of thought, that quest should be counted one of great value.

In the end, we will find that the quest of God in Akanland is a quest of their culture, their politics, their economics and the spirit of their art and life. It is a catholic quest to discover the discipline attained by the Akan in their contact with the rough edges in nature and the attempt or effort to hew and fashion those edges into something harmonious, beautiful, satisfying and true under the control of the Akan mind and for the service of their kind.

*   *   *   *   *

It was mentioned in the preface that parts of this work, contained in four books of twenty chapters, were lost in a midnight fire which destroyed the typescripts and the notes upon which they were based. Those chapters covered an examination of certain facts in Akan life upon which the conclusions in the present book were based. In the fifth and sixth books, which were saved from the fire, the essentials of the Akan world view, what the Germans call *Weltanschauung*, were set forth as a deduction from the facts. Section One, Book V, Chapter 21 of the original MSS. now follows as Chapter II of this book. It embodies an examination of what two of the three European writers abovementioned, had taken to be the nature and place of the Akan God, or, in their language, the Akan Supreme Being.

CHAPTER II

CRITIQUE OF THE DOCTRINE

I. RATTRAY AND WESTERMANN

CAPTAIN (later Dr.) R. S. RATTRAY, had been a political officer in the Gold Coast who, through his own efforts and interest, qualified for appointment as Gold Coast Government anthropologist. His study of Akan thought was confined almost exclusively to one of the principal branches of the race, the Ashanti, but what he found and said of them is in many cases of general application to the entire race. Rattray attained academic distinction through his devoted work ; the degree of Doctor of Science was conferred on him by the University of Oxford ; he was a member of the International Institute of African Languages and Cultures, and his labours earned academic recognition also in France. His works were published by the Oxford University Press.

Dr. Diedrich Westermann is, however, the more famous, more international of the two European writers on the Akan. As professor of African Languages and Cultures at the University of Berlin he has had plenty of time and practice in the study of African thought, and as Director of the International Institute of African Languages and Cultures, several institutions and governments in Africa and elsewhere have had occasion to seek his advice and guidance in their measures directed towards " improving " the lot of the African in the light of his thought. Westermann's views examined in this chapter are to be found in his Duff Lectures delivered in Scotland in 1935 and published by the Oxford University Press in 1937 under the title " Africa and Christianity."

The two men may therefore be taken as fairly typical of European and other thought concerning the Akan in Africa, and, although not in many respects conventional (the " fetish " to them is not the true Akan Supreme Being as is conventionally believed in Europe), they may be said to express the most far-reaching of all the attempts Europe had made in the last hundred years to understand the Akan in particular and the African in general.

2. RATTRAY'S ''ASHANTI''

First as to Rattray. How did the Akan conception of God appeal to him ? What, upon his enquiry, did he discover had moved the Akan to embark upon God-worship ? And what sort of a God or Supreme Being did he consider the Akan to have discovered for themselves ?

One definite answer he gave was this. The Ashanti, or Akan, said Rattray, was moved to worship his dead ancestor through " fear, pure fear." Westermann, as we shall presently see, built up a theory exactly the contrary of this doctrine of fear.

But, again, Rattray went on to state : " The Ashanti regard the Sky and the Earth as their two great deities. The Sky-God is ' Nyame,' " (p. 214, " Ashanti." Except where otherwise stated, the quotations are from Rattray's " Ashanti ").

At another place Rattray states : " It is hardly an exaggeration to say that every compound in Ashanti contains an altar to the Sky-God (142). . . . Anotchi [1] told Osei Tutu and all the people that this Stool (Golden Stool) contained the Sunsum (soul or spirit) of the Ashanti nation, and that their power, their health, their bravery, their welfare were in this stool (292). . . . The Golden Stool was and is far more than that ; it is the shrine of the sunsum or soul of this people, something for which they have fought and for which, I believe, they would fight again. . . . I believe it will be found to be the case that all the obedience, the respect and great loyalty we (British Government) have been given by the Ashanti is given through and by reason of the Golden Stool (293). It is not, however, the Sky and Earth deities who in Ashanti are held to be the prime factors in shaping and influencing the actions and destinies of mankind. These great unseen powers are generally too remote or perhaps too mighty to be concerned very intimately with the individual clan, and the predominant influences in the Ashanti religion are neither ' Saturday Sky-God,' ' Thursday Earth-Goddess,' nor even the hundreds of gods (abosom) with which it is true the land is filled, *but are the Asamanfo, the spirits of the departed forebears of the clan* (216). Quite apart from these ceremonial occasions, I do not suppose that a day passes among any of the old folk upon which some little offering is not cast upon the roof of the hut or placed on the altar beside the door to ' the great God of the Sky ' who is ' of all the earth, the King and Elder ' (144). . . . It has already been recorded how Ta Kora's temple, unlike so many pantheons, did not contain a single fetish. I sometimes think that, had these people been left alone to work out their own salvation, sooner or later, perhaps some African Messiah would have arisen and swept their pantheons and their religion clean of the suman (fetish). Then West Africa might have become the cradle

---

[1] *Okomfo* (priest) Anotchi, was priest and minister to Osei Tutu, king and founder of the Ashanti Confederacy. He is often spoken of as the Cardinal Wolsey of Ashanti.

of a new religion, which acknowledges one Great Spirit, who, being one, nevertheless manifested himself in everything around them, and taught men to hear his voice in the flow of His waters and in the sound of His voice among the trees." . . . "In a sense, therefore, it is true that this great Supreme Being, the conception of whom has been innate in the minds of the Ashanti, is the Jehovah of the Israelities " (141).

3. WHY RATTRAY MISSED THE AKAN "SUNSHINE"

The Supreme Being, the Saturday Sky-God, the Thursday Earth-Goddess, the Asamanfo or Spirits of Departed Ancestors, and Ta Kora or Tanno—these, when one comes to think of them, must be accounted great discoveries. It is a great discovery in the centre of West Africa, the proverbial land of fetish, that the great God of the Sky, is daily worshipped or acknowledged as " King and Elder." It is a great discovery that with their knowledge of this Great Sky-God or Supreme Being, the predominant influences in Ashanti religion are, however, the Asamanfo, or *Nananom*, the spirits of the departed forebears of the clan. Ta Kora, indeed, is not called by Rattray " fetish." He calls him " god " (*obosom*). But his name tells us what he is. *Ta* is a short form of *Tanno*, and Tanno is the name of a river. *Kora* means the keeper or adjuster. He is not an ancestor god or *osaman*. He is the type that other people call " fetish," but Rattray confines that name to the *suman*, the amulet or charm which people wear as a mascot for luck. Tanno is a god of sorts to the Akan (but they do not call him " Nyame," which name is reserved for spirit gods, or the God who is Supreme).

But great as Rattray's discoveries make him in our estimation for the immensity of thought he brought to his quest, his conclusions, however, confirm the view that while he saw shafts of light here and there in the Akan religious dawn, he just missed seeing the whole sunshine.

He had discovered, by what must be the fruit of serious and long cogitation, that the predominant influences in Ashanti religion were the Nananom or Asamanfo enshrined in the Golden or consecrated Stool ; this Nana having once been king or elder (*opanyin*), and subsequently deified. He had also seen that the Sky-God or Nyame was a great deity of the Ashanti whom they, at least the old folk, daily acknowledged and worshipped, and that this Nyame was also King and Elder, the Jehovah of the Ashanti. But, probably being against the grain in the mind of a Christian, Rattray could not bring himself to comprehend what was the most obvious core within this growth of thought, namely,

7

that the Ashanti had found a bridge over the gulf between the worshipful king and elder (Nana) and the fatherly and divinely creative king and elder (Nyame, or Sky-God).

Rattray had, indeed, urged against Ellis, in "Ashanti Proverbs," that the Ashanti conception of Supreme Being was the monotheistic. But the speculative effort to connect the Ashanti "Jehovah" with the Golden Stool as the sacramental link or covenant between the deified Nana and the Deity Himself, just slipped through his fingers.

Instead, he would recommend the Akan sweeping the counterfeit pantheons clean of the multitudinous abosom or animistic spirits for the advent of an African Messiah, the anointed of the god Tanno. Rattray's failure consists in his inability to realize that if a real prince or elder, anointed as an exemplar for the people must come, his gospel must be of a Nana or elder, a father "Nyame" of the people, not certainly of a fetish, or god, called Tanno, who, so far from representing the monotheism implicit in Nana or Nyame, is only one among many gods of very uneven propensities.

And so, to the very last, we search Rattray in vain for that basic conception in his interpretation that should show Akan thought to be susceptible of linkage with other thought in order to give it value in the organon of truth, or of that knowledge so far accepted as true and proved in the world of thought. Had Rattray discovered that basic reality, he would, instead of speaking of a new West African religion, have spoken of a new light on truth, from the West African standpoint.

Rattray's failure, notwithstanding the value of his great work, leaves one abiding impression on our minds : When all is said and done, the Akan, to readers of Rattray, must be seen as a people who either have no true religion at all or have one too many.

No wonder, then, that Rattray, unlike many of the European interpreters of the Akan before him, spoke, at one moment, of the Supreme Being as remote and, at another, of Him as a daily object of religious worship. He had searched long and well but, failing to see the link between the Akan *sunsum* or spirit and the Akan *okra* or soul, with the interconnection between both the *sunsum* and the *okra* and the pre-existent soul of being, Rattray failed, too, to see the Akan God as already in full bloom and established. Not something as yet to be unearthed with the coming of a new West African religion, a Messiah of the god Tanno, whom others call the great fetish.

4. WESTERMANN AND AFRICAN BELIEFS

We turn to Westermann for a more provocative speculation. It is true this great teacher of Europe concerning the African wrote of all Africa in a bulk, just as one would write of all elephants in a bulk, and his justification for so treating all African religions as fundamentally homogeneous, was that they all started from a common motive : a motive found by him in a dictum by Tertullian, *Anima naturaliter christiana*, " The (human) spirit is naturally Christian," which Westermann placed at the head of his chapter on " The Religious Heritage."

He added, with respect to his quotation from Tertullian, that " Every one of the phrases quoted by Tertullian as current among his pagan contemporaries is literally the same as those in daily use among West Africans to-day, and it is more than likely that the religious views lying behind them also do not differ much between the modern pagan African and the citizen of the Roman Empire who lived in the second and third centuries of our era : namely, the belief in a Supreme Being or a personified power who, in a general sense, rules the world, maintains its order, and to whom man owes the essential institutions of his life as well as his cultural achievements, but who is too vaguely conceived, or, according to the native creed, too great and too far removed, to be concerned about the personal fate of an individual " (64–65).

This, so far, is to give us a good start. But Westermann goes on to state : " People acknowledge him (the Supreme Being), but neither *fear* nor *love* nor *serve* him, the feeling towards him being, at the highest, that of dim awe or reverence. He is the God of the thoughtful, not of the crowd ; of people whose mature observation, personal experience and primitive philosophy have led them to postulate a central and ultimate power who is the originator of everything existing and in whose hands the universe is safe ; it is in sayings of these people that sometimes the figure of God assumes features of a truly personal and purely divine Supreme Being " (65).

(Obviously, in examining this passage, we have to disregard the distinction which Westermann essays to draw between the ideas of West Africa's thoughtful people about God and the ideas of West Africa's crowd about God, for the simple reason that it is illogical to separate a people's philosophers from the philosophy of that people. Every people have the philosophers they deserve. The philosophizing of the philosophers is, in fact, derived from the common ideas current among the people who are called the crowd.)

So far, then, in the above-quoted passage, the nature of God revealed to the reader is one of which no Christian need be ashamed : the Supreme Being as a personal God who rules the universe and is so distantly placed from mortal man that even some thinkers have described Him as " otiose " ; yet powerful

9

and awe-inspiring as the ultimate originator and creator, that people not only acknowledge Him, but entertain towards Him a " feeling of dim awe and reverence " as, above all, says Westermann, One *in* whom they *believe*.

The " Christian " and the " African " therefore share between them a Supreme Being of like nature. Except in one respect. And that respect, if Westermann's theories are accepted, is both vital and fatal for the African viewpoint.

The exceptional difference is found in the religious significance, to both the " Christian " and the " African," of the states of mind called awe, reverence, fear and love, and the activity called service or worship. In respect to these, Westermann suggests, the attitude of the African is different from that of the Christian.[1]

Now, by positing this difference, what Westermann seems to say is that whilst the Christian may be said to have or to entertain " fear for, or of, God," the African, although aware of this same God as creator and a spirit of power or might, has not, on his part, a fear of, or for, God. Only he reveres Him. The difference between fearing another and standing in awe of him is probably as potent as the difference between the gymnastic of high jump and long jump, and if that were so, credit might be accorded to Westermann's distinction. But the fact is the psychologists seem to say quite a different thing from what Dr. Westermann says concerning the relation between fear and awe.

What they say is that awe is a fusion of admiration with fear ; that reverence is awe blended with tender emotion ; that tender emotion is an essential constituent of the system of emotional dispositions called love which is a sentiment ; and that, in fact, the emotions that play a principal part in the religious or worshipful sentiment are admiration, awe and reverence. All this may be found authoritatively stated in W. McDougall's " Social Psychology," at pp. 123 and 302.

The total impression one gathers from reading McDougall is that awe is a better kind of fear, reverence the best kind ; that fear arises to the height of love when the ingredients of awe and reverence are dominant in it, and that it is when fear is transformed into awe and reverence that it begins to have any religious value.

In plain language, reverence and awe, even " dim awe," for God, are not, as Westermann holds, a sign that the person having

[1] Against the term " Christian " Westermann opposes only one term, " African " Religion. It did not seem to occur to him that the Christian religion had been, for generations, even before Rome became officially Christian, an African religion as well. The tendency for certain Europeans to think of Christianity as a European product is greatly to be regretted.

such feelings, be he African or Christian, does not fear God, nor
love, nor worship him, but that, on the contrary, in holding God
in awe and reverence, he is showing for God a tender emotion and
several other emotional dispositions which make up the sentiment
called love.

But Westermann would have none of this : The West Africans
to-day, he maintains, acknowledge God, " but neither fear, nor
love, nor serve him, the feeling towards him being, at the highest,
that of dim awe and reverence." Is this a West African dogma,
derived from an admitted attitude towards God, or merely a mistaken doctrine as to what the West African seems to feel and
know about God ?

Nor is this all. Westermann's further suggestion that any
human mind could come to acknowledge God as *the* truly personal and purely divine Supreme Being, a God whom " he finds
no difficulty in trusting " (95) and in whom he believes (64) but
whom he nevertheless does not love, nor fear nor worship is, to
say the least of it, quite impossible to swallow.

Could any man really meet death face to face and live ? Could
any man really know God and perish ? It is true that in ordinary
parlance we speak of some men as being without fear for God or
respect for man, but what we really intend to say in such cases is
that such men do not know, *i.e.*, do not acknowledge, the essential
beauties or values in either God or man. But to posit, as Westermann does, that some one has acknowledged God, and believed
in him and trusted him, can only mean one thing : that that
person accepts or has faith in God.

If Westermann is on the other hand right, that acknowledgment of God is possible without either fear or love of him, then
Calvin must be wrong when he states at p. 37 in volume one of
" Institutes of the Christian Religion " that he who knows God
" restrains himself from sin, not merely from a dread of vengeance,
but because he loves and reveres God as his Father, honours and
worships Him as his Lord, and, even though there were no hell,
would shudder at the thought of offending Him." Or probably
the reply of the Professor of African Languages and Cultures
would be that whilst what Calvin says might be true of the
Christian, it might be quite obviously untrue of the African or
West African in his feeling and knowledge of God. And this
would be tolerable only on the assumption that what the West
African takes to be God is not the knowable God. Which would
be quite contrary to all the facts. For it is known as a fact that,
from Augustine to Calvin, the nature of God to the Christian has
suffered and undergone more variation in value than has varied
the African's conception of God, be he acknowledged merely as

a Father and therefore Superior or Supreme of All, or as the Supreme Being because he had created the Thing, or the world of Being. But, perhaps, here, we are anticipating our main result.

5. "MY WILL BE DONE"

Leave, for the moment, the question whether the African is unable to know God emotionally although he is thoroughly acquainted with him intellectually, and ask the other question, namely, how near is the African to God ? Is God a reality and a near thing to the African's personal needs ?

Westermann's answer cannot be stated in two words, nor in one sense, for he often speaks with various voices. Thus, he states at p. 73 : " While fully admitting that, as a rule, God does not live in practical religion and that the ideas concerning Him are often nebulous, it cannot be overlooked that he is a reality to the African, who will admit that what he knows about God is the purest expression of his religious thinking and, in individual cases, also of his religious experience."

This God, about whom the African has some nebulous ideas, and who is a reality to the African, is also spoken of by Westermann as a remote and an indeterminate sort of God : " The African's God," he states, " is a *deus incertus* and a *deus remotus* ; there is always an atmosphere of indefiniteness about him " (74). " The Bible also speaks of a hidden God whose doings are inscrutable ; but the Christian's answer to the unanswerable questions in his life is : ' Nevertheless I am continually with thee ' ; he knows God to be *his* Father, and his conviction that all things work together for good to them that love God gives him the courage and freedom to say, ' Thy will be done.' Whereas the Alpha and Omega of a pagan's religious action and prayer is, ' My will be done,' and when this request is not fulfilled his religion has failed him " (74–75).

Which is to say, from beginning to end, the conviction of the pagan towards " the Supreme Being or personified power who, in a general sense, rules the world, maintains its order, and to whom man owes the essential institutions of his life as well as his cultural achievements "—from beginning to end, the pagan's feeling of dim awe and reverence towards this Supreme Being, even when he prays or religiously petitions to him, is of the nature of a spell, the instrument of magic.

The pagan, or the African (the two, to Westermann being one and the same), neither loves nor fears not worships this God-Creator in whom he believes, but he has the impudence, if I understand Westermann rightly, to put his magic spell on Him, requesting Deity to do his will, failing which, God is relegated to the background of forgotten " fetishes " as a useless Being on whom man has no profit in life. " ' My will be done,' O Deity and God-Creator, in whom I believe, and if it be not done, then so much the worse for Deity and so much the better for me," prays the pagan.

This, in effect, is what Westermann states to be the case, in the following passage : " It (the African's religion) cannot but fail him in relation to the Sky-God, for unlike the lesser deities and ancestors he cannot be moved to action by human effort ; he is absolutely sovereign ; and *this is the reason why* he is not approached in prayers and with gifts. He cannot be made subservient to man's wishes. Moreover his remoteness makes it impossible that personal confidence or personal relation of *any* kind should exist between him and man " (75).

In effect, says Westermann, the African is able, by means of some mysterious power as yet unknown to science, to move the ghost or spirit of his dead and deified ancestor and the lesser deities to action by a certain superior human effort, but when it comes to using this same effort in the direction of Deity the effort fails of utility. If that truly is the case God truly must be inscrutable not only to the African but to all who believe in Him. But has science any evidence why God should be unmovable by a pagan's prayer and petition ?

And if, indeed, the African has the power to achieve the tremendous effect of moving the ancestor, dead 150 years or so ago, to action by mere human effort, is he not justified in being impatient and indifferent to the intractable Sky-God ? Says Dr. Westermann : " How should he come to love a God who is not concerned with an individual man but with the *universe ?* " (75). How, indeed, could he, or could any one, for that matter ?

But this is to introduce another inscrutable ability of the African, his ability, namely, intellectually to apprehend God as one concerned not with an individual, but with the universe ! How, one may ask, did the African, in all his pagan simplicity, come to utter this terrific truth, the truth, namely, that God, as absolute Sovereign, or the Absolute, objectifies Himself in the whole, but is indifferent to the individual ? How did the African who only feels God dimly, come to give articulation to this great insight of a Kant or a Plato or a Hegel ? Are we really being just to the African when, although he happens not to inherit the same spiritual background as anthropological professors may possess, we ascribe to him attributes and qualities and names whose implications go far beyond what is psychologically possible for the human mind to attain ? Can the African, in the presence of a Deity concerned with the universe, have the freedom and courage to say, " My will be done ? " Who, then, is he, this African so supremely confident in the unlimited capacity of his own volition ? Can he be human, or like anything human we know of ?

6. THE AFRICAN'S FEAR AND HOPE AND THE MORAL OBLIGATION

Turn now from the knowledge of God in Himself to the cause of the obligation that man feels in relation to Him. Here, too, what Westermann takes to be the case is clearly put : " It is recognized (by the African) that the principles of good and evil are rooted in God, his will is that man should be good, and he hates evil-doings," but the African's assent to the moral demands of God " is no more than a platonic acknowledgment, it is not a sanction which guides him in his actions. Moral obligations are rooted in social bonds, not in God " (75–76).

That is to say, although the African, like John Calvin, is aware that God, his Creator, is one whom one might not offend without shuddering, yet when it comes to finding a reason for doing good, and avoiding evil, he altogether leaves God out of account, treats Him platonically, and rejects moral obligations as things in which the God in whom he recognizes that " the principles of good and evil are rooted," is not at all interested. The African, apparently, says in effect, " I know God expects me to be good, but I would do good irrespective of God."

Of course, it is by no means a bad thing, nor a disgraceful moral guide, to seek to do good whether God is interested or not. It promises to be certainly far better than the Roman's *video meliora proboque, deteriora sequor*, for it is a higher kind of morality which seeks to do good for its own sake, and not for the sake, or on account of, divine approbation, in the form of rewards and punishments or otherwise. The morality which is done to please can be very superficial sometimes. Milton gives quite a good example of this type of morality, which he called the " dividual movable," in the " Areopagitica." It was the story of a man who found religion to be a traffic so entangled, " and of so many piddling accounts, that . . . he cannot skill to keep a stock going upon that trade. . . . What does he, therefore, but resolves to give over toiling, and to find himself out some factor, to whose care and credit he may commit the whole managing of his religious affairs : some divine of note and estimation that must be. To him he adheres, resigns the whole warehouse of his religion, with all the locks and keys, into his custody ; and indeed makes the very person of that man his religion. . . . His religion comes home at night, prays, is liberally supped, and sumptuously laid to sleep ; rises, is saluted, and, after the malmsey, or some well-spiced bruage . . . his religion walks abroad at eight, and leaves his kind entertainer in the shop trading all day without his religion." [1] To such men, indeed, God has become a luxury, a *satis superque*. It were far better to leave God and religion out of account, and do good whether religious or Godly or not, than to hand it over to a factor or agent for his kind care.

All this, in the view of Westermann, is probably beside the point. According to him, the reason for the African seeking to be religious is not because he regards certain beings as deserving of worship or reverential regard, such as the ancestral Nana or the creative Nyame who is Father, but because " the belief in God is too weak a weapon in man's fight for life, and it is in this struggle that he needs religion. . . . Normally his attitude towards his visible and invisible environment is that of guarded caution, and sometimes one is under the impression that he is afraid, like a child in the dark. The enemies of life are many. . . . He is—not unlike European statesmen—engaged in a constant search for security and safety " (76).

This large theme, the proof of which is nowhere forthcoming, affords an equally large basis for Westermann to expand himself on the inefficiencies of the African in coherence of thought and action. He goes on : " It is no exaggeration to say that the African suffers from a constant feeling of insecurity . . . (79). Above all, there is the fear of death, ' the mother of all fears.' Life is the one great thing which matters. To preserve life is the real aim of religious practice. True, there is an existence after death, but it is *not* life, it is rather an object of fear, *never* of hope. There is also a belief in reincarnation, but it is far too vague to be a means of overcoming the horror of death. . . . The African negro is *not* heroically disposed. . . . The ideals which make it imperative or glorious to sacrifice one's life *do not* exist for him, nor is death the gate to a greater life, but rather the *end* of *all* things—how should he not be afraid of it ? " (80).

Precisely, one should say. For granting the premise that the African, like a child in the dark, is afraid of an existence after death, which he regards as a hopeless condition of non-life, how should he entertain anything but an unheroic horror for death ? Rattray speaks somewhere of the European's blood-thirsty fondness of life, clinging to it with all claws out in the certainty that what comes after cessation of life is not worth having. But can we really get at the truth of human anthropology by calling each other names ? Is it a worthy thing to suggest of the African that

---

[1] " Areopagitica," 55. Quoted by Mackenzie, " Ethics," p. 357.

his fear for the future—of the after-life—paralyses his courage and his hope ?

But, again, Westermann states : " It would be wrong to look at the African as nothing but a victim of fear, whose philosophy ends in idle resignation. On the contrary, he has always fought against his foes and has never lost hope or courage. . . . Nor has he been unsuccessful in his endless fight. . . . They gave him that strength of body, intellectual mobility and a degree of self-assurance which made the Negro a virile race " (81).

If then the African has hope and does not resign himself to the consequence of the so-called inevitable hopelessness of the after-death condition, and if the African has not been unsuccessful in his fight, are we justified in saying of him that in his attitude to good doing and not the contrary, he leaves God out of count ?

Indeed, one feels driven to utter exasperation in a search for reconciliation of the different things Westermann sees fit to say of the African in one purposeful breath, now this, and then that ! We are told by Westermann that the West African does not love God because He is not concerned with an individual man but only with the universe, but it is Westermann also who states of the West African :

" To the African the supernatural and the invisible are *realities* as genuine as things which he can see and grasp. He finds no difficulty in *trusting* in a God whose presence he can experience only by belief. He feels no need to see him, be it only in the form of an idol or some other symbol. The idea of a mediator between God and man is not foreign to him. The West African nature gods are said to be children or servants of God, sent by him as his representatives in human form ; they can be seen, whether in the natural phenomenon or in a symbol placed in their shrine, and so it is easier for man to approach them with offerings and prayer than the invisible high-god. It is true that the prayers are concerned with only material welfare and their form is conventional, but nevertheless they are *sincere* and there is *true devotion* in them " (95–96).

Westermann has made a life study of the African and has carved of him for the European mind a certain portrait in stone, and I see the problem this way : it helps no one to carve a black portrait of the African heart if that heart is indeed white. (The search in anthropology is for truth, not for what is false, and if the vision of what one sees is false, it were better left unsaid than to blur the perspective of a true light on truth.)

Indeed, there are glimmerings and vivid lights of great brightness in Westermann's Duff Lectures, but there is also a be-clouding of the true vision, resting upon a nebulous tradition which, for centuries, had elected to look upon the African as a being with a " mind " the direct opposite of what Europe, through untold years of struggle with the Hebrew mind and the Dark Ages and the Reformation or Renaissance and the reactionary consequences of modern times, had only just dimly discovered for herself. And it would appear to some Europeans strange and probably " undesirable " that what had taken modern Europe some 2,500 years to discover or achieve in the knowability of God could have been discovered or achieved independently by the African without waiting for others from abroad to bring him the new gospel and teach him the right knowledge of God. It seems quite an impossible proposition for certain European writers to accept that just as the Hebrews, unaided by modern Europe and Rome and Greece, were able to discover for themselves all the God that there was and could be, so, too, even though the African had not Moses and the prophets, he was able to discover for himself all the God that there was or could be, gradually coming upon that discovery in the quietude of the dark recesses behind the Sahara oases and dunes, undisturbed by the busy bickerings of the nations east and west of Suez !

7. MUST THE MISSIONARY BE RUTHLESS?

The jealous nature of God demands that there should be no other Gods before the true God. But this need not mean that there should be aggression of God against God, jealousy going mad even in the camp of the one true God. But, unless I wrongly interpret Westermann, that is just what he admonishes the Christian missionary to do, although, in other parts of his book, the author of the Duff Lectures would appear to suggest that the missionary had better leave the African's God alone !

Westermann says : " However anxious a missionary may be to appreciate and to retain indigenous social and moral values, in the case of religion he has to be ruthless . . . he has to admit and even to emphasize that the religion he teaches is opposed to the existing one and the one has to cede to the other " (94).

But, as against this totalitarian admonition to ruthlessness in Africa, Westermann admonishes the missionary that " it is not his business to prescribe in detail the forms of Christian community life " (103) because, apparently, Christianity has nothing new to teach the African in the matter of " fellowship with others in mutual service " (102), because in that the African with his altruism, his rooting of the religious obligation in social bonds and not in the will of an external uninterested spectator, seems to lead the " Christian " quite a long way ahead in good doing, for its own sake. " Christianity," says Westermann, " is inseparably bound to the Church, the *ekklesia*, that is ' the gathering.' Here we have one of the most important and most far-reaching points of contact between the indigenous and the new Christian form of religious life : both are eminently social. African religion finds expression in social forms. There is personal devotion and there are religious acts of personal character, but religion as an institution is social and serves social purposes ; the performance of religious rites is a matter of the group headed by its spiritual leader. It is exactly the same in the Christian Church. . . . Christian communities (in Africa) are sometimes weak and show a lack of cohesion, because they are new and are not governed by those stern sanctions which maintain a group based on community of blood and soil : it is therefore all the more indispensable for them to seek contact with those binding forces on which African life has rested in the past and to let them find a new life in the Church " (103).

But, if so ; if, that is, there is something indigenous in African religion which has successfully cemented his social life in the effort to produce harmony, why first be ruthless with it and then later rebuild ? Not that there is any suggestion that the African is himself incapable of maintaining the old against the new, but for the interference of those whose business is not, says Westermann, to prescribe in detail the forms of Christian life desirable in Africa. Says Westermann himself : " Native religion has not disappeared ; it may even in some of its features rally new forces under the pressure of modern conditions, but the destructive powers have become too formidable for it to fulfil its functions as a life-giving factor. Christian missions are partly responsible for this destruction " (94). Is it wise then to admonish them to continue with their ruthless aggression ?

CHAPTER III

THE POSITIVE DOCTRINE

I. WESTERMANN'S CONTRIBUTION

PASSING now from criticism to constructive statement, we find Westermann quite at home with the African, as near as may be, in his statement of what the much spoken of, but little known, African " religion " really is in its African habitat. It is here that we find Westermann's work of the greatest value in the approach to the true Akan doctrine of God. That doctrine, if we follow the teaching of Westermann closely, would appear to be, indeed, not alone Akan, but truly *African* in at least the geographical sense of the word, for it pervades and permeates a large part of Africa, as indeed Edwin Smith and Cullen Young have also discovered in East Africa. That doctrine, simply stated, is the cult of God as the Great Ancestor, with all other ancestors in between as the Mediators. God, says the doctrine, is the Father of all diverse men of one blood, and the good chief of the tribe is exemplar of the chief good.

The originalness of this conception with the African may not be accepted by the world of the learned unless stated in its most primitive form, and I think it better to do so in the words of Westermann :

" A cult of the dead is found throughout Africa . . . the worship of ancestors may evolve in the same direction " (assuming features of a high-god) ; " the terms *Mukuru* and *Unkulunkulu*, which in South Africa designate the high-god or sky-god, mean literally the ' old one,' that is the ancestor or original founder of the social group, whose Mana is still present in his descendants, in particular in the *leader* of the group, and who is not only the *national hero* but also the ever-existing protector of all his children. Other names for the high-god, such as *Muzimu*, *Modimo*, *Mulungu*, mean the spirit of a dead person, the term being in a special sense applied to the spirit of *the first ancestor* who is held in reverential esteem, or it may express all the ancestors of the group as a collective spiritual whole, which is at the same time an agglomeration of Mana by which the life of the present generation is over-shadowed. Many tribes make a significant distinction between a true high-god (sky-god or sun-god) and a high-god who is really an ancestor or the first man : the former create men and animals, while the ancestor gods cause men and animals to come forth out of something already created, a tree, a rock, water, or reed. And, on the other hand, the idea of a tribal or clan ancestor is so closely bound up with the ancestor high-god that *the living chief*, as his earthly representative may be identified with him " (92–93).

This statement of doctrine is based on facts available to Westermann from a study in South Africa. Readers of Rattray will be aware that the names *Mukuru, Unkulunkulu, Muzimu Modimo,* and *Mulungu* have their equivalents in the Akan *Nyame, Nyankopon* and *Nana,* and that in meaning or intention—*e.g.,* the living chief or the *Nana* or leader or national hero, looked upon as the earthly representative of the ancestor high-god, or the spirit of the first ancestor—the similar terms in Akanland bear the same values as in South Africa. We shall return to this theme presently.

It behoves us here to emphasize that in the above statement of doctrine we are brought close to the scene as partakers and spectators of an emergence or movement which is the genesis of all the highest religions, except perhaps the Moslem. We see arising among the African, tucked away from the world east and west of Suez beyond the Sahara, the conception of God as father, the " old one," the first man, the ancestor, the creator of the family, the tribe, the race of man, and, indeed, of all things, or as the phrase goes in Akanland, Creator of the Thing, the universe of being. As we shall have occasion to discover for ourselves later, no doctrine of the true God is a true doctrine which gives him qualities adverse to the qualities which a good and original father should have. Hence we make exception of the Moslem doctrine because whilst it elects to call God a Sultan it denies to him the name of Father, thereby cutting man off from the Divine Head ; from all kinship with Him in blood or spirit or breath. To this, too, we shall have occasion to return as the argument develops.

2. THE FATHER-GOD IS NOT A MANA

In his statement of the African doctrine of God, or the Father-God, Westermann suggests that the spirit of the " old one " still present in his descendants is a manifestation of Mana, and that the spirit of the highest ancestor or of the agglomeration of ancestors is also an agglomeration of Mana. I consider it necessary that the incrustation of Mana in the mind of anthropologists should not be allowed to complicate the African idea of the ancestral spirit, lest it lead to a confusion of thought and to undesirable misunderstanding.

The term " Mana " is a Melanesian idea. In its original·form as translated from Oceania to Europe by Bishop Codrington, it implied some supersensual power or influence which is not itself personal though dwelling in persons and in things. " You find a stone of an unusual shape ; it may resemble some familiar object like a fruit ; you lay it at the root of the corresponding tree, or you bury it in a yam-patch ; an abundant crop follows ; clearly, the stone has *mana*." [1] But, says Carpenter, the *mulungu* of the Yaos, east of Lake Nyassa, is dissimilar. It is a widespread term in the eastern group of Bantu tongues, " and is said to have the meaning of ' Old One ' or ' Great One ' ; and in this sense it has been employed as the equivalent to God." [2] It does not imply personality, but " sums up at once the creative energy which made the earth and animals and man, and the powers which operate in human life. . . . It is sometimes dimly conceived as a spirit within ; sometimes regarded as a universal agency in nature and affairs, impalpable, impersonal ; sometimes rising into distinctness as God." [2]

We feel entitled to conclude upon this evidence that we go slightly wrong when we speak of the ancestral spirit as a manifestation of " Mana." In the African, and the West African or Akan sense, the ancestral spirit is essentially a creative energy, a soul if you wish, and can often impress us as an over-soul, the " Old One " or the " Great One " of Being. Anything, according to the Melanesian idea, may have a manifestation of *mana*, but, according to the African idea, all things have one (creative) *mulungu*. At any rate, in Akan conception, the *Okara* (or *'Kra*) which links one being to another in Nyame, is only possessed by human spirits, or spirits who can bear or realize intelligence. It has nothing of the character of *mana*.

3. WHY THE FATHER IS GOD

Let us now put two and two together and obtain a summary. Rattray says : " The predominant influences in the Ashanti religion . . . are the Asamanfo, the spirits of the departed forebears of the clan." And Westermann says " The terms . . . which designate the high-god or sky-god, mean literally the ' old one,' that is the ancestor or original founder of the social group . . . the spirit of a dead person . . . the spirit of the ancestor who is held in reverential esteem . . . a true high-god who is really an ancestor of the first man. . . . And, on the other hand, the ideal of a tribal or clan ancestor is so closely bound up with the ancestor high-god that the living chief, as his earthly representative, may be identified with him . . . ancestor high-gods (who) cause men and animals to come forth out of something already created, a tree, a rock, water, or reed . . . whose Mana is still present in his descendants, in particular in the leader of the group, and who is not only the national hero but also the ever-existing protector of all his children."

This God the Akan call *Nyame* (the " Shining One "), or *Nana*

[1] Carpenter, " Comparative Religion," p. 80.
[2] Carpenter, *op. cit.*, p. 82.

Nyankopon ("Grandfather 'Nyame' who alone is the Great One "), ancestor of the first Akan, the primordial ancestor, or of all ancestors in one supreme idea, head and cause of the family, who are his grandchildren. In its highest form, he is the Final Ancestor, the Creator of the First Progenitor, who made all diverse Akans of one blood, the True High-God.

This Nyame lives in the social group and operates as the beneficent ancestor through his representative or exemplar, the head or chief of the family, the judge, hero or prince of the ancestor's people, the *opanyin* or elder who, living in the manner of Nyame, is called a *Nana*, grandfather, in his life or in death, the ideal of the beneficent life of the group.

Among Gold Coast tribes the term *Nana* is so bandied about in all forms as titles or appellations of persons, that its intrinsic value is often swamped. *Nana* is probably best derived from *e-na*, mother, grand-mother being *e-na*'s *e-na*, that is *nana* (there being no apostrophe " 's " in Akan), and it means literally begetter, root, seed, producer. The patriarch of the family is *nana*, the Paramount Chief of the State is *nana*, the grandchild named after the " old one " is *nana*, male or female. Among the Ga the male form is *Nil* or *Nini*, *Nana* or *Naa* being reserved for the female. Among the Ga-Adangme the form is *Nene* or *Nee*. And all the tribes call God by the same designation : *Ataa Naa Nyonmo*, " Old One Grandfather 'Nyonmo " (Ga), and *Nana Nyankopon*, " Grandfather Nyankopon " as aforesaid. In fine, the Akan or Gold Coast Nana, begetter, root, seed, who is head of the head, the Ultimate Ancestor of the contemporary ancestors, has the same signification as the like terms among the South and East African Bantu, as discovered by Westermann, Edwin Smith and Cullen Young.

We venture the view, therefore, that taking Africa south of the Sahara in a bulk, in the manner of the anthropologists, the ancestral idea holds a predominant place in African religious thought, and the African who declares the father or the high-father as God or the High-God, would probably lead the way when all mankind comes to recognize that the revelation, through Paul, that God made all men of one blood, and therefore all men are of one family, is not a doctrine for mere lip-service, but an actual living principle of the possibility of one human harmony of life, that all men *are* one family, and can only see God or be like God when they live as members all of one body, descendants of one Great Ancestor.

This God, in the language of Westermann, is, furthermore, the social centre of African life. He is the Alpha and Omega of that experience, and his omnipotence is conditioned by the fact that he is the Great Ancestor of that life and its participants. Social obligation is rooted in him because he is the head of that society, the " Old One," or, as the old people of Sumer and Akkad would say, the " old Anu, father of the Gods " ; the gods here being the deified partriarchs and kings in whose descendants operate

PLATE II

NYAME NWU NA M'AWU (or NYAME BEWU NA M'AWU) (" Could God die, I would die "). The name of " a small inextirpable trailing plant " (Christaller).
The plant is Commelina Nudiflora or Benghalensis.

the stern sanctions and binding regimentations of blood and soil. This God is truly father, and men, in all things, are his children, because He created them.

4. THE FATHER'S ''OMNIPOTENCE''

The conclusion in the last paragraph, which is simple enough in all conscience to assent to, holds, however, consequences which may not so easily obtain universal assent. Is the high-father omnipotent ? Or, put the other way about, are all men omnipotent ?

The antithesis, perhaps, admits of a simple solution : If all men are not omnipotent it is because all men are not the creator.

23

But solution of the thesis itself is not so easily forthcoming. Is the high-father omnipotent ? It was assented to in the last paragraph of Section 3 that the omnipotence of the high-father is conditioned by the fact that he is the great ancestor or begetter of the life of the community and of those who participate in it. This ought to afford a solution which is final, but the prevailing popular conception in Western Europe is that the high-father or the High One is Absolute Omnipotence, a monarch absolute in his own right. The Moslems also look upon him as a great sultan, external to his own creation, standing over against the will of the faithful and poor creatures, and commanding them to do his will irrespective of the conditions operative in the living society of created mankind.

It is obvious that such a conception would be entirely foreign to the " African " or Akan idea of an ancestral creator, and would leave quite a lot of suffering and inequalities in man's society absolutely unexplained. The Akan idea is of an ancestral creator and head of the very real and near community, continuous with the past, present and the future of his relations of blood. The omnipotence of the high-father cannot be greater than the reality of this community. A father, of necessity, is of what all his children are. Otherwise tradition is of no intrinsic value. The claims of the past must be at least as real as the hopes of the future—the " bliss " we wish to attain.

Everything would seem to depend on whether we consider *Nyame* or the Supreme Being to be father or not father. In several of the divine conceptions from the Near East and, more pronouncedly, in the Moslem form, the fatherhood of Nyame is a late development, or, to be exact, in Islam God is denied the function of fatherhood altogether. Of the ninety-nine names traditionally given to God or Allah in the Koran, not one is Father. A Moslem poem speaks of God as

> " God alone, not begotten,
> For he begets not."

In other words, apart from there being no one before God, there is also no one after him ; he can own no one as his son, nor any people as his children. His obedient subjects are all, after the pattern of a sultan and his slaves, to be ordered about according to his supreme will.

The consequence of this unconditioned omnipotence is an ideal of life in which submission of the self to the external will is an imperative demanding complete self-surrender and annihilation of the individual's self. Here, the humble and the meek and the lowly enjoy exclusive exaltation and blessedness as against, for example, the Grecian pride of self, the Akan exaltation of the family as above all supreme, the dignity of the head of this family, called *opanyin* or Nana, the unqualified loyalty to the clan, the country, " the honour of a name, the glory of a tradition." All this is summed up in the old, old Akan saying : *Animguase mfata Okanni-ba*, " A thing of dishonour befits not the Akan." Dishonourable conduct is a cap the Akan would not wear. At all times, the Akan, or son of the Akan, is expected to maintain the dignity of the traditional Akan.

This is not self-pride, the kind that " goeth before a fall." It is the far greater thing, the honour and the dignity which consider the greater self—the family, the community (of whatever size)— as standing for a value in itself so noble as to deserve the name divine. Lowly submission of the self to external power in prejudice to family or community honour, is a sacrifice of the greatest experience of human life, man's possibility of divine nobility.

If there is divine pride, this is the Akan version, and it accords his tradition and race a religious value which is to take a possession of divinity, a value akin to God.

5. THE ABSOLUTE AND MAN'S EXPERIENCE OF FREEDOM

Granted, as the Moslems sing, that God should be God alone, or Alone God, classical Monotheism or Absolutism would go a little wrong were it to force on the paternal nature of God this " aloneness " to the final extent of loneliness or solitude. God and man, in the Akan, as in other doctrines, do not stand apart like the moon and the tides, the one doing the will of the other, irrespective of the conditions of a moral and religious life, a life which in man is not only social and elevated but is also profoundly material. God and man are for ever linked, in a relationship that is communal from its first beginnings at a lower level of which we sometimes do not like to be reminded, up towards the subsequent elevation to which it can rise, and has indeed risen.

But complete absolutism, as familiar to us in certain Northern and Eastern doctrines, places God and man at times in a polarity of subject and object, or in the old Akan terminology, *owura* and *akoa*, master and slave ; to such an extent that some detractors of Christianity have dared to call it a slave religion, solely because they have been told of, or they have elected to see, God as supremely omnipotent and not as above all a Father.

Climate probably has a lot to do with this fashioning of doctrines. All conditions of life contribute to man's native way of thinking. The Northern idea is centred in the cold and spiritually snow-covered and bleak arctic, where everything is pure and white and quiet, and life itself seems at its best when most bereft of converse, and is lived in the manner of the ideal man of that doctrine, the secluded saint.

In contrast is the Akan idea, wherein we feel the warm coloured south with its luxuriant green and yellow foliage, the blue sky abounding with sunshine, the blue sea reflecting this sunshine, the seasons tinctured with variant hues, the vivifying complexity of life's panorama presenting a scheme of variegated colours from which the true and azure colour of the good, the true blue, is to arise. Here, in the south, active good doing, the give and take of beneficence, and not any one-sided activity of charity or grace, is that by which the balance of harmony is maintained. In the north, the good is ever at par with itself, and the striving to produce and maintain a satisfactory moral order is frigidly unnecessary, for the good is given. Here, in the south, there is need for continual striving to keep the good from putrefaction or deterioration. The great heat of the sun and the great humidity of the dark tropic nights between them make this life one of continuous unbalance, requiring daily attention in contact and in converse with the men of the family, the insurance of the communal life. Hibernation in such a life is virtually impossible, and any one who in the pursuit of sainthood through seclusion cuts off the world from contact with him, would find the south conditions supremely unfitted for the realization of his aims. To keep the good fresh in the south, continual adhesions of strength and vigour must be forthcoming, and the warm conquests, which accompany the effort, increase the zest in life's struggle, even a hundredfold.

The difference, which indeed there is, lies in this : The quiescent and blissful life is preferred by those who prefer it because those who enter into it happen to be saved, or are chosen by grace. The southern life is avoided by the saint because, to him, it is that from which he is to be saved.

Now, the acquisition of grace which is not earned, but is conferred, is itself charitable, and charity is its measure. Deny this as much as they will, Christian apologists must agree that Calvin spoke a profound truth for the Christian doctrine when he said : "Whom God passes by He reprobates, and from no other cause than His determination to exclude them." [1]

This, if true of the true God, would be the most terrific fate fore-ordained for mankind. One can only hope that Calvin over-states the case, and that quite a number of those chosen, from the number called, will comprise the majority of good men. The Akan way is to set up an *obra* or *abrabo* (ethical life) not for a chosen individual only, but for the universe of the blood. In this

[1] Quoted by Hobhouse, "Morals in Evolution," p. 502.

26

other form of choice, salvation is meaningless, for goodness is an acquisition, not a gift. It is earned by each individual's own *obra* or manner of life, and not by the favour he obtains by uncensored grace.

God, in the Akan sense, is Himself at the centre of experience, is Himself Experience, in the sense that F. H. Bradley frequently used the term. But this Experience can also be an Absolute in a sense that Bradley did not probably intend, namely, the Interminable Being—interminable for as long as there could be any being in being (End), and as from the time (if conceivable), any being was in being (Cause).

In this way, and in this only, can we hope to resolve the difficult poser presented to us in our Akan saying :

> " He went far away ;
> He went long ago ;
> He went before any one came.
> Which of them is the eldest ? " (Maxim 1730).

Which is the beginning, which the end, and which the new or old ? The There, the Then and the Now-There, which of them is the eldest ?

The solution is that in a Father-Ancestor-Creator you need not go a-searching for the young, and the aged, and the eldest, for a father cannot be other than the continuous being of his son, looked at from the production end, nor can a son be other than the continuous being of his father, looked at from the produced end. The one's omnipotence is necessarily conditioned by the other's limitation, and *vice versa*.

And, seriously talking of omnipotence, would not a truly omnipotent being be a fearful thing to live with, not to speak of serving, and also of loving him ? Only a terrific damnation or a terrific bliss can be the portion of those who come within the vortex of such a potency, and the will of any so elect could never count for anything. Nothing that they willed could ever be executed unless it was by the potency also willed.

That cannot be the true nature of God. We must presume God as assuring a far greater measure of freedom to men. Otherwise men become little else than the tides, to ebb or to flow at the potent mercy of a power independent and outside of this ocean, the vast ocean of humanity.

6. SUMMARY VIEW OF THE DOCTRINE

Akan knowledge of God teaches that he is the Great Ancestor. He is a true high God and manlike ancestor of the first man. As such ancestor He deserves to be worshipped, and is worshipped in the visible ancestral head, the good chief of the community (of whatever size). All ancestors who are honoured as such are in the line of the Great Ancestor. Every head of a community, because he is in such line, must live according to the dignity of the first. To fall below that dignity is a falling below the dignity of God. The elder or head of the family is the nearest of such ancestors.

He is called Nana, as even God, the first ancestor, is called Nana. The Chief of the tribe, race or nation is called Nana even as he is in the footsteps of the Great Ancestor. Ancestors do not live for ever ; they die and are honoured and deified for having lived in the dignity of the Great Ancestor. The deification makes them worshipful, even as the Great Ancestor is worshipful.

The Great Ancestor is the great father, and all men of the blood of that ancestor are of Him, and are of one blood with all other men created of His blood and breath. Life, human life, is one continuous blood, from the originating blood of the Great Source of that blood. The continuance of that blood in the continuance of the community is the greatest single factor of existence. It is an idea worshipful in itself, and the purpose of *community* is that the value of that life should be continuously kept abreast of the dignity of the ancestor. Anything short of that ideal makes life a degradation, a contradiction of what men of the ancestral blood, one in the Great Ancestor, should be inspired by.

Apprehension of the Great Ancestor is a definite community act and results in a singular name for the being of the ancestor. He is called Nyame, or Onyame, the " Shining One." And as He grows to be worshipped and to be intimately known He is called Nyankopon, or Onyankopon, in comparison with other competitors, and distinguished as the Greater " Shining One." He created things, the *Oboo-adee*, or *Boadee*. The community is of Him, the entirety of it. He is " *Borebore a aboo Adee*," the great builder or excavator, who created the Thing ; the Odomankoma, the creator *par excellence*, beyond whom there is nothing, the Supreme of the Thing, of all that is in being.

This singular and eternal ancestor and creator has therefore three names under which He is objectified in the life of the community, Nyame, Nyankopon, and Odomankoma. He is, like the human being, objectified in the community in relation to the Nana. The human being is an *Okara*, Soul, with an *Nkra* (" Intelligence " or Nous), who looks to the head of the race, the *Nana* (The Mediator), to take him to Nyame, on the way, *obara*, of God. The way of the ancestor is the way of the *okara*, of each and every *okara*, and the exemplar for that way to God, to the ancestor, is the visible ancestor, the *Nana*.

The rest of this book will be devoted to an analysis of how this apprehension of God came about, and where it is likely to lead the race, whether to perish within itself or to expand within the community of all men of the like blood, creation of the Great Architect, the first and ultimate father. *Onyame, Onyankopon* and *Odomankoma* on the one hand, and *Okara, Nkra* and *Nana* on the other. What are the postulates to justify their truth ?

SECTION TWO

THE AKAN MEANING OF GOD

CHAPTER I

ONYAME, THE AKAN DEITY

I. IN WHAT SENSE A "SKY"-GOD

THE most used name of God in Akanland is Onyame, often pronounced Nyame, and modern anthropologists say He is a "sky" God. I feel convinced from internal evidence that the appellation is misleading and does little credit to Nyame Himself.

As already noticed, the Akan designate the Supreme Being by three distinctive names, Onyame, Onyankopon and Odomankoma. Onyame, we shall show presently, corresponds to the basic idea of Deity as commonly understood in Christian theology. Next is Onyankopon, who is more appropriately described as Supreme Being or Supreme Deity in the sense of a personal religious God. The third, Odomankoma, corresponds to a conception of the Godhead as the Interminable or Infinite Being.

Common to each of these is the appellation of *Boadee* (*Booadee*), Creator, and specifically to Odomankoma is that of *Borebore*, Excavator, Hewer, Carver, Creator, Originator, Inventor, Architect. Each of the three names of God is recognized as possessing certain qualities characteristic of its function. One of the best known of such qualities is that of Onyankopon who is called *Kwaame*, or *Kwaamen*, that is, "He whose day (of birth, or of worship) is Saturday." It is for this reason, namely, that the day of birth of Onyankopon is known, that under this name He is made the object of religious adoration to a far greater extent than either Onyame or Odomankoma.

Now, until anthropologists left Europe to study "native" races the idea of a "sky"-God was not commonly associated with the Supreme Deity. He was, to them, either the God of Heaven or the Celestial Godhead, or in Milton, plain Celestial. But, for one reason or other, it has become the fashion to designate the high-gods of "native" races as "sky" Gods, and one's admiration cannot but be stirred by the studied insistence to dissociate the Akan Onyame from "heaven," keeping him pinned, as far as bearable, to the rather funny idea of "sky."

There was, of course, some justification for this linguistic acrobatic to jump one godhead over the other in precedence within the firmament. According to Rattray, he was told that

Onyame was " some power usually considered non-anthropo-morphic which has its abode in the sky " ; that Onyame was derived from *onya*, to get, and *mee*, to be full, satiated ; that " long, long ago Onyame lived on earth, or at least was very near to us, and not then high up in the sky, and that it was much later that ' he took himself away up in the sky.' " [1]

In other words, Onyame was not, or of, the sky. Originally he was some one staying on the earth, or near the earth, who later acquired new quarters in the sky, like some of the Greek gods did. Before the Akan God acquired this new domicile his name or nature was, according to Rattray's guides, that of giving satiation or satisfaction. (It should be noted that I do not subscribe to the interpretation of the word *Onyame* to be derived from *onya*, to get, and *mee*, to be full, satiated. *Onya* does not mean " to get " ; it means " he gets." *Nya* is the infinitive form, " to get." For the purpose of argument, however, it seems convenient to work with Rattray's own premises.)

I believe it ought to have struck Rattray that if indeed the Akan had wished to look upon Onyame as " sky "-God, they would have changed his name as soon as he changed his domicile from the earth to the sky. But apparently they did not think the change of domicile made any difference to the nature of Nyame, for whether he lived on earth or in the sky, he was known to the Akan as Onyame, and remained to them as such.

It follows that, to the Akan mind, the fact that Onyame, for some reason unstated, was elevated to the sky, did not thereby cause his native quality to be altered. The Akan people appear to have looked at the matter this way : If a hunter, living in a mud hut with his family, subsequently changed the form of his dwelling and went to live in a grass house, or a glass house, he would not thereby have exchanged his trade to acquire a new name or characteristic. He would still remain to his fellow-men the hunter, or the ex-hunter, who now lives in a grass house or glass house. But no one would think of calling him grass or glass hunter, for it would be meaningless in the context.

So, too, I think, the designation of the Akan Nyame by the term " Sky " God is meaningless, solely upon the evidence that He had left the earth and gone to live in the sky.

Indeed, if Rattray and the other anthropologists were looking about for a proprietary character to distinguish the Akan Onyame from the other types of Akan gods, they could not have done better, with the information at their disposal, than to have called him the " Satiation or Satisfaction God," following the supposed etymology of the name given Rattray by the " natives."

[1] " Ashanti Proverbs," pp. 18, 19 and 20.

31

But this was not to be. From now on, and to the very last, the Akan Onyame (as also Onyankopon), became to the anthropologists not " God of Satisfaction," or " Repletion," but " Sky " God. And thus was the mental horizon of European students of the Akan religion definitely " set " for them by the limitations they had chosen to impose on the workings of their own minds. The fixed firmament, possibly only the near-side of it, became for these students the limit of the horizon the Akan could be supposed to have reached in their search for Godhead. Is it any wonder, then, if students of Akan thought were progressively hindered in their effort to *understand* what the Akan were thinking about most of the time when they talked about God—Onyame ? What these anthropologists and scientists did was, of course, to create confusion for themselves and others, for first they caused a mis-understanding and then called it learning, which is not a bad parody of the aggressor's conception of a new order : to make a solitude and call it peace.

It would not matter much to the Akan were such learned mis-understanding to be confined to field anthropologists, but, as in this case, the " Sky " God idea became so widespread that even the great Marett, of Oxford, after critically reading Rattray's " Religion and Art in Ashanti," and writing a treatise upon it, and after acknowledging that the Akan conception of Supreme Being was that of a *living* God, maintained, nevertheless, in addi-tion, that to the Ashanti or Akan, God was a " Sky " God : Whereas, in truth and in fact, a God cannot be a " living " God if He lives in the sky.

2. SOME FALSE MEANINGS OF ''NYAME''

A similar fusion of incompatible ideas would seem to have led Dr. M. J. Field in her " Religion and Medicine of the Ga People " (p. 61), published in 1937, to follow Rattray's style and describe *Nyonmo*, the Supreme Being of the Ga people, as " certainly . . . a sky-god " because in the Ga language " the word Nyonmo means rain. The only way of saying that it is raining is to say that Nyonmo is falling." In the major part of her book the Ga Nyonmo therefore remained sky-god and rarely a rain-God. Which, one must think, is a peculiar way of interpreting a people one is supposed to know to others who are not supposed to know them.

Probably Dr. Field is better justified in her interpretation than the anthropologists of the Twi or Akan people. For she, at least, gives the Ga word for rain, which looks like being the same as the word for the Supreme Being, or what she elsewhere calls " Nature." The Akan anthropologists do not quite do the same thing.

All the same, Dr. Field is not less wrong than any others in calling a Gold Coast God a " sky " God, even on the evidence of the similarity of the names for rain and for God. Mr. E. A. Ammah, of Accra, a poet of the Ga race and an authority on the language, has explained to me personally that the term *Nyon* in Nyonmo does not mean rain. *Nyon* is found in other compounds where it appears to mean bright, light, shine, day, or the firmament. *Mo* is the Ga suffix for person acting or doing. Thus *Nyonmo* (God) possibly means " The Master of Light " or " The Actor of Light," etc. Other words in the Ga language using *Nyon* in the sense of light or brightness are *nyon-tsele*, " moon," *nyonten*, midnight. Mr. Ammah adds that the Ga word for rain is best written without the middle " *n* " or " *ng*," *nyomo* and not *nyonmo*, the first " *o*," of course, being the broad " *o*," as " *oa* " in *broad*, and not the " *o* " in " *told*." For the benefit of the research student it may be useful to add that the " *tsele* " in *nyontsele* means " brightening up " ; *tse* often means *neat*. (*Ehe ntse*, he is neat, holy, or attractive) ; also the " *ten* " or " *teng* " in *nyonten* means " the middle of." So that *nyontsele* primitively meant, probably, " Nyon is brightening up," and *nyonten* also meant " The middle period of Nyon," whatever Nyon may mean. In any case, there is here evidence which points to the conclusion that the " Nyon " in *Nyonmo* belongs to a certain fundamental general idea covering all the elemental changes in the firmament, and not alone concerned with rain. If we may venture an opinion, it would be that the *Nyon* in these words refers to the firmament as a place associated with the " Shining One."

As regards the Akan Onyame, it may be useful to note first that the principal syllables are or are nearly the same as in the Ga, and the primitive consonants are much the same, NYNM. Students of other African languages, east and west, would discover other similarities in the different tribal names of God. Some of the East African tribes, according to Edwin Smith, call God Nyambi or Nzambi, and we are taught in philology that *b*, *m* and *n*, as also *y* and *z*, often assimilate. Moreover, Father Williams, S.J., in his " Hebrewisms of West Africa," has suggested that the *M* in the Akan Nyame is the old *W* in the Hebrew Jahweh, and Dr. Field has further suggested a certain similarity between the Ga Nyonmo and the Hebrew Jahveh ; Captain Rattray also, we recall, made the same suggestion concerning the Ashanti Nyame, that He is the Jehovah (Jahweh) of the Israelites. Dr. Williams' view, in fact, is that the Hebrew Tetragrammaton is no other than these African names of God : JHWH, NZMB, NYNM. But this is probably a problem best left to the philologists.

As regards Onyame, we may note, in the second place, that

Rattray and others were ignorantly following the "man in the street" interpretation when they said that Nyame meant the "Sky" God. There is no doubt that in poetry and other language the sky is often referred to as the *onyame*, but the Akan name for sky, as such, is not *onyame* or *nyame*, but *ewie* or *ewim*, which is clearly so stated in Christaller's "Dictionary," 2nd edition, p. 576. The word *ewim* is obviously from *owia mu*, "in, or, at the place of the sun," *owia* being the ordinary word for sun. Literally, *ewim* means "Where the sun reigns." There is another word, *ewie*, which means "the overhanging firmament," and it or *ewim* usually means the air, atmosphere, heaven (Christaller).

Ordinarily, the Akan word for the upper part or parts, or any space above, is *osoro*, which, at p. 472 of Christaller, is given to mean the upper world, what is above, upper regions, sky, heaven. Throughout his edition of the great Twi Bible never does Christaller use the word *onyame* as meaning heaven or sky. At all times he translated heaven by the word *osoro*, *e.g.*, the angels are called *osoro-abofo*, messengers of heaven.

As already noted, the word *onyame* is used in poetry and the maxims metaphorically to mean the upper parts, heaven, even the clouds, as of rain, but not to such an extent as to lead a scientific investigator to identify the God-idea with the sky-idea exclusively. The whole effort is a sad story.

It is well known that for nearly 2,000 years at least, and for 4,000 years at least, among the Europeans and the Hebrews respectively, the idea of a heavenly or celestial God, located at a certain distance in the sky, has been a fixed one among these nations. And they always called this God the heavenly God, the Celestial God, or the God of Heaven. How anthropologists hailing from these countries came to locate another class of gods, sky-scape, or sky-ward "high-gods" in Africa, and among "native" races generally, must be merely a curious geographical and psychological study.

Part of this sad story must be ascribed to the fact that the Akan had chosen to leave the study of their thought to foreign nationals who were imperfectly acquainted with the language and ethos of the Akan. A little knowledge of the Akan language made each of such men an authority on the Akan. The same sad story might be written of an Akan who, taking up a study of native European languages and cultures, came to discover that the word God for the Supreme Being was a Teutonic word derived from Guth or Gud or Goth or Ghen, which, in its turn, is derived from a Sanscrit root, *gheu*, to invoke, to pour, the latter being the sense in which the word was used by the ancient Teutonic races in sacrificial offerings. Now, if any Akan anthropologist in Europe was, for this reason, to call the Teutonic God a " Pouring God," would not research students pick a quarrel with him for mistaking the root of a word for its present usage or meaning ?

PLATE III

OBI NKA OBI (" One shouldn't bite another ").

Indeed, if we are to pay due compliments to one another's gods, we should call them by none but their proper names.

As regards the suggestion by Rattray that the Akan God or Supreme Being is conceived to be a Satiation God or God of Fulness, looking at the form of the name (*Onya-me, mee*), it is perhaps, enough to point out that the highest authority Rattray discloses for that derivation is that it was " given by natives."

Now, of course, no scientific enquirer would be satisfied with the merely popular or " man in the street " interpretation of a highly technical theological term like Nyame of God. Doing that could never bring us exact knowledge. Like the popular belief that the English word God is associated with " good " must be this explanation of the similar Akan word given to Rattray by " natives." Unless we are told who the natives are —their ability or opportunity for giving a correct interpretation— it must be obvious that the evidence may be quite worthless.

As to " satiation " there can be no doubt that any one who " gets God " (*onya me*) would be full or satisfied, in the same way as any one with whom God abides (in the phrase " God be with you," corrupted into " goodbye ") would be good, or expected to have God with him. But both interpretations are ignorant popular etymologies, and Onyame no more originates from " Obtain-and-be-satisfied " than God is from " Good."

3. THE TRUE MEANING OF NYAME

The question has been seriously put to me in discussions with Mr. K. B. Ateko and Dr. J. W. de Graft Johnson that if Dr. Williams is right in suggesting that the Hebrew tetragrammaton is the same, discoverable in several of the African tribal names of God, then what is the explanation for peoples so distantly separated having a similar name for one idea ? And, further, does the etymology or derivation of the Hebrew Jahveh or Jahweh, agree with the etymologies in the several African names for God ? In other words, does, *e.g.*, the Akan group of consonants NYM stand for a meaning similar to the Hebrew group JHVH ?

These are difficult questions. The first is mainly historical, namely, whether the African tribes have at any time had such connection with the Hebrews, in Egypt or elsewhere, as to have led the one to borrow an important word from the other. It is well known that Moses had not a name for God when he met the angel of the Lord on Mount Horeb. He had married Zipporah, daughter of Jethro, a Midian priest, and had been staying with the family for some period until " in the process of time, the king of Egypt died." At a loss for a true name for Adonai who had sent him to go to the Israelites in Egypt, Moses may well have adopted from his father-in-law the name for God that Jethro was in the habit of using as a priest. At any rate we are told in Exodus iii. 14 that God told Moses His name was I AM, that is *Jahveh*, in Hebrew.

Now, the Akan word for *I am* is *Eye me*, or *Meme Me*, and it is quite impossible for us to say here whether, like the Hebrews, the Akan people turned EYEME into NYAME, or that the Ga people turned MIDZI-ME into NYONMO. It is enough to say that in most of the tribes in which NYNM or NZMB appear in the name of God, *ye* or *dzi* is the indicative of the verb " to be," *am*, and that the personal pronoun (nominative) is *me* or *mi*. Where the English would say, " I am what I am," the Akan would say, " *Me ne nea me ne*," or " *Me ye nea me ye*."

But, as aforesaid, these are very difficult and complicated issues, requiring considerable research, for which the present writer is not well equipped without a knowledge of Hebrew, little only of African languages, and much less access to the original books and other sources. Meanwhile, by going back to Christaller, our sure and certain guide, we may hope to arrive at a certain fundamental meaning of the word Nyame, by appealing mostly to the best form of evidence, internal evidence. It is just possible that in all the languages in which the NYM, or NYMB or NZNM formula is found for the name of the Supreme Being, the root meaning is I AM, as in the Hebrew JHWH, but I have not enough evidence to be certain.

The other evidence obtainable from Christaller unmistakably shows, to my mind, that Onyame or Nyame is derived from the word *onyam* which means glory, dignity, majesty, grace, etc., as in the phrase, " *ohye ne ho nyam*," he glorifies himself ; " *mehye m'anim nyam wo Farao so*," " I will be honoured upon Pharaoh " (A.V.), or " I shall be glorified in Pharao " (Douay Version), of Exodus xiv. 4. Another example is, " *n'anim ye nyam*," " he is honourable, illustrious, dignified, respectable."

It is from the same source that we obtain the Akan word *anuonyam* (Fanti, *anyim-nyam*), literally, " splendour of the face," glory, splendour, brilliancy, excellency, celebrity, honour, dignity ; or the phrase *hye anuonyam*, to glorify, to honour. An *onuonyamfo* is an illustrious or distinguished person.

In fact, all such words eventually derive from the verb *nyam*, to move quickly or rapidly, to wave, to brandish, flourish, as in the phrase *onyam gya*, he waves a firebrand. It means also to wink or squint, and *nyama*, to beckon, to move to and fro, would seem to be connected with the same root.

The reduplicative of *nyam* is *anyinnyam*, connected with *nyinam*, to glimpse, to appear by glimpses, to flash, to glitter, gleam, giving the noun *anyinam*, lightning.

Obviously, from the above evidence, we are driven to one only conclusion, namely, to say with Christaller that the word *onyame* as meaning heaven or sky was " probably called so from its splendour or brightness."

Christaller went on to add that this derivation was similar to the use of " the root *div-* in Sanscritic languages," such as the name *deva* in ancient Indian mythology which " denotes the shining powers of the upper world, the radiant dwellers in the sky " (Carpenter, " Comparative Religion," p. 210). The evil spirits were called in India *asuras*, a word which in Iran (Persia) was, conversely or perversely, made the name of God the Lord (*Ahura*). As already remarked, among the Indo-Iranian peoples the opposition of light and darkness, good and evil, was central for the understanding of their religious doctrine. This opposition led to the Iranian philosopher, Zoroaster, elevating the conception of the *Ahura* and degrading the Indian *deva*, *dæva*, or *daivas* to the rank of malicious powers and devils. And this unfortunate confusion all English-speaking peoples have inherited in the use of both " divine " and " devil," which are derived from the same root, *div-*, the " devil " meaning simply the little god, or the little of " that which shines," *div-*.

Here, it may be said, we have veered round to the point where we had left the " sky " God school, namely, that the Akan God is so described because of a certain connection between his nature and the brightness of the sky or heaven. Obviously. But there is a certain distinction, and it is a distinction with a great amount of difference.

It is legitimate to infer from the evidence Christaller affords, that the name Onyame as meaning Heaven or Sky arose because the thing so named (the high expanse or firmament) is the bright or shining place, the place of the sun and lightning, the glorified or illuminated place. This is not the same as saying Onyame is called Sky God because he lives there, or has gone to live there. The Akan, it must be urged, should be credited as having, from the very beginning, conceived the idea that if there is to be a God, then He must have qualities and powers which are illustrious, glorious, luminous, shining and bright, and the *association*, but not identification, of Heaven or the Firmament with that idea is a natural and highly instructive one.

The point of this argument may best be seen in the Maxim 227 : " *No one points out the onyame* (*i.e.*, the luminous place) *to a child*," or, as Rattray comments, " little children who lie sprawling on their backs looking up to the sky do not need to have it pointed out to them " (" Ashanti Proverbs," p. 24). The obvious reason for the maxim is that the thing, heaven or sky, yields its own significance and meaning : Where it is brightest. The native and attributive power of Nyame, God, is that he is a shining living being elevated above, beyond the ordinary reach of man, but manifest to them through His light which is visible even to a child. The fact that He is not identified with the sun, nor with the moon or stars, although associated with the firmament above, and that mind or intelligence is attributed to him, gives him a personality that must be something divorced from the impersonal sky or the firmament.

To Him is attributed also the providence of rain, sunshine and growth, and indeed, of life generally. Now, once such a beginning is made by any intelligent race, the idea of the Bright One being the source or creator of life, or of Being, or of all things, could not be long in coming to the apprehension of the race. Says Christaller, " according to the notion of the natives," Onyame or God is " the Creator of all things," and " God never ceases to create things."

Further, Christaller suggests that originally the word Onyame had no plural, but that in recent use the name had come to mean a " god of polytheists, with a newly introduced plural, *a-nyame*." " The heathen Negroes are," he goes on, " at least to a great extent, rather monotheists, as they apply the term for God only to the Supreme Being."

Now, the remarkable thing is that these words were first published by Christaller as far back as 1881 and are retained in the 1933 edition of his classic dictionary. Yet European anthropologists of the present century, in reckless or more probably ignorant disregard for what this great pioneer had discovered and established before them concerning the thought or mind of the Akan, perpetually go on creating a spate of literature about the Akan, most of it based upon a misunderstanding, but put forth to the world with a great show of profound learning as result of having " lived with *the natives* " for a tour or couple of tours.

In consequence, among Europeans, the popular idea of Akan " religion " is as part of West Africa's " fetish " cult. Actually, Akan religious doctrine knows only one God. Everything else found in the land, in the form of religion, is nothing else but superstition, and one may even make a study of the many ramifications or " systems " of such superstitions—just as many have made a study of witchcraft among the European nations—but, in justice to the Akan, the cults of the private man desirous for short cuts to satisfy the natural craving for some religion, should not be ascribed to the Akan as their racial or national conception of God. To some extent, it must be admitted, the Akan themselves are to blame for having no native literature, their own religious doctrine being embodied in certain traditional forms and sayings which, of course, are not easily comprehensible to students of anthropology, armed, as most of them are, with the belief that everything in Darkest Africa is dark, and without the " Christian " light. But at least Christaller should have been a warning, and it is much to be regretted that so much misunderstanding has been suffered to pass under the umbrella of learning, or " anthropology."

Be that as it may, our conclusion in the present section must be as follows. That *onyame* was made the substantive name of a power, living and personal, by the subjunction of the usual pronominal prefix *O-* to *nyam*, and the addition of the suffix. *-e* to the final *m* in *nyam* to give the verbal balance for a proper name. Hence O-nyam-e is from Nyam, shining, glory or bright, and there are still people who pronounce Nyame, *Nyam'*, in poetry and elsewhere. The Fantis always say Onyam, and the view is held that the final *e* in Onyame is probably an Ashanti and Akim refinement of dialect, in much the same way as the Fantis say *ohin* (king) and the Ashanti and Akim say *Ohene* (king). In a word, the Akan root name for Deity is Nyam, the Shining One.

4. THE UTILITARIAN NATURE OF NYAME

The nature of Nyame is that he is the Shining Power, but that does not explain his functions. We gather the sum and substance of these from his appellations or strong names. He is called *Amowia*, the Giver of Light or Sun ; *Amosu*, the Giver of Rain, and *Amaomee*, the Giver of Repletion, that is to say, Sufficiency of Good.

Thus to Onyame are ascribed many of the utilitarian or pragmatic qualities in Deity or Providence which man appreciates as making essential provision for the primary economies of life, making the day-to-day life possible for each of us.

Onyame is, in this sense, pre-eminently the useful God, a God suited to the pragmatists because He works, He gives to life a hum and a song. In the most material and matter of fact sense He opens up for man an appetite for life, makes life worth living for him.

For the purpose of comparative religion and psychology, we would discover, upon inquiry, that the Akan Nyame corresponds to the appetitive nature of man which the Greek philosopher, Plato, found to be the first element in man's being, what he called *To epithumetikon* (τὸ ἐπιθυμητικόν). Modern psychology would discover in the nature of God, Onyame, the feeling or affective nature ; in the realm of being, the ontologists would say Onyame corresponds to that which is known or experienced ; in the physical realm, Onyame would correspond to the *phusis* (φύσις) or framework or ground plan, what the Akan call the *nipadua*, man's stem. In previous books we spoke of an Akan conception of a fundament spirit or power called *E-su*, which is at the root of the universe of being, and Onyame would correspond to that idea in the religious sense, he being the irreducible minimum of the Deity idea.

In contrast to this quality would be that of Nyankopon, the Greater Supreme Being, whose comparative nature would correspond to *Sunsum,* the personality behind Deity, sunsum being derived from e-su.

In brief, in so far as the Akan system may be said to have developed in line with other theological ideas, Onyame would be the foundation of Akan Deism. He would be the darling of the busy man of action, the materialist who wants to get things done for particular uses.

But this utilitarian quality is carried higher in the Maxims having particular reference to Nyame, excluding Nyankopon or Odomankoma. Indeed, it would be dangerous to draw a sharp and fast line between the functions of the three Akan conceptions of the Godhead, but distinctions are just discernible. We have already noticed one of these in Maxim 227 : " *No one points out the Nyame to a child,*" which, on the surface, looks like a simple reference to the wide expanse, but can be seen to bear the deeper meaning already explained in Section 3. The higher metaphorical significance is noticeable also in Maxim 1653 : " *When the fowl drinks water it shows it to Nyame,*" suggesting that even the lowest of our domestic animals are conscious of the utilitarian providence of Nyame.

In the remaining Maxims, however, the references to Nyame's functions and powers in relation to man and other created beings show a much deeper significance than the merely utilitarian. Consider Maxim 2538 : " *There is no by-pass to Nyame's destiny,*" meaning, it is not given to man to subvert the order of nature. In this, and in the following five Maxims, we pass from the consideration of Nyame in relation to the traditional " sky " idea to a higher order of his nature :

234 : " *No one teaches smithery to a smith's son ; if he knows it, it is Onyame who taught him.*"

2436 : " *All men are Onyame's offspring ; no one is the offspring of Earth.*"

2777 : " *Says the Hawk : ' All Onyame did is good.' *"

2787 : " *The earth is wide but Onyame is chief.*"

2855 : " *The order Onyame has settled living man cannot subvert.*"

These maxims refer to qualities which many other races have also attributed to God : 234 identifies Onyame with mind or nature, 2436 makes Nyame the Father of all men ; 2777 shows

41

Nyame as Creator and as one whose nature must be good ; 2787 shows Nyame's supremacy over the totality or sum of creation, and 2855 shows the orderly nature of Nyame, his supremacy over men, and his interest in the final destiny of man, his religious relation to Nyame.

In fine, the most common name for Deity in civil conversation among the Akan is Nyame, especially in all cases where the reference to divinity is not specific as to a particular exercise of His power, or where it is not necessary to look upon him as a Person, but as a universal immanent Power only. I feel that, in this sense, it may be justifiable to render the Akan word Nyame or Onyame by the English word Deity or Godhead, reserving, as aforesaid, the name Nyankopon for the reference to divinity as a personal God.

This conclusion is further supported by the form of the three main strong names or honorifics specifically assigned to Nyame in contradistinction to those of Nyankopon and Odomankoma ; namely, *Amowia, Amosu* and *Amaomee.* In all three cases the particle *A,* and not *O,* begins each name, the idea having become so abstract that the appropriate pronoun would be It and not He, where Onyame is concerned. We may exemplify this by reference to two words in the language, *Owia,* the Sun, and *Awia,* Sunshine, or sun's time. " *The sun is shining* " is expressed thus : *Owia (no) abo,* but " *It is sunshine,*" *i.e.,* it is day time, is expressed thus : *Awia abo.* Here *Owia,* because of the *O* prefix, suggests a personification of the entity implied, where *A* in *Awia* connotes for the Akan mind an abstraction (It) and not a person (He). It is the same with the use of *Amowia, Amosu* and *Amaomee* in relation to the definiteness or otherwise of Nyame's individuality. He is Deity or pervasive divinity, not God or the religiously inclined personality. It is wrong to speak of Him as " The Sky God," and it is correct to consider His nature as that behind or beneath things, the ultimate irreducible Godhead, the blue print of Akan Divinity.

CHAPTER II

ONYAMKOPON KWAAME, or THE GOD OF SATURDAY

I. THE ''GREATER'' NYAME

RATTRAY was one of the first to recognize that the Akan have a particular name for the God of religion, who is called " He of Saturday," *Nyankopon Kwaame*. Any Akan male born on Saturday is called *Kwaame* or *Kwaamen* (female, *Ama* or *Aba*). Saturday is recognized by the person born on that day as particularly appropriate for soul worshipping or " washing." Those born on other days of the week observe the equivalent ceremonies for their souls as the Saturday-born do for Saturdays. The God of religion is therefore called " He of Saturday," either because he is supposed to have been born on Saturday or that Saturday is the appropriate day for his worship. On every fortieth Saturday, called *Dapaa* or *Dapaada*, Open or Free Day, special ceremonies are performed in respect of Saturday's God. There are nine *Dapaa* days in the Akan calendar.

Onyankopon, like Onyame, may be written or pronounced without the O, -Nyankopon. The obvious meaning of the word is : " Alone the Greater Nyame," for *-pon* is an Akan suffix for great, and *-ko* is from *okoro, biako*, single, alone, one.

There are several variants of the name of the Saturday God. Christaller's view is that Onyankopon or Nyankopon is the settled form, it being also one of the Akim forms, a dialect which, he holds, is the purest Akan, being " dainty and affected," Ashanti being " broad and hard " and not as " soft and delicate " as the Akim. My own view is that it is because of a prevalent poetic strain in the Akim tribes (the Akim Abuakwas, Akim Kotokus, Akim Soaduros and Ashanti Akims) that 'the dainty and affected forms of the Akan language are so noticeable among them.

These other ways of writing or pronouncing Nyankopon are : Onyankompon, Onyankoropon, Onyankorompon, Onyankoropono, Onyankorompono, and, again, the same words without the prenominal O-. The Afutu (Winneba) tribes speak of *Onyankome* and the Ga (Accra) people speak of *Nyankomli*.

In Akan mythology and folk tales the name *Ananse* or *Ananse Kokuroko*, Gigantic Ananse, often replaces the use of Nyankopon. Ananse (spider ?) is the ubiquitous hero of the Akan mythos, noted for his great skill and ingenuity, and for bringing knowledge and science to man. It is to *Ananse Kokuroko* that reference is made in the following mythical ditty as the middle or second

Person of the Trinity through or by Whom creation came or was brought into being. The first of the three is *'Te (Ote)*, *i.e.*, Hearing, signifying speech or word, a reference to Onyame, an idea similar to the Greek *Logos* (Word). *Ote*, in the sense used in the ditty (Hearing), may probably be rendered better as " Understanding." The ditty below is played on the *Ntumpan* or Talking Drums, and also sung on the Speaking Horns (*Asese-ben*) :

> *Hena ko se,*
> *Hena ko se,*
> *Hena ko se,*
> *Hena na oko see 'Te,*
> *Ma 'Te ko see Ananse,*
> *Ma Ananse ko see Odomankoma,*
> *Ma Odomankoma*
> *Boo Adee ?*

Meaning :

> Who gave word,
> Who gave word,
> Who gave word ?
> Who gave word to Hearing,
> For Hearing to have told Ananse,
> For Ananse to have told Odomankoma,
> For Odomankoma
> To have made the Thing ?

That is to say, how did the idea occur to God to create the Universe, the Thing ? The process must have involved first a " hearing " or a taking of notice, *i.e.*, understanding ; then a knowledge or cognition involving experience ; and then an insight or apprehension of the entire idea or concept. Not at all an easy matter as an exercise in epistemology. Of the three Persons in the Trinity of Godhead who first thought of creation ? Or, in simple human terms, how did *thinking* come about ?

These are some of the problems that a delving into the significance of Akan thought are likely to present to us. We need not go into this particular problem of the origin of thought at the present juncture, but there will be plenty of work to do when the time arrives.

We consider here the significance of the name Nyankopon. Apart from recognizing that Nyankopon is " He of Saturday," it did not seem to appear to Rattray that Nyankopon was given qualities that could not be confused with those of Onyame. He called both of them the " Supreme Being " or " Sky God " without distinction. An attempt was made by one eminent Gold Coast writer, Joseph Ephraim Casely Hayford (Ekra Agyeman) in his " Gold Coast Native Institutions " to give a derivation of

Nyankopon. He said it was derived from the beautiful idea of " Great Friend," taking *Nyanko* in the name to be the equivalent of the Fanti *nyanko* (*nyonko*), friend.

I believe Casely Hayford was wrong in this effort, and it is much to be regretted that a whole generation of College boys, at Achimota and elsewhere, has been taught to believe that Nyankopon means, by etymology, " The Only Great Friend."

To begin with, nyanko, or nyonko, does not mean friend in the usual acceptation of the term. It means neighbour or the other fellow. A friend is a person joined to another in intimacy and mutual benevolence apart from sexual or family love. A fellow is a comrade or associate, a neighbour, the dweller next door. It seems to me most unlikely that the Akan Nyame or Shining One should suddenly take on the form of " the other fellow," or the near neighbour, ceasing thereby to be the dear and near God, Creator and Father. Finally, if *nyanko* in Nyankopon means " friend " or fellow, what does the *nyan* or *Nyam* in Onyame signify ? Casely Hayford's explanation does not help at all. In the Akan language, as aforesaid, *m* assimilates to *n* in compounds, and it is the same *Nyam* in Onyame that becomes *Nyan* in the compound Nyankopon.

My own view is as already stated : Nyankopon is correctly and most obviously derived from *Onyame* and *koro*, from *biako*, one ; and from *-pon*, great, such that the entire name means, by etymology, " The Only Great Onyame," " The Only Great Shining One," or " He who alone is of the Greatest Brightness." Nyankopon is the only Great Nyam, the Greater God.

2. NYANKOPON, THE ''RELIGIOUS'' GOD

How did the idea of a Greater Nyame come about ? The first obvious inference is that the idea of Nyankopon is a development of the idea of Onyame, for the term " greater " implies it. It suggests comparison. It suggests also that, originally, Nyame must have been in competition with some other concepts of gods, for instance, elemental gods like *Asase Afua*, the Goddess of Earth whose Day is Friday. Onyankopon would appear to have risen triumphant over all other competitive gods as the Great Shining One, the Great Div-, as the Indo-Iranians would say.

This leads to the quite interesting speculation that the Akan probably started life with a great number of competing Gods : the Shining One of Heaven, the Earth Goddess of production and fertility, with probably the Moon God or *Obosom* taking the middle place between the Shining One and the Earth. But this is purely speculative, although it is of interest to remark that one ancient people, at least, the Babylonian Akkad or Akana, had a

45

divine trinity of similar nature : the Shining One or Old Anu (Adu) ; the Earth Goddess or Bel (Enlil), and the water God or Ea.

But if that is so then Nyankopon must have asserted his supremacy early over all his competitors, especially against the Earth, his near neighbour in the triad, for this is seen in the Maxim 2787 already quoted : " *The Earth is wide but Onyame is Chief*," or Maxim 2436 : " *All men are Onyame's offspring, no one is the offspring of Earth.*" Indeed, this view of the early supremacy of Nyame must have been firmly established even before the development of the greater Nyankopon idea, for both Maxims use Nyame, not Nyankopon.

As to the relation of Nyame to Nyankopon, Christaller most carefully shows that though they are both much of the same nature, there is some perceptible distinction. Whilst the common name, *onyame* means " heaven, sky, probably so-called from its splendour or brightness, from *nyam*," the common name *onyankopon* is given as " the visible expanse of the sky, the apparent arch or vault of heaven, the heavens which are expanded all over the earth." That is to say, even at this level, where they both are metaphorically taken to mean the firmament, the longer name has a deeper connotation.

Then, secondly, there is Onyame as the name of Deity, which Christaller shows to mean " The Supreme Being, the Deity, God, the Creator of all things . . ." who " never ceases to create things," and above that it is Onyankopon who is " God, the Supreme Being, the Creator and Sovereign of the Universe, perhaps ' the Shining and Only Great One . . . Onyankopon Kwaame.' " We should be blind not to recognize that even in the mind of Christaller, there was a distinction between Nyame and Nyankopon, how much more in the mind of the Akan thinker who brought the two concepts into common usage ? The first, Onyame, to my mind, refers to a Supreme Being who is Deity, and the second, Nyankopon, refers to a Supreme Being who is Sovereign God of the Universe, with the distinctive name of Kwaame, a personality not an abstraction : a concrete knowable person, and not an abstract distant notion, what the Germans call *Begriff*.

Finally, there can be no two opinions that the God who is most objectified in Akan religious ceremonies is Nyankopon Kwaame. It would, indeed, be hard for the Akan to do any worshipping of " Onyame," for his personal name not being known (because he has none), his " ancestry " is equally unknown (because it does not exist), and therefore he cannot be *addressed* in religious ceremonies. But that of Nyankopon is known, he is *Kwaame*. This alone is sufficient for the Akan worshipper. If God is Kwaame, then his religious appellation or strong name is *Amen*, for every Kwaame, probably taking after the original of that name, is *addressed*, in salutations, etc., as *Amen*. Further, if Nyankopon is Kwaame then he can be called on the Talking Drums *Atoapoma*, meaning, " *He has fired* (his gun), *but it is loaded*," *i.e.*, " *The Ever-ready Shooter*." And, again, if Nyankopon is Kwaame, then he can be addressed in religious ceremonies as *Oteanankaduro*, meaning " *He who knows the antidote for the Serpent*."

But the Akan Nyankopon has many other names of far greater import than these, and I consider it necessary to give a separate paragraph to these other significant names.

Meanwhile, it may be of interest to subjoin here a note on the use that the Akan make of a person's natal day name. As already remarked, there is a specific name for each person according to the day on which he is born. That name is that by which he worships, for it is by that, the natal day name, he is known to the gods. Among Christians a person's baptismal name is that by which a priest calls him, *e.g.*, at a marriage ceremony, at an ordination, or during burial. So, to a far greater extent, is the Akan natal day name used. It is each person's godly or religious name.

And, apart from the name, there are strong names or appellations or honorifics, attached to each of the seven. Thus Kwaame is described as *Odaa Amen*, " He whose dependence is an Amen," whatever *Amen* may mean. The table below gives some idea of what a natal day stands for :

Day		Natal Name		Honorific	Child of :—	
English	Akan	Male	Female	Tutelar god	Akan sense	Classic sense
Sunday .	Kwasida	Kwasi	Akosua	Awusi	(Under) the Sun.	Sun.
Monday .	Dwowda	Kwadwo	Adwoa	Awo	Peace	Moon.
Tuesday .	Benada	Kwabena	Abenaa	Abena (Ben)	Fire or Heat	Mars (war).
Wednesday	Wukuda	Kwaku	Akua	Aku (Okuning)	Fame	Mercury (Woden).
Thursday .	Yaoda	Yao (Yaw)	Yaa	Aberaw	Strength	Jupiter (Thor, Jove).
Friday .	Frida	Kofi	Afua	Afi	Growth	Venus (Freya).
Saturday .	Memenda	Kwaame	Ama	Amen	Most ancient (Seasoned)	Saturn (Amon of Egypt).

Corresponding to each person's natal day name is his attribute or secret name, by which he is addressed on the talking drums or on the horns, and at religious ceremonies. Thus (1) Kwasi (" He of Sunday ") is known as *Bodua*, " Tail of the Beast " ; (2) Kwadwo (Monday) is known as Okoto, " Suppliant " ; (3) Kwabena (Tuesday) is *Ogyam*, " The Compassionate " ; (4) Kwaku (Wednesday) is *Ntoni*, " The Champion " or " Vicarious Hero " ; (lit. " He buys and decides for you ") ; (5) Yao is *Preko*, " The Aggressor," or " Eager for War " ; (6) Kofi (Friday) is *Okyin*, " Wanderer " ; and (7) Kwaame (Saturday) is *Atoapoma*, " Ever-ready Shooter," and also *Otanankaduro*, " Master of Serpent's Antidote."

It is from this class of appellations and secret names that Nyankopon, too, came to be called Kwaame, with all that the name implies for religious and ceremonial purposes.

3. NYANKOPON TWIADUAMPON

Nyankopon Kwaame is also called *Twiaduampon*. This, perhaps, is the most potent name of God in the language for invocation purposes. Many, including Rattray, have given it the significance of Almighty, or the Dependable God.

The name is usually written Tweaduampon, and some insist that the *e* is a nasal vowel. It must be frankly admitted that great variations prevail in the pronunciation of the name. My own father,[1] from whom I obtained my first impression of the genuine in Akan tradition, usually pronounced it Twieduampon. Some say it is Twireduampon. Those who use the simpler form (with the nasal *e*) suggest that the name is derived from (1) *twe*, *adi*, and *amoon*, or (2) *twe*, *aduan*, and *ampon*. Christaller himself added a prevalent suggestion of his time : *tweri dua a, wompon.*

I believe Christaller was not satisfied with any of these suggested derivations of the name, for, as was his custom, whenever he did not personally approve of a derivation, he avoided giving an English translation of it in his dictionary. He gave none for the above suggestions.

Nothing of any value can, indeed, be gathered from the suggestions above. " *Twe adi ampon* " possibly means " Pull out what is worth greatness," or " Pull out and eat (*i.e.*, use) the great," but both are ridiculous. " *Twe aduan ampon* " means " Pull out food the great," which does not make sense either. " *Tweri dua a, wompon*," where the *e* in *tweri* is the open and not the nasal *e*, makes better sense if translated : " If you lean on a tree you do

[1] Emmanuel Yao Boakye Danquah, called Yiadom (the " Deliverer "). Till the age of 40 he was *Okyerema* or Court-Drummer, *i.e.*, interpreter of the traditional history and poetry to the King of Akyem Abuakwa. Then when the Basel Missionary Society came, he joined the Mission, became an evangelist and a great and fervent preacher of the Gospel. He died in 1914.

not fall," but I can't think of a God's name in the subjunctive mood.

Rattray's own suggestion was not very helpful. He apparently accepted the derivation about " leaning on a tree " and said: " The derivation of Tweaduampon is almost certainly *twere dua ampon*, leane on a tree and not fall." I cannot myself support Rattray in this. It does not sound like a name, but rather like a prohibition or exhortation, not certainly as assertion of a quality. I doubt whether Rattray himself was satisfied with the suggested derivation. He is careful to qualify his assertion with " almost certainly."

I suggest that there is confusion because the name was not correctly transcribed by earlier writers. It is wrong to write it Twe-adu-ampon. It is correct to write it Twi-adu-ampon, and I say so upon the evidence of how I heard my old father pronounce it and from the fruit of research. How does this come about ?

(1) *Twi* : We are familiar with this word in this book. It is the ancient, almost forgotten, name of the Akan race, or of a race originally wider than the Akan race and of which the Akan formed a part. It is often written Twi, but it is always pronounced as if the *i* were double, Twii.

(2) *Adu* : This word is a variant of Anu, the labial *n* being substituted for the dental *d*, a common operation in the Twii or Akan language. We have already seen that Anu was the name of the God of an ancient people, the Akkad or Akena of ancient Babylonia, the Old Anu, Father of the Gods, a Shining One of the Sky.

(3) *Ampon* : This is a variant of *-pon*, a suffix meaning great. We recognize the same suffix in *dupon*, great tree ; *Akropon*, great town ; *obopon*, great beast ; *amaniampon*, great neighbour ; *ohempon*, great king, etc.

Now who were the original Twi (or Twii) people ? I consider this one of the most interesting questions in Akanland to be settled by research. It would be discovered to be of the same value to the Akan as the discovery of Sanskrit as the basis of the Indo-European languages was for the Teutonic and Aryan peoples. Sanscrit helps to give a proper background and a balance to the modern European in comparison with the great civilizations of Egypt and Mesopotamia and China. So would Twi also show the Akan a way back to his ancestry.

In a monograph on the origin of the Akan and Twii races, I offered evidence to show that the word Twii was a corruption of the old and hallowed African ethnic name *Cush*, or *Kush*, which the Egyptians corrupted into Ethosh or Thaush, the Abyssinians

49

into Itiopijwan, the Greeks into Ethiopia, and the Romans into Tutzis. I have not been able to discover what the primitive form of the name was. *Kush* or *Cush* was the Hebrew form, made familiar to the English-speaking nations through the Bible. The primitive form may have been *Ku* or *Tsu*, but that is only a guess. In the Douay (Roman Catholic) version of the Bible, Kush or Cush is written Chus, which is near enough to Chui or Twui.[1]

One of the most difficult feats for a European in the Gold Coast is to pronounce the word *Twii*. Its nearest sound is like the French *oui* with a *T* or *Kw* placed in front. In the mouth of an Akan the " T " sound is not outstanding. " T " sounds more like " Ch " and not " Tw," provided the " Ch " is followed by " u," with a " j " or " k " initial sound.

English and German writers have variously transcribed the word as Tshi, Etwi, Otwi, Chwee, Tyi, Oji, Otyi, and Otshui. Another variation given me by Dr. J. W. de Graft Johnson is Octhi, from an old French MSS. That " Tw " can, in the dialect of the Akan people, be a softened form of " Ku " is evidenced by the fact that Twiforo, name of one of the Akan states, is, up to the present day, pronounced by the Fanti as Kwiforo, the *Tw* being thus interchanged for the *Kw* or *Ku*. Europeans write Twiforo indifferently, such as Juffer, Tufel, etc. (Christaller, p. 555).

In some of the old Greek texts Cush or Kush is often written Chum. Twum is a common Akan name. Actually tradition has it that Twum and Entwi were two ancient or mythical rulers of Ashanti.

This relation of Chum to Twi, the evidence of how the ancient peoples of Egypt and Abyssinia and Greece gradually softened the hard Ku to Th or Tu, and the great difficulty of arriving at a settled sound for the name in Akanland, provide ground for saying that if the ancient Akan also softened or hardened that same sound to Tw or Chu or Tsh, the change would be within the bounds of philology. We only find it difficult to reconcile ourselves to this conclusion when we insist that the Cush or Kush of the Hebrew was the primitive form, but no one can be certain as to that. Moses could not have written the first five books of the Bible until some time after 1,500 B.C., and long before that period men

---

[1] In most Bible commentaries Cush is said to mean " black." He was the eldest son of Ham (meaning " warm "), son of Noah. His descendants spread along the tracts extending from the higher Nile to the Euphrates and Tigris. In all passages of the Bible, except Gen. ii. 13, the name Cush refers to an African country. Sometimes it is translated Ethiopia. Cush was the father of Nimrod who was founder of Babylon, Erech (Arach), Akkad (Accad, Achad) and Calneh (Chalanne). Nimrod, or Nimrad, is referred to in the cuneiform tablets of Akkad as Nimrudu, a common form of African name, Anim, Ayim, Ayimadu, etc.

had lived and moved about Africa and Egypt for upwards of 6,000 years. The problem opens up another. Were the Akan ever in touch with the known " Kush " races in the East of Africa. The answer is implied in the conclusion already suggested, that, to my mind, Twii or Tshi is a softened form of Kush or Itiopijwan, or Ethaush, or Ethiopia. How or when or where it came about, we need not go into now.

It is well known that Anu was " the high one " or God for the Akkad or Akkadians, the ancient people, who, with the Sumerians, lived in Mesopotamia before Sargon the Great, and long before Hammurabi. As Anu is clearly a variant of Adu, the name Twi-Adu-Ampon must have been given to Nyankopon by a neighbouring race of the Twi who, comparing Nyankopon to Anu, the high one of Sumer and Akkad, must have said of him that he was " The High One of the Twii," that is to say *Twi-Adu-ampon*. To those not acquainted with the cuneiform language of Sumer and Akkad, the temptation to say this explanation is far-fetched will be easy, but there is the further evidence that basically, in grammatical formation and development, in the similarity of words and their meanings, the language of the people of Akkad or Akana was the same as the language of the Akan to-day.

Further support is lent to this bold solution by the still further resemblance between the worship, or the almost lack of worship, of Nyankopon by the Akan, and the worship, or the almost lack of worship, of Anu by the people who owned him as their high God. According to one authority, the Babylonian Anu was a purely theoretical God, " and in the annals and votive inscriptions as well as in the incantations and hymns, he is rarely introduced as an active force to whom a personal appeal can be made. His name becomes little more than a synonym for the heavens in general and even his title as king or father of the gods has little of the personal element in it." [1] As Clement Wood [2] points out, after the early Babylonians passed out of their animism, their next form of worship took on the character of the matriarchate, when primitive women ruled and fatherhood was unknown. The female God, Ishtar, was their principal god. Ishtar was the Semitic name given by the invading Semites to a native Babylonian virgin heaven goddess Innini, daughter of the heaven god, Anu. The principal seat of her cult was Kish. She had various names in Akkad and Sumer and her name Innini was often rendered Inana, Nanna or Nana. She was called the Supreme Goddess, or queen of the gods. She is said to have had as many as forty-two names of which one was queen of the mountain, by

[1] " Encyclopædia Britannica," 13th Ed., Vol. II., p. 89.
[2] " The Outline of Man's Knowledge," p. 506.

51

which the Sumerians meant queen of the earth, which, in Babylonian theology meant, " land of the departed."

This community of ideas about the qualities and relations of
the High One of the two races appears to me to suggest that the
hypothesis of Nyankopon having been called Twiaduampon
because of a certain geographical or racial connection between
the Akkad or Akana and the Akan is not as far-fetched as was
previously apparent. First is the common idea of Nyankopon or
Anu as the heaven god of the bright place ; next is the idea of a
Nana standing between the heaven god and mortal men and
pleading for them or serving as an exemplar, and who was, in
consequence, more frequently appealed to in worship than the
high one himself. And finally is the conception of the Nana as
originally feminine, or at least female, under the name *Nana*,
common to both races in the same, or nearly the same sense.
There are, of course, differences in detail, but they help to
emphasize rather than diminish the similarity. For instance,
among the Sumerians Nana was a name assigned to an ancestral
divinity who was a female, whereas among the Akan to-day the
name is applied to the deified ancestor who is in most cases male.
But—and Christaller points this out—the Akan name Nana can
mean both grandfather and grandmother. As a fact, it appears
to have derived from *e-na*, mother.[1] Further, the Akan head of
the family or State, though male, derives his blood by right of
female descent, not of male descent. Among the Ga people, we
have had occasion to point out, Nana is reserved for the female
only, Nene or Nini or Nii being that for the male, and in all such
cases the term means the grandmother or grandfather. And yet
a third point of difference in resemblance is that the old Sumerians
and Akkadians looked upon the Nana as ruler of the land of the
departed. They called her queen of the mountain, deemed to be
living though dead, and acting or supervising as goddess, and she
was said to have been a daughter of the High One. The Akan, whilst
sustaining a similar order of ideas, cut off the " Earth," as such, from
the heavenly order, reserving for the residual Nana (the patriarch or
head of family) all the honours that would otherwise have gone to
her as the Earth Goddess, daughter of the Heaven God.

Probably the pursuit of this line of thought would complicate
the issue for the reader. Suffice it to say that judging from the
nature of the name, there can be no doubt that the true derivation
of Twi-adu-ampon is " The Great Adu (Anu) of the Twii," no
matter how the derivation came about.[2]

---

[1] The Sumerian or Akkadian word for mother was *e-na* or *e-ma*.

[2] As to the Gods and religion of Sumer and Akkad, useful reference may be
made to Will Durant's classic summary, " The Story of Civilization," pp. 118–
124, 127–130 and 232–244 (" Our Oriental Heritage ").

As already remarked, Twiaduampon is a potent name for invocation. This is the reason why it is so often heard of in prayers. Even in the modern-day Christian Churches, *Awurade* (Lord) Twaiduampon is often heard in eloquent prayers and sermons from the pulpit. It bears a certain magnanimous meaning hard to find in God unqualified or in Almighty as translated in the vernacular, " *Otumfo* " (He of Power). Only the grand tetragrammaton, Jehovah, can equal the magnanimous proportions of Twiaduampon in the language of the Akan ecclesiastics.

In some of the oldest prayers known to the Akan (before Christianity) the invocation of Twiaduampon is often met with. Rattray gives a good example at p. 23 of " Ashanti Proverbs " :

> *Osee! Yei!*
> *Yei!*
> *Twiaduampon e e e !*
> *Yeda w' ase o !*
> *Amen !*

Meaning :

> Hurrah, hurrah !
> Oh, hurrah !
> Oh Twiaduampon
> We thank you,
> Amen.

Rattray heard this song on the occasion of the installation of a new chief, when all the women and girls of the new chief's family paraded the town and thanked Twiaduampon that the choice had fallen on a member of their family.

As has been pointed out, most worship of God is done through the ancestors who are the intermediaries between God or Nyankopon and man. But Twiaduampon, as ever, is the supreme title of the supreme godhead, the High One who, above all, is known to man, and of whom the Akan poets ever sing. There is no altar to Nyankopon or Twiaduampon in Akanland. In fact, altars or shrines to ancestral and divine gods are unknown things with the Akan. The nearest to a symbol of God fashioned by man is the triadic altar called *Nyamedua*, God's Tree, placed in the temple, *Nyamedan*, God's Room, often found at the entrance of a king's palace, or placed in the inner courtyard of the palace. To this temple (in Ashanti situate at Mampong), the king retires once a year to sleep in it for a week, after the completion of the ceremonies for the ancestral gods, the Nananom, at the turn of the year.

Of Twiaduampon the Akan poets sing that *Oboo Nyame*, He created Nyame, the God. One such piece is recorded by Rattray at p. 269 " Ashanti," Stanza VIII :

Asiama Toku Asare,
Twiaduampon 'bo Nyame.
Opontenten asi akatabaa,
Asiama Nyankopon,
Odomankoma Kyerema se,
Oko babi a,
Wama neho mere so oo,
Wama neho mere so.
Akoko bon anopa,
Ako tua bon,
Nhima, hima, hima.
Yerekyere wo,
Nso wo behu.

Meaning :

(Spirit of) Asiama Toku Asare,
Twiaduampon who made God,
The Long Table has settled authority.
Asiama (of) Nyankopon,
The Odomankoma drummer says :
If he went elsewhere,
Behold, he has risen up,
He has risen up.
The Cock crows at dawn,
The Cock crows with intent,
Early, early, early.
We are telling you,
And you will understand.

It is worthy of note that to Twiaduampon, too, the personal name Kwaame, belonging to Nyankopon, is appropriate. The Akan speak of Twiaduampon Kwaame, or Nyankopon Twiaduampon, or Nyankopon Kwaame, but not Nyame Kwaame or Odomanoma Kwaame, nor Oboade (Creator) Kwaame. Only Nyankopon is Kwaame and the name is extended to Twiaduampon in view of its being Nyankopon's potent appellation.

4. OTHER NAMES OF NYANKOPON

It is natural that Nyankopon, the personal God of religion, should be glorified in knowledge of him by man under several manifestations of his goodness or power. One of such names is *Totorobonsu,* or *Tetrebonsu,* or *Toturobonsu,* of which the first is the established form. The Hebrew poet, Job, would call *Totorobonsu* the Leviathan, a behemoth of land and sea.

In its elevated divine sense, Totorobonsu bears the meaning which Christaller found for it, namely, " He who causes rain to fall copiously and makes waters (rivers) overflow." This meaning is evident in its derivation. *Bonsu,* the last two syllables of the name, means the whale, and is often taken as a metaphorical name for a sea conqueror. Thus the Ashanti king (Osei) who conquered the lands up to the sea coast was called Osei Bonsu, the Conqueror of the Sea. The other syllables in the name also have to do with water. *To* means to fall, as rain, and *to-toro* is a triplicative of *to* (*to-to-to*). *Bonsu* may also be further derived from *bo*, to create, and *nsu*, water.

Nyankopon as Totorobonsu is therefore taken to be an unfailing copiousness of the source of the waters, that is to say, a flowing or outpouring of all those things which water or ease the lot of man, or, on a larger view, of being. Indeed, the more we study the names of Nyankopon, the greater increases the impression of the generous and magnanimous overflow of his great being.

(2) Another name of God Nyankopon is *Brekyirihunuade* (*Brekyi'hun'ade*), that is to say, He who knows or sees all, whether the thing (*ade*) known or seen is facing him (*hunu*) or behind him, *i.e.*, after he had left the scene (*brekyiri*). In the language of the schools, Nyankopon is All-knowing or Omniscient.

(3) Yet a third name of God Nyankopon is *Abommubuwafre*, that is to say, He upon whom you call (*wafre*) in your experience (*abo*) of distress (*mmubu*) : A Consoler or Comforter who gives salvation.

(4) God Nyankopon is known also as *Nyaamanekose*, that is to say, He in whom you confide (*ko se*) troubles (*amane*) which come upon you (*nya*).

(5) A fifth suggestive name of God Nyankopon is *Tetekwaframua*, or, He who is there now as from ancient times, *i.e.*, says Christaller He who endures for ever.

(6) Further, God Nyankopon is *Oboadee* (Oboo-Ade), He who created the Thing, a name which is also assigned to Nyame as well as to Odomankoma.

(7) God Nyankopon may also be referred to as *Opanyin*, as a form of address, meaning, prince, grandee, chief, elder, superior or sovereign of all, even of the wide or expansive earth (Maxim 164). He is therefore easily *Otumfo*, the man of Power, majesty ; from *tumi*, power, " he who is able to do."

(8) God Nyankopon is also addressed as *Nana*, the grand ancestor. This gives him the full title, for religious purposes, of *Nana Nyankopon Kwaame*, "The Great Ancestor Nyankopon whose day is Saturday," a description which entitles him to the honorific or strong name of *Amen*, already noticed.

Of these several appellations of God Nyankopon only Nana, Opanyin and Otumfo are also legitimately used of exalted men, such as kings and heads of families or commanders of armies. The rest are only appropriate of Nyankopon. I know of no specific name in Akan which describes Nyankopon as Omnipotent, unless we take *Otumfo* as meaning the all-powerful. But many would think *Otumfo* as rather a mild name for omnipotence, unless omnipotence be limited, which is a contradiction of terms.

5. THE MAXIMS OF NYANKOPON

There are some ten Maxims which specifically dilate on the powers and qualities of God Nyankopon, and a study of these throws a flood of illuminating light on the nature of the God of Akan religious hope.

2434 : *If all men suffer Nyankopon together, the individual does not suffer.*

2023 : *I face upwards and can't see Nyankopon, but what of you sprawling downwards.*

2543 : *Because Nyankopon wished to save us (ogye yen), he let Macarthy land at " Save us " (Gye-yen).*

(This, clearly, is a modern maxim. It refers to Sir Charles Macarthy, the English Governor-General of British possessions in West Africa, who landed from Sierra Leone to fight the Ashanti on behalf of the coast Akan in 1824. Macarthy (called in the Akan vernacular *Mankata*), in his second expedition, lost his head to the Ashanti.)

2544 : *" Feign-not-to-die " is name of Nyankopon's son.*

2545 : *Let living man empty your goblet of wine, Nyankopon would refill it. (Literally, if God gives you a goblet of wine and a living man kicks it down, God makes it up to the brim for you.)*

2546 : *Unless you die of Nyankopon, let living man kill you, and you will not perish.*

2547 : *If the plucky sparrow got nothing else from Nyankopon, it got dash |*

2548 : *To save fraud, Nyankopon gave each person a name.*

2656 : *If you would tell Nyankopon, tell the wind.*

2825 : *If you would serve Nyankopon, be thorough, attaching no conditions.*

Contrast these Maxims with one at least of the Maxims that refer specifically to Odomankoma, and it is easily realized that in this third name of God we are introduced to an entirely new order of reality, something above the run of the merely mortal man. One of these Maxims is 964 :

" Odomankoma ; he created Death, and Death killed Him."

Here we see the juxtaposition of Being to Non-Being, of the Supreme Living Authority to his counterpart, the non-living, or

56

Death, and we are told that the Living God who created Death died Himself and is yet alive.

Up till now we have studied the nature of God as the Shining One, *Nyame*, and the Great Shining One, *Nyankopon*. What, then, is the condition of this new Akan teaching concerning God, that he is related to Death ? What are the implications of this ontological doctrine of God ?

To this problem, perhaps the most original of the Akan attempts to hew the rough edges of nature into a harmony of the living with the non-living, of life and its after effect, we now turn for an answer. We can, at least, now say that there is something very brilliant and hopeful and comforting about the Akan doctrine of Divinity : it promises immortality to man. If the living God can die and be still alive, cannot His children also enjoy the like immunity ? Obviously. But what sort of immunity from death are we thus promised ? Is it personal, individual and of right, or is it divine, dividual and meritorious ?

ODOMANKOMA, or THE INFINITELY MANIFOLD GOD

I. GOD, THE MANIFOLD

THE first distinctive mark of the exalted and distinguished comprehensiveness of Odomankoma, in comparison with either Onyame or Onyankopon or both, is the recognition of him as *Borebore*, the two others being usually referred to as *Boadee*, *simply*. *Boadee* (*Oboo-adee*) means creator, but *Borebore* means the excavator, hewer, carver, originator, the architect. That is to say, Odomankoma, who is properly so called, is conceived as creator in a sense neither Nyame nor Nyankopon is supposed to achieve. Every one of the Akan conceptions of God is creative, but Odomankoma, somehow, goes into the root of things and, as Rattray says of him, " invents." The Akan express this quality by an intensifying of the creative activity, in this case to the fourth (really *n*th) degree. *Bo* means to create ; *bore*, to scoop or dig, is a duplicative of *bo*, the particle -*re* being the Akan grammatical manner of expressing a continuous or repetitive action, *e.g.*, *oko*, he goes, but *oreko*, he is going, or keeps going, progressively. Now in *Borebore* we have as many as two *bo*'s and two -*re*'s, and that, possibly, is as much as the human mind can stand for intensiveness.

Odomankoma is thus he who continuously and interminably or progressively excavates and creates. He invents or hews out, as it were, carving out creation into being. It is interesting to recall in this connection that the Hebrew word for " create " also means to hew out : *Bara*, from BeRITH, hew out, carve, create.

Odomankoma is Borebore, the creative genius of the Thing. But he must be substantially something over and above a conception of God as the Shining One, or the Great Shining One, and we must look into the substantive of his name to discover the lesson it bears.

Rattray confessed to difficulty in tracing or knowing the derivation of Odomankoma, and stated that " the word is used somewhat as the equivalent of inventor." [1] Christaller did not attempt to give a derivation, but treated the word as being an adjective as well as a noun or substantive. As adjective he found it to mean " the many, manifold, plentiful, abundant, copious," exemplifying these meanings by the phrases " he did not thank him for his *manifold* benefits " ; " God (Nyankopon) made all

[1] " Ashanti Proverbs," p. 19.

things *manifold* (Odomankoma) " ; " a *world* (odomankoma) of palaver." That is to say, anything prolix, incessant, perpetual, interminable, endless, infinite is *odomankoma.*

These words are not to be understood in the simple plurality or severalty senses. There are ordinary words available in the language to express those ideas. Such as *bebree* (many) ; *pii* (plentiful), *peewa* (copious), etc., and when *odomankoma* is used in the sense of manifold it must be understood in the deeper sense of infinitely manifolding.

Let us now do the work which Christaller, obviously, must have left to us, his students, to carry on where he left off. From what roots is the name Odomankoma derived ?

We may conveniently consider it from two aspects : *Odom* and *ankama* or *ankoma,* being one aspect, and *Doma* and *nko-ma,* another.

First as regards *odom.* There are two distinct words in the language similarly spelt : *odom,* meaning grace, and *odom* meaning a tree, the bark of which is used in a particular ordeal. In a previous work I ventured the suggestion that Odomankoma might be derived from *odom* (grace) and *ankoma* (always full of), such that the term could be taken to mean " He who is always full of grace," but the subsequent discovery of the use of *doma* in compounds like *mmoa-doma,* " the world (or family) of animals," " the animal kingdom " ; *adomakwadee,* " all sorts of things," " medley," " odds and ends," completely threw my first hypothesis out of gear, and it has to be given up. Odomankoma does not mean " he who is always full of grace," despite the great temptation to take *odom* in the compound word to mean grace.

Let us, then, take the other aspect : *doma.* Upon close inspection, this word is found to be so rich in meaning, or meanings, that we should go warily with it lest we are tempted to hasty conclusions, as I was tempted with regard to *odom,* grace.

The word *doma* is made up of *do* and *e-ma,*[1] and *do* may be pronounced either with the open " o," as in " close," or with the broad " oa " as in " broad." *E-ma,* which admits of a simple meaning, signifies full, full of, filled up ; to make full, to fill. The same word can also serve as a substantive, meaning fullness, and as an adverb, plentifully, very.

What of *do ?* In both senses, it has no less than some twenty meanings :—

    (i.) To increase in quantity or number, to multiply, to become numerous ;

    (ii.) To bring forth abundantly ;

[1] It is possible that the word is derived from *dom-* and *-a, i.e., edom,* host, army, and *-wa* diminutive, " armylike," " little host," *i.e., edom-wa.*

59

  (iii.) To produce, attract, gather ;
  (iv.) To sink under water, sink down ;
   (v.) To become deep, to deepen ;
  (vi.) To fill, to become full ;
 (vii.) To enter, lose one's self in ;
(viii.) To go abroad to foreign countries (with *mu*) ;
  (ix.) To enter deeply into ;
   (x.) To take refuge with, have recourse to ;
  (xi.) To swear by ;
  (xii.) To love ;
 (xiii.) To like ;
 (xiv.) To become hot ;
  (xv.) To be of importance to, excite an intense interest or
        sympathy in ;
 (xvi.) To have an appetite, a longing, desire for, lust after ;
(xvii.) To become wild, fierce, frightening ;
(xviii.) To dislike, to be bashful of ;
 (xix.) To suffice, be sufficient ; and, (of course),
  (xx.) To be cruel, hard-hearted.

The vast vista of combinations thus opened up can know of no small end. If we took *doma* as derived, for instance, from *do* to multiply and *ma* (to be full of), or from *do* to love, and *ma*, to be full of, we should be forced to say *doma* means " to be full of the multiplied," or " to be full of love." But this may cause the orthodox anthropologist to raise his eyebrows in irritation and ask : " How possibly could a primitive people in Africa have conceived of a Godhead as *full of love ?* "

And there is this to help the critic of the primitive Akan in the stand he thus takes : That whilst *doma* in *odomankoma* has the open " o " which is often nasalized, the " o " in *do*, to multiply, or to love, is of the broad kind, therefore the word *doma* could not have been derived from *do*, to multiply or to love.

To that, however, the Akan philologist answers : That when *do*, to multiply or to love, enters into a compound, it loses its broad " o " and becomes an open " o," like the " o " in *doma*. For example, the reduplicative of *do* (multiply or love) is *dodo*, with the first " o " as in *doma* and the second " o " as in " broad." For instance, in *Wo dodo won ho won ho*, " they love one another," the sounds in *dodo* are as if the word were written " *dowdor*," that is to say, the first broad " oa " had become an open " o " or " ow," and only the second retains its original form. Consequently, *doma* taken to mean " full of love " is not an improbable derivation.

But I have, I believe, given enough evidence for saying that the best and unquestionable derivation of *doma* is to take it to mean *abundance* (of anything), whether it be love or cruelty or a medley of things, as in the phrase *mmoa-doma*, " the *world* of animals," the *entire* animal *kingdom*. In fact analysis of the twenty odd meanings of *do* suggests that there is an underlying feeling of *overwhelming intensity and depth* discoverable as the special quality in each of the said meanings.

It is this feeling of overwhelming intensity and depth that I choose to translate in connection with the name *odomankoma* as " the many, the manifold, the interminable, the infinite."

As regards the other half of the name—Odomankoma—namely, *nkama* or *nkoma*, our task is simplified by what we have seen already in the name Nyankopon, that *ko* is often a compressed or abbreviated form of *koro*, *biako*, one, only, alone. Christaller took it to be an adverb meaning alone, only, apart, aside, exclusively. The other syllable *ma*, is, of course, our old friend, *e-ma*, full of, filled.

Further, the distribution of stress and accent in the long word *odomankoma*, requires a pause between *doma* and *nkoma*, and that, in Akan, suggests the slurring over of a peculiar word or particle in the language, *ara*, which is an intensifying, particularizing particle, usually added to or compounded with pronouns, or, following after adverbs, is often combined with other adverbs, and has the meaning : " even," " this very," " just," " self," " same," " merely," " only," or, for the particular case in point " on and on," " by degrees," " continually," " continuously," " uninterruptedly."

This particle (*ara*) is very often slurred over when combined with words having the vowel *a* or *i*, as in *oyiara*, " this very man," which is usually abbreviated or compressed into *oyia* ; or *obiara*, " any one-soever," compressed into *obiaa*.

In fine, with these derivations and particles granted, the term *odomankoma* written out completely is *O-doma-ara-nko-ma*. This gives us the full-dress meaning of " He who" (or " That which") is un- interruptedly, infinitely and exclusively full of the manifold, namely, the interminable, eternally, infinitely, universally filled entity.

English and German philosophers, considering the word " God " endlessly overworked and nearly ab-used and mis-used, go off at a tangent, and describe an idea such as the Akan Odomankoma seems to imply by that most obstreperous of words, the Absolute. That is to say, *That* with nothing outside it or beyond it. *It* fills all things, and all things fill *It*. If, in that sense, there is really an Absolute, namely, the total content and container of reality or the thing in its absolute sense, the Odomankoma is such an Absolute.

2. GOD, THE INEXHAUSTIBLE

Not only is Odomankoma manifold and universally filled, but, judging also by the full definition provided by Christaller, he is also inexhaustible. In both depth and extent, he is undimensional. Christaller found the following as the meaning the Akan assign to God Odomankoma :—

"ODOMANKAMA, or ODOMANKOMA, *God, the Creator* ('*He is much above all*, oye bebree, woko baabiara a wohu no' (*i.e.*, '*he is many, wherever you go, you see him*'). Onyankopon Odomankoma abo ade nyinaa, *God, the creator, has made all things*. Odomankoma boo nna-mmerenson, woto ade a, wontua kaw? *Since God has created seven days, has it not always been so (is it not equally true) that, what is bought, must be paid? i.e., Why is it that you have not paid me for such a long time?* (Fanti : Nyankopon no Domankoma ba, *the Eternal Son of God;* Nyankopon onye Odomankoma Sunsum, *God is an Eternal Spirit.*"—Parker, "Mfantsi Grammar.")

The word as a name of God seems to mark him as *the boundless, infinite, interminable, immensely rich Being,* (also as *the Great One, the Mighty One ?*), or as the author, owner and donor *of an inexhaustible abundance* of things. *Cf.* Onyankopon—Odomankoma owuo, "*death (ordained) caused by God* (not by poisoning or an accident). The etymology in 'Mfantsi Grammar,' p. 72, 'the sole benefactor' is untenable."

(*Note.*—This last sentence does not appear in the 1933 edition of the Dictionary, but appears in the 1881 edition.)

The inspiration of the above definition is sufficient to fill a cyclopædic book. But I do not feel equal to the energy to use up all my inspiration, at any rate not for the present. It may suffice for the purpose of the present book to select a few salient features in the definition and direct attention of the reader to their significance and implications. Other issues which arise, such as death, immortality and the like, will receive treatment fully in other parts of the book. We have now ground for saying that God Odomankoma is all the things that follow :—

    (i.) Odomankoma is many and is visible everywhere.

    (ii.) He is "Onyankopon Odomankoma."

    (iii.) He created "Ade Nyinaa" (All the Thing).

    (iv.) He created "Nna-mmerenson" (*lit.* Days of the Seven Eras).

    (v.) "Nyankopon no Domankoma Ba" (Eternal son of God is Nyankopon).

    (vi.) "Nyankopon onye Odomankoma Sunsum" (The Being or Individuality of God is Nyankopon).

    (vii.) The boundless . . . immensely rich Being.

    (viii.) Author and donor of inexhaustible abundance.

    (ix.) "Odomankoma owuo" (*lit.* God's (kind of) Death).

(i.) *He is Many and Everywhere Visible.* The Akan guide told Christaller : "Odomankoma is many (*oye bebree*), and wherever you go, you see him (*woko baabiara a wuhu no*). He did not have access to a phrase such as this : Odomankoma is manifold and omnipresent. He used the simple language of the Akan : He is many, and is visible to you wherever you care to see him."

There is one important logical consequence of this thought. If Odomankoma is visible everywhere and is many, is there need for an image of him in any shape or form ? The Akan answer is No! Hence, search as long and as far as one can, there is met with nowhere in Akanland the least representation of God Odomankoma. Not because he is an Unknown God to the Akan, but because, like one's own mother or one's own father (if known and near) there is no need to keep a picture or image of her or of him for the purpose of keeping her or him in mind. It is an ideally perfect thing to see your mother in every mother, to see your father in every father, to see your fellow man in every man. So, to the Akan, is Odomankoma : He is everywhere, not in one form, but in the Thing—one and manifold. He is God in you and in others you see. He is God, even, in the things you see— the shining firmament, the wide solid earth, the unfailing source of the waters. *Odomankoma ye bebree, woko baabiara a wuhu no.* " Odomankoma is many, and is everywhere visible."

(ii.) *Onyankopon Odomankoma.* The " Greater Nyame " is Odomankoma. This is to say, Odomankoma is inclusive of the Greater Nyame. The latter is not of a final nature which could not find its justification in the former, but since God is not three persons or three ideas, but suggests to the Akan mind a threefold idea or notion, it follows that Odomankoma must have personality if he is to include the personal God Nyankopon. And mind is in that personality, ensuring a unity which is many, manifold, plentiful, abundant, copious.

It is this identification of copiousness with a theistic God, with God Nyankopon, that arouses the most lively association of contraries in the contemplative mind. The solution of this distemper of contraries can only be found in the Maxim 3680, the last of all the maxims : *Nsem nyinaa ne Nyame,* " God is the justification (End-Cause) of all things." If God is all things, or all the Thing, then God Nyankopon, who is the End, must find his Cause in the all-embracing, all-pervasive, copious and inclusive Odomankoma. All the Thing is Odomankoma. All of All (of all things) must find their justification in him. God Nyankopon is not outside of Odomankoma, or he could not be at all. All that is is in the All in All, the all-embracing. We cannot serve God and Mammon, but also we cannot serve God Nyankopon without serving God Odomankoma, for God Nyankopon is not without God Odomankoma. *Nyankopon Odomankoma,* God, the copious, interminable, all-inclusive is God the personal religiously Supreme God.

(iii.) *Oboo Ade Nyinaa* (" *He Created the Thing* "). Odomankoma, says Christaller, created all things. But this is going a little beyond the Akan original. It is absolutely imperative that the student should, from the very beginning, see into the depth of the Akan mind and recognize that the phrase is not " *Oboo nneema nyinaa*," " he created all things," but rather, " *Oboo Ade Nyinaa*," " he created all (the) thing." There is no distributiveness about the created universe of Odomankoma. If there were, it would not be spoken of as a *uni*-verse, a single thing turning upon itself, a wheel within its own gigantic wheel. And yet the Akan speaks of the undistributed, undimensional " Thing " with the adjective of plurality or severality—*all, nyinaa*. Ordinarily, all, *nyinaa*, goes with the plural *nneema*, things, not the singular *Ade*, Thing. But the Akan considered it superfluous to force a comparison where there is indeed none. The intention is to call attention to the underlying unity of created universe : it is the Thing, the absolute Thing, beyond which there is nothing else, apart from nothing itself, that Odomankoma created.

Under this creative attribute of Odomankoma, he is often referred to in the poetry of the Ntumpan drummer as *Borebore*. Borebore, as we have seen, is an excavating, hatching, hewing, scooping, unfolding, carving, maturing quality. One half of the word alone means " hewing out " (*bore*, like the Hebrew *bara*). When it is repeated, Christaller suggests, it takes on the meaning of finding out, devising, that is to say, in the language of Rattray, inventing, or, in a word, evolving, or, more probably, originating an organism, that is to say, the Thing.

We shall perhaps never know how things came into being, or how God came to be. Not until we have had in review all the Akan theories, mythological and traditional, can we evolve from such ideas a comprehensive view of the Akan concept of the origin of the Thing in association with the Great Architect, Odomankoma. We have such familiar theories as that the Creator came down from heaven and made men and things with earth and water. There is the theory that men came out of cavities from the soil. There is the theory of Nyame moving upwards from the earth because he felt that for his own safety he must keep himself apart from men. There is also the story of how the magic stone, *Duko* (Eleventh), whirled by Death across the river, called on the winds, " Winds, take me and set me on the other side," and winds took Eleventh and set him on the other side, and thereupon Duko came to life and became the first god, a god evolved out of the non-living, Death. There is also the story of a man and a woman coming up from earth, and a man and a woman coming down from heaven, and the couples being paired by *Enini*, the Python, whereby they gave birth to the first human clan, uttering for their parents the magic word : " *Kus* " by the waters of the Muru, or Buru, giving name to that first clan, the *Mmuru ntoro*.[1]

There is a large literature of these stories and theories, all enshrined in the testament of the people, the tradition and folk-lore, or philosophy, of old, but these have not been yet correlated into one connected story, and until work on them has advanced to a high stage, all we can say or accept is that the Akan conceived of their highest idea of the Creator as originating or hewing out *ade nyinaa*, evolving " all the thing " into being.

(iv.) *Oboo Nna-Mmerenson* (" *He created the Seven Eras* "). Odomankoma created the Days of the Seven Eras, *nna-mmeren-son*. Obviously, creation of any other " thing " in the universe is not other than creation of the " days." The Akan mind probably loves to simplify these things. " Time, too, was created " is the significance of the saying, and, too, it was created by Odomankoma. The idea fulfils the condition of Odomankoma's eternity : he has no beginning in time, and of course, no beginning in space, nor end. He is there always, was there, and ever will be. *Odomankoma boo nna-mmerenson, woto ade a, wondua kaw ?* " Should obligations (or debts), too, be left undischarged for eternity, like the duration of Odomankoma's days of seven eras ? " The answer must be " No, or life would be intolerable."

And what are the seven eras ? That is not a matter of current interest. It is enough to say the Akan, unlike some *African* and *Wiro* or *European* tribes of anthropology, have always had the seven-day week. We have explained elsewhere that they have for each of these a particular tutelar god whose nature, in a measure, corresponds to the Indian and Babylonian and Egyptian planetary names for the seven days which later became current in Europe. The Romans until a late period in their history counted days by the *nones* or by the eight-day weekly periods. The Greeks counted in periods of ten days. The Anglo-Saxons counted by fortnightly periods. Some African races had only a five-day week, others four days, the days of the great markets. But the Akan have the seven-day week and their system bears evidence of great antiquity. It may be, in fact I believe, that they gathered it from the Egyptians or Babylonians, but that must have been long, long ago.

[1] See Rattray, "Ashanti," p. 48. Note also the resemblance of Buru or Mmuru, to Nimrod, or Nimruddu, son of Kush.

It is possible that the seven-day week, with its seven names and distinct appellations and honorifics and attributive powers, may have suggested to the Akan mind this idea of seven eras of undimensional duration ; of that we cannot be certain without further evidence, but the fact remains that the idea is prevalent and common. The phrase *nna-mmerenson* is thus made up : *nna*, days, from *da*, day ; *mmere*, times, from *bere*, time or period ; and *nson*, seven, from *ason*, seven.

(v.) *Nyankopon no Domankoma Ba* (" *The Eternal Son of God* "). The eternal Son of God Nyankopon : *Nyankopon no Domankoma Ba*. This phrase was used by Parker in his Mfantsi (Fanti) Grammar. Obviously it is a late or modern conception, of indubitable Christian origin. It was employed to elucidate the position of Christ in relation to Nyankopon, who was taken by the Christians to correspond to their conception of God, the Almighty, Father of our Lord Jesus Christ.

Its value, in this connection, lies in how it came about for an English scholar, who had studied the Fanti thought, to appreciate and relate the position of the Odomankoma idea to the position of the Eternal Spirit as conceived by the Christians and Jews.

Nyankopon no Domankoma Ba, literally, The (*no*) God's (Nyankopon) Always (*Domankoma*) Son (*Ba*). It serves to emphasize for us the meaning of Odomankoma as not only manifold, but also timelessly subsisting, even in his Son. It implies, of course, a reversal of the Akan order of priority (in man's sense) of the Trinity among themselves. The Akan would say that Nyankopon is the middle term of the Trinity, the object of religions experience, not Odomankoma. But for this reversal, the Akan is not responsible.

(vi.) *Onyankopon, onye Domankoma Sunsum* (" *God is an Eternal Spirit* "). This also is taken by Christaller from Parker, and he translates it, " God is an Eternal Spirit." But we now know the notion which corresponds to the Akan " Sunsum," namely, not " spirit " as such but the personality which covers the relation of the " Body " to the " Soul " (*Okara*), we can take therefore the literal translation of Parker's phrase as a guide to its true meaning : " God (*Onyankopon*) is (*onye*) the Infinite God's (Odomankoma's) Personality (*Sunsum*)."

This is one of the most difficult notions in the Akan doctrine of God, of psychology and epistemology, and it requires very close attention in the reader to appreciate its true significance in Akan thought.

Sunsum, we know, is basically the *e-su* (phusis) which provides the possibility of the incipient individual's appearance in Nyankopon's presence, then and there to obtain his *nkrabea*, destiny or intelligence, his "message" to earth, to realize the essence or capacity of his particular soul (*okara*). If, then, we are now told that Nyankopon is the *e-su* or *sunsum* of Odomankoma, we come face to face with the same dual entity in the Godhead which we had encountered in the study of the nature of the individual, namely, a being with an *okara*, soul, as well as a *sunsum*, individuality or personality, through the latter of which the *okara* or soul manifests itself in the world of experience. That is to say, man, and also God, is both an experiencing being (*sunsum*), and also a being who is to live the objective and destined life, or "intelligence" of the *conceived* or spiritual being, the soul or *okara*.

On this level, Odomankoma is apprehended as the Soul (*Okara*) of the totality, namely, The Thing, of which Nyankopon is the *Sunsum*, or the experiencing individuality or personality. Odomankoma is therefore to be taken as transcendent where he is made to stand in a relation to Nyankopon. But he is not other than Nyankopon because apart from him he is only Soul and not an experiencing being, an Individuality or Personality. It is *sunsum* that experiences, and its end is *okara*, the ideal to be lived or experienced.

As we saw in the case of the human individual, it was in the harmonizing or re-integration of the experience of the *Sunsum* with the ideality of the *Okara*, that we get *Honhom*, the spirit of pure ethereality that identifies or links up man with the Ideal Spirit, pure *Honhom* ; not a Holy Ghost in the Christian sense, but a Spirit in reality—*spiritus realitas*.

Here, as often happens in philosophical idealism, we encounter a thesis and an antithesis which seem to baffle all satisfying human solution. It would seem as if the pursuit of perfection is ever to elude the grasp of man.

First, we have had Onyame as the fundament of a universe-idea, the Thing as it was. Then, we had the conception of a personal being, a Nyankopon, with personal sovereignty over his creation, and which worships him. Eventually we were confronted with the idea of an Odomankoma hewing out or originating the Thing interminably. Now, over and above all, we are to have *Honhom*, the Spirit of pure ethereality which appears to be both the *informing* ideal that the Thing is " to become," as well also as the Thing in its final perfection as, in fact, it is hoped to be realised. Are there then four in the Godhead, and not three ? Onyame, Onyamkopon, Odomankoma, and Honhom ? The answer is of course, no. For Honhom is not a " thing " at all. It is the " Spirit " of the " Thing " itself. It is the " in " in the

Thing. The Greeks had a name for it. They called it *idea* ($\epsilon\mathit{\iota}\delta\eta$)[1] ; the Akan call it *Adee*.

A similar baffling antithesis confronted sponsors and friends of the conditional creation idea, and they found the final solution by denying altogether the omnipotence of the Disposer, and substituted for it " the evolutionary conception of a Spirit striving in the world of experience with the inherent conditions of its own growth and mastering them at the cost of all the blood that stains the pages of history, and all the unremembered tears that bedew the lone desert places of the heart." [2]

Purged of its metaphors and metaphysical exactitudes, this passage means, in plain language, that the Absolute itself is " a becoming," an embryo ; that the given is not perfect, but that it has every possibility of ever and always becoming the perfect inherent in the given.

Hence arises, we may presume, the Akan idea of the necessity for re-incarnation if the effort of the human material is not to be wasted upon the short span of three score years and ten.

The Akan see the situation thus : In *nkrabea*, destiny or intelligence, both the *sunsum* and the *okara* are immeasurably involved, and it is within their approaching and perfect identification that *honhom* supervenes for a taking-up into the Source of Perfection, or (which is the same thing) the End thereof.

Equally so in the world of the Thing, or the Universe of Being. Here, too, the Odomankoma is conceived as the Okara of which Nyankopon is the Sunsum or Experience, and the idea to be fulfilled is the evolved and completely realized Honhom or Spirit of the Thing.

In other words, just as an individual personality has a *sunsum* for experience, so, too, the Thing has a Sunsum for Experience.

Hence man, as living in the world of Experience, the world of Nyankopon, has most need of that " experience " in his religious and moral day-to-day life. Man needs Nyankopon or he could not have experience of experience. It is by living a life patterned on " experience," of Nana Nyankopon, that man may hope to reach the supreme and final Source, Honhom or purest perfection, in an identity with what Honhom is in the whole.

The vital and final solution we achieve is therefore this : That Odomankoma is best known to man in Nyankopon, in the domain or " house " of experience (Sunsum). Further, it is in the realization of Odomankoma that Nyankopon identifies and unites the universe of experience with the universe of the ideal—

---

[1] " Plato, Timæus," 51 (*d*) and (*e*).
[2] Hobhouse, " Morals of Evolution," p. 506, quoting Professor Adams Brown, " Christian Theology in Outline," pp. 207-209.

the Sunsum with the Okara of the Thing. And the Thing is truly itself as perfect Spirit or Honhom, not a new being, but the " in " in the Thing, the informing Spirit of the Odomankoma that is and was to be. *Onyankopon onye Odomankoma Sunsum* : " Nyankopon is the Sunsum or Personality through whom Odomankoma experiences," but Odomankoma in himself is Okara, and the ideal is Honhom—pure ethereality.

(vii.) *The Boundless . . . Being.* Odomankoma, the Boundless . . . immensely rich Being. Christaller's interpretation must, in the view of the above, be accepted as correct beyond question, namely, that the term Odomankoma " as the name of God seems to mark him as the boundless, infinite, interminable, immensely rich Being, the Great One, the Mighty One." Beyond the Thing, indeed, beyond the totality of the All of All, it is impossible to conceive of anything else as falling outside the being of Odomankoma. As already pointed out, *doma*, as in *mmoa-doma*, can mean " the world of," the " host of," the word being in this sense the same as is found in *edom*, army, host, thus suggesting as contained within the word the implication of " He who is full of all the Host," that is to say, " The All of all of the Host," of the entirety of things, or of the Thing.

Such a conception must imply a being who, surely, is immensely rich in all things ; it must imply a being who is not bounded by anything ; it must imply a being who is not even limited by time or space, and is therefore infinite ; it must imply a being who is not subject to the ordinary limitations to which man is accustomed, and is therefore interminable. Nothing is exaggerated to call such a being Mighty or Great, for anything greater or mightier than " The All of all of the Host " is inconceivable.

(viii.) *Odomankomo as Author.* Here, again, Christaller must be taken to have divined rightly the true being of Odomankoma, for the creator is inevitably the author. As creator he cannot be himself the product of another author ; as he owns all, nothing can be owned outside of him and he cannot be owned by another ; as he gives all, " all " has all that can be given, nothing can be given outside of him. He is the donor, not the donee. He is the world as it is, the Thing, *Adee*, and not, in the final analysis, things, or *Nneema*. Isolated things are not outside the entirety of the Thing. And the Thing, *Adee*, as we have seen, is, in the last analysis, an *Idea*, a Honhom or Spirit of all that is. Odomankoma is the creative genius, the Universal Spirit of the entire Thing, he who made it to be.

(ix.) *The Quintessence of Odomankoma's Creation.* The last associative idea Christaller found to be suggested by the Odomankoma concept is death : *Odomankoma Owuo*, God's (kind of) Death.

Other races speak of " natural death," the Akan of Odoman-koma's death. It is the line of least resistance to suggest that the two ideas are one and the same. But we find nothing in traditional Akan ideas to justify such identification. The Akan speak of *owu pa*, proper death, and of *owu bone*, improper or accidental, or poison, or witch-caused, death, but nature as such is not mentioned, though possibly, it may be held to be implied. Here, however, when Odomankoma's " death " is spoken of, we have to look for a deeper significance than is implied in " natural " death. The Akan speak of Odomankoma as having created Death, and it is in relation to that conception that I suggest the phrase Odomankoma's death may best be understood.

The suggestion appears in one of the best known drum stanzas :—

(1st version) :

Odomankoma,
Boo Adee,
Borebore,
Boo Adee.
Oboo deeben ?
Oboo Esen,
Oboo Kyerema,
Oboo Kawu Kwabrafo,
Di tire.

Meaning :—

Odomankoma,
He created the Thing,
" Hewer-out " Creator,
He created the Thing.
What did he create ?
He created Order,
He created Knowledge,
He created Death,
As its quintessence.[1]

Now, what is given above as the " meaning " of the 1st version of the stanza should not be taken to be literally so. What I have done is to give the stanza a realistic meaning, something said in the way an Englishman would say it. There are, however, some " literal " translations of the stanza, one of which is found in Rattray's " Ashanti," at p. 282, stanza XV. The piece so translated differs slightly from the 1st version above. It adds two fresh lines :—

[1] *Di tire* should be in literary Twi *di ti* (*Odi ti*), *i.e.*, he is first, or (in Latin) *princeps*, head, but drum language of the Akan came into being before the Akuapem literary Twi. Equally *Adee* should be in literary Twi *Ade*, but in both cases the drum version is retained.

(2nd version) :—

> " The Creator made something,
> What did he make ?
> He made the Herald,
> He made the Drummer,
> He made Kwawuakwa, the
>   Chief Executioner.
> They all, they all, declare that
>   They came from the *Ate* pod."

The last two lines read in the Twi :—

> *Ye(n) nyina nyina se ye firi tebena*
> (" They all claim to have come from one pod.")

In a footnote Rattray explains that the *ate* pod, or *teena*, is derived from *ate*, a creeper of that name, and *bena* (*bona*), husk or shell. The *ate* is a hard round nut used by the young in a game of marbles.

Again, at p. 137 of " Ashanti Proverbs," an earlier book than " Ashanti," in which Rattray shows many signs of immaturity, he gave the vernacular of a third version, thus :—

(3rd version) :—

> " *O-do-man-ko-ma, bo-o, a-de, Bo-re Bo-re bo, a-de, o-bo de-e-ben, o-bo-o e-sen, o-bo-o, kye-re-ma, o-bo-o, Ku-a-ku Ak-wa, bo-a-fo ti-ti.*"

This was translated by Rattray as follows :—

" The Supreme Being created things, the Creator created things. What things did he create ? He created the Herald, He created the Drummer, He created *Kwaku Akwa* (meaning unknown), but chiefly He created the executioner."

It must now appear clear to the reader why a literal translation of the 1st version would have been of no real help to him. The following is such a literal translation of the 1st version :—

(1st version) :

>   Odomankoma
>   Created (the) Thing,
>   Borebore,
>   Created (the) Thing.
>   He created what ?
>   He created Court Crier (Herald),
>   He created Poet-Drummer,
>   He created " Touch-and-die," the big Executioner,
>   As principals.

Now, what is a Court Crier ? What is a drummer ? Who is " Touch-and-die," the Executioner ? Rattray rightly translates the term *Esen*, Court Crier, as " Herald." English readers of ancient British history may recall that the herald was an officer who (1) made state proclamations, (2) bore messages between princes, (3) officiated in the tourney, (4) arranged various state ceremonials, (5) regulated use of armorial bearings, (6) settled questions of precedence, and (7) recorded names and pedigrees of those entitled to armorial bearings. The Akan herald, in addition to performing all but the seventh of these duties, had to keep and maintain order, *i.e.*, officiate in the assembly of an Akan king as an orderly. He is seen, even to-day, wearing his fur cap, with gold or silver top. His duty as such is to keep order in the assemblies. From time to time he utters the words : " *Tie ! Tie !* " meaning " Hearken ! Hearken ! " or " *Yentie, Yentie !* " " Let us pay attention, Let us pay attention," or " *Berew ! komm, komm !* " " Quietly, Orderly, Orderly." The quintessence of his function is therefore that of keeping order.

Order, it is said, is heaven's first law, and when the *Esen's* name is mentioned *first in the list of things God created*, it is obviously an attempt by the Akan to symbolize in the *Esen* the primordial orderliness of Creation itself.

The duties of the Akan herald or *esen* are indeed many, but they all boil down to the underlying principle of giving or maintaining order. Rattray tells us that the functions of the Esen include " the privilege to drink first from the wine cup, before the king, before any chief, and even before the spirits themselves " (" Religion and Art in Ashanti," p. 279). Evidently, the Esen tastes the drink first to certify that it is in order before the same is offered to the spirits. A Court Crier or Esen is sometimes also employed as tax-gatherer and he stands at the main cross-roads to intercept commerce and gather tolls and duties. He also, as herald, functions as officer of the Court for proclaiming at the high places of the town the orders and decrees issued by the king.

All these senses are implied in the Akan use of the term *Esen*, when the Akan poet speaks of him metaphorically as the first in the three " things " created by God. God, says the Akan poet, first created *Order*, the Esen, the paragon or type of Order, Order, Heaven's first law.

Next the drummer, or poet drummer, of the Ntumpan or Talking Drums, the *Kyerema*. The drummer is not, as in other orchestras, merely the " big noise " man. The Ntumpan drummer, called Kyerema, is both poet and historian. His mind is a storehouse of the tribe's traditional knowledge. He could not play a single bar on the Ntumpan or Talking Drums unless he knew what the " talking " was about, playing the appropriate stanza on the appropriate occasion, or for the appropriate person. The *kyerema* is from childhood trained in the poetry and lore of the people, and there is not a knowledge of nature or of man which

is beyond his comprehension as the language of the talking drums
testifies. He is therefore the Akan symbol of knowledge, Heaven's
Second Creation.

Then there is the Executioner. He clearly symbolises death,
and he was created by Odomankoma—third in the Order.

The Akan name for " executioner," *obrafo*, is, as I pointed out
elsewhere, closely connected with *Obra* (*Obara*), the Akan name
for the moral ethos, and with *mmara*, the Akan name for the
positive law of the community. Both words derive from the same
root, *ba, bara*, come, or " becoming." To suggest a " becoming "
is to imply its ceasing to be—emergence and submergence, life and
death, " becoming " and " non-becoming "—Death.

Obviously, and as has been pointed out repeatedly, the three
notions of God in Akan theology seem to stand to one another in
an ascending relation, involving the three modes which form the
quintessence of Odomankoma's creation. First, there is Onyame
who represents the fundamental nature of the Thing, Nature in
its *natural Order* (Esen) ; next is Nyankopon who represents
experience, or the *knowing principle* (Kyerema) ; and finally,
there is Odomankoma himself, who is *interminable both in life
and in death* (Executioner), for we know him as the creator of
death, as, of course, of life. In his one being, he suffers and
enjoys the two contraries usually regarded as opposites. Consequently Odomankoma is both being and non-being, both life, or
the living principle, and death or the survival principle. This is
to raise the question of immortality, and we cannot go into it at
this point. It is sufficient to say, if there is to be survival it
cannot be considered out of relation to the total being of Odomankoma, and since Odomankoma is All in All, immortality will not
be possible for the individual unless he be immortal in All. Those
only can be immortal who can share in the divine nature. A subsequent section is devoted to this subject.

Meanwhile, it must be obvious to the reader that had he been
content with the conventional mode of translating " native "
sayings into English, he would have been deprived of an opportunity of getting to know the inside mind of the Akan when he
talks about the *Esen*, Court Crier, the *Okyerema*, drummer, and
the *Obrafo*, executioner, as the quintessence of the Thing Odomankoma had made. We can understand the feeling of the Akan poet
when he thus salutes God at dawn —

> " The sky is wide, wide, wide :
> The earth is wide, wide, wide.
> The one was lifted up,
> The other was set down,
> In ancient times, long, long ago.

Nyankopon, Twiaduampon,
We serve you.
When Nyankopon teaches you something,
You profit by it.
If we wish ' white ' we get it ;
If we wish ' red ' we get it.
Twiaduampon,
God, Good morning.
God of Saturday,
Good morning." [1]

In the midst of this amplitude of Odomankoma's universe, man
stands overwhelmed by the mighty infinity of God, Odomankoma who made the Thing. Let man make the least move, even
to imitate Odomankoma in art, but he finds all filled by Odomankoma : he is there ; he is here ; he is everywhere, long, long ago,
before man came on the scene with his art and his skill. And so
the Akan poet sings again :—

Okwan atware asuo,
As uo atware 'kwan,
Opanyin ne hena ?
Ye boo kwan
Kotoo asuo yi.
Asuo yi firi tete :
Asuo yi firi
Odomankoma,
Aboo Adee. [2]

Meaning :—

" The stream crosses the path,
The path crosses the stream,
Which of them is the elder ?
Did we not cut a path
To meet the stream ?
The stream had its origin,
Long, long ago.
The stream had its origin
In Odomankoma.
He created the Thing."

The mere mortal, man, may only ask : " The living Odomankoma, and the surviving Odomankoma who knows Death, which
of them is the elder ? " It is the certainty of the response to this
question that gives man all the comfort there is in life for him.
The living and the surviving are not one and different. They are
one and the same. Life ends in its own beginning. Odomankoma
is life. He created its quintessence—Order, Knowledge and

---

[1] Rattray, " Ashanti," pp. 101–102.
[2] *Ibid.,* p. 273, XVI.

Death, and survives all three—even Death. He is immortal. So man must be, who is son of Nyame.

3. ON THE WAY TO A SYNTHESIS

There are now sufficient data for saying that the earlier contradictions which the idea of Onyame, Onyankopon and Odomankoma seemed to suggest would receive a complete and satisfactory solution in the foregoing analysis. In our common human experience we know and believe that liberalism is the opposite of conservatism, that progress is the opposite of the settled life, the more knowledge, whether of the Tree in the Garden of Eden, or in the growing child, the greater the disturbance of man's sense of order, leading, as in the traditional case of Adam and Eve, to death.

There is the triad—Order, Knowledge and Death. There is also the divine triad, Onyame, the naturally given, Onyankopon, the experience of the given, and Odomankoma, reconciliation of the given and experience of the given, of being and the effort towards non-being, i.e., knowledge. If Odomankoma contains both in himself, then there is no real contradiction, but simply an appearance, what *seemed* merely to be contradiction.

The Akan conceive of this difficulty in that hardest of all Akan sayings : " *Odomankoma created Death, and Death killed Him.*" And, as they say in fiction, Odomankoma and Death lived happy ever afterward. In the union of a paired opposite arises life. They are revealed to be mere contrasts of thought, not opposites in reality. In effect, the maxim means that the mystery of life does not end in death but in life, the life that conquers and supersedes the *dead*.

And as for the suprasensible world of being, so for the human being. His natural body (*onipadua*) or blood (*mogya*) is the basis of the order in his own nature ; his *sunsum*, or personality, is the superstructure of that basis, that through which experience or knowledge comes to be ; and finally we have the *Okara* (Soul), operating towards a *honhom* (spirit), through which, after death, a complete knowledge of, or indentification with the Source is gained, the incarnation cycle being completed. In ethics and religion we have the same triad in Nkara as the given, the Nana as the experience, or example for the experience, and the Nyame as the final goal.

These ideas are not easy of comprehension unless one has made a study of the elementary basis of the Akan conception of life. But, at least, on this level, we can feel certain that the first of the given is Order. That is the *thesis*. The *antithesis* is knowledge and experience of that order. Knowledge analyses, separates, complicates, and, by its own effort, seeks for new adjustments for a new and completed harmony, a striving for development of a whole within which the basis of knowledge, mind, seeks expression.

What then is the *conclusion*, the reconciliation ? It is found even in the most simple fact of physical growth. Life is a harmony in which individual experience, the seed that is planted, must first perish, in order to find itself in a new ripened order. At the risk of some tautology, I shall put it this way : The individual dies to himself in order to find himself in a whole that is completely ordered. Logical knowledge comes through the combination of a *major* and a *minor* premiss, in the disappearance of which, the third premiss, the conclusion, which is *true* knowledge, supervenes. So it is with the divine order ; so it is with man's order ; so it is with the religious and the moral orders. A thesis, an antithesis—then, at the cost of the first two, the reality is found again, in a *therefore*, an *ergo*, a finality that gives satisfaction.

If we look at Plato's psychological system we find the same principle in operation. The rational synthetizing element would correspond to Odomankoma. It is that element that brings the naturally given, the appetitive element (Onyame) into conflict with the spirited element in which man has the courage to venture for experience (Onyankopon). The rational, the Odomankoma, brings the two into a harmony of the rider of a horse whose intelligent and masterly management of its reins leads the chariot into desired ends, the destination of the journey.

We find the same principle also at work in the terms of modern psychology. Feeling, desire and reason. The third transmutes both to end in the resurrection of the final idea, truth. Equally, in the realm of values—Beauty, Goodness and Truth—there is the self-same pair with a third serving as the crowning glory. Beauty is Order ; Goodness is Life's experience ; and Truth is that which neither beauty nor goodness can deceive. " What is Truth ? " asked jesting Pilate, and would not stop for an answer. Truth is truth. Just in the same way as Odomankoma is Odomankoma, the All in All, the totality of both being and non-being, in the discovery of which there is the end of all search. Beyond Odomankoma, there is neither non-being nor being. If there is anything worth finding, it is within Odomankoma where neither life nor death, nor their instrument, knowledge, can be superseded. He is the absolute end-cause of which the last of the Maxims speaks. The end of all of all.

4. MAXIMS OF THE OPPOSITES

A glance at the Maxims of Odomankoma shows at once how the consciousness of opposition and the need for reconciliation underlie each of the root conceptions.

963 : *Odomankoma created the rich man, but he created the poor man as well.*
964 : *Odomankoma created Death and Death killed him.*
965 : *Odomankoma created death before he created prophecy (priesthood).*
966 : *It was none but Odomankoma who made Death eat poison.*
967 : *Odomankoma having died, he left his affairs in the hands of the Counsellor.*
968 : *Would Odomankoma (universal) Death venture to take man if he were the type to be scared by Discord (Opposition) ?*

The answer to the last poser must be No. Relentlessly the order of nature advances, irrespective of the particular desires and disapprovals, contentions and discords, oppositions and contradictions in man's unstable and inharmonious world. Just as man has his own *hyebea* or decree, so, too, the Thing must have its Hyebea or Decree within itself, and life and death, or being and non-being, Spring and Winter, pass and repass before the eyes of man. It is not his either to approve or disapprove, but to carry out his part, in the mode of the Absolute Thing—Odomankoma.

SECTION THREE
ETHICAL CANONS OF THE DOCTRINE

CHAPTER I

CONSERVATION OF VIRTUE

I. RETROSPECT

THE main interest which had inspired this treatise was the ethical motive. It had appeared essential for the Akan point of view to be stated and, if possible, related to current modes of thought on the value of man's place as a living organism in the social universe. Positing a social universe necessarily dovetailed into a quest into the Akan attitude to the worshipfulness of certain suprasensible values in that universe, which opened up the perennial question of religion. The gods of religion came up for review, and we have just seen that, eventually, in the Akan view, there can be only one sort of unity, the interminable unity of Odomankoma.

Into the many consequences of this revelation and its relation to other racial thoughts on the final nature of being, we cannot fully enter without making it difficult to keep this work within reasonable proportions. Epistemology, psychology and ontology ; or science, philosophy and metaphysics ; are all subjects which that " single unity " conclusion would help in elucidating the relationship of the Akan viewpoint to other ideas on those levels. Not that it is held, here, that there is a different *kind* of epistemology or psychology which the Akan are ready to contribute to the accepted body of knowledge, but that when the Akan viewpoint is known, it may throw considerable light on the advances so far made, and possibly aid solution of some of the major unsolved difficulties.

But all this is not work for the present. We have our hands full with the ethico-religious problem, and in regard to this the solution will be that a common ground is found in a unitary conception of life as itself a unit that cannot be lived in sections or compartments without doing damage to its human usefulness.

One way of setting forth the Akan viewpoint may be by contrasting it with the nearest example that Western European thought presents to the modern British West African on the subject : the tenets of the Christian religion. This is not intended as a cross-examination of St. Paul or St. Augustine, of Dean Inge, of Bishop Barnes of Birmingham. I accept the main principles of that religion and would state them in the most favourable light for a true comparison without offence to either the Akan or the Christian.

Christian anthropologists delight in describing the Akan cognition of God as remote, that, in fact, God, if worshipped at all, is treated like a disillusioned magician would treat the worn-out spell of a great name. Westermann said God was not worshipped by the African for the reason that he (the African) believed that

PLATE IV

MUSUYIDE (" Evil Diverting Talisman "). " A cloth with this design stamped on it lay beside the sleeping couch of the King of Ashanti, and every morning when he rose he placed his left foot upon it three times."

God was not really concerned with his affairs and would not yield or succumb to his magic and other spells. God to the Akan, according to Westermann, may not be taboo, but He is, on this view, otiose, even a luxury.

This is not an easy problem. It is not as if one could make a counter-assertion that Nyankopon is neither remote nor magical, and leave the matter there. The problem had appealed to Christain writers as a striking feature of Akan religion because they had seen the Akan God being treated in a way that Christians would not treat their God. From their Christian traditional point of view, they were, if we may say so, quite justified in dealing with the matter according to their own lights. But, as it happens, there are other lights besides the two-thousand-years old ancient lights which have had their dawns and sunrises and sunsets and dark ages and eventual renaissance and modern reactions in the Europe of the Romans, the Holy Roman Empire, the feudal age, the industrial revolutions, racial and geographical nationalisms, and the more topical totalitarian dictatorships of our own time.

What these other lights are, comparative religion is there to reveal. That which concerns us here is to make an enquiry into what the attitude of the Christian is when he comes to consider his own relation to God.

2. THE CHRISTIAN DIKTAT

In the main, the predominant feature of the Christian view is that, to the Christian, God is One whose Will must be obeyed. Not only that. He is *the* One with any Will to be obeyed. God is both law-giver and king. If moral obligation has any source or root it must be found in God's Will. His Will is that which must be done. If a practical rule is needed for life it must be God's Word as revealed in religion. No Christian hopes for any salvation or for anything else worth his while in religion unless he fulfils this *diktat*.

According to the Christian view, life is an unpleasant process of sins and remission of sins, beginning in sin and directed to eventual salvation through grace. This salvation, so precious to Christians, is needed because, according to the Christian faith, every man, woman and child is born in original sin and deserves eternal punishment even before he is old enough to know the difference between sin and sinlessness. This original sin was caused by the fall of the first parents from grace, and the obligation is imposed upon every Christian from birth till after death, to suffer in all perpetuity unless each man, woman or child is saved, not alone or at all by his own works or faith, but through God's abounding grace.

So to Christians, unlike the "remoteness" of God to the Akan, Deity is an ever commanding and ever near presence. In whatever they do, they are either doing God's Will or acting by their own secondary will ; and acting against the Will of God, in any respect, is sin. Further, this universe of man is worldly and not God's world or kingdom. Those who would inherit God's kingdom must deny themselves of worldly goods and seek the heavenly treasure. It is, as Westermann has said, a religion " full of high-blown idealism," a looking-upward task in which those are held most sinless or regarded as nearest to Deity who belong to the Church (Catholic or Protestant) and act according to God's Will as interpreted by that Church. This has the further consequence that those who would not accept the Church have no standing in the Grace, for, as Hobhouse infers from this tenet, the necessity for belonging to a Church has not made it possible for the Christian to hold that it is the good man through his goodness who is nearest to God.[1] No amount of goodness done is any good unless the doer shared, in a real sense, according to doctrines of the particular Church, in its membership or fellowship.

Secondly, the so-called Akan attitude of " remoteness " to God (really it is obliteration of difference) does seem queer to the Christians because it seems to them to amount to a total indifference in man's relation to God. In the Christian religion, although there has been an atonement through the death of Christ for " original sin," salvation assures nearness, but a further condition is required before salvation could be won. That condition is faith. Or some say, works. Without that faith, even the best of the heathens who had no means of knowing the Gospel are irrevocably lost. Thus said St. Augustine : " All who are strangers to the religion of the one true God, however they may be esteemed worthy of admiration for their reputed virtue, not only merit no reward, but are rather deserving of punishment because they contaminate the pure gifts of God with the pollution of their own hearts." Even Luther and Calvin, modern enlightened critics of the older pronouncements of the Fathers, appear to have changed but little, and sometimes the little was for the worse. They also held that " outside Christendom there is no forgiveness and can be no holiness." The Anglican Article XIII denies that " works done before the grace of Christ " are pleasant to God—" yea rather, for that they are not done as God hath willed and commanded them to be done, we doubt not but they have the nature of sin." So that even if the modern Christian, with the evolutionary background as his guide, appears to have advanced to a stage slightly removed from the former stern and austere cause of obligation, it is still the case that, unless through baptism he belong to a Church, his salvation from original sin and benefit through the Atonement, avail him nothing. It is not enough even, according to St. Augustine, to die for Christ. To attain salvation the man must, in addition, accept the doctrines of the Catholic Church. That need, namely, for salvation, overshadows all men and all values. " Conduct, and not only conduct, but the whole ethical attitude of a man, his character, his soul as expressing itself in his life and in his relations to other men, fall into the

[1] " Morals in Evolution," p. 514.

second place," comments Hobhouse at p. 509 of the book already quoted. Not perhaps in so many words, but it has been said also that the justice of the Church, as established, will be the justice of the final reckoning.

3. THE AKAN SOLUTION

Now, to anyone who has followed the delineation of what the Akan attitude to religion, to life, and to God is, this doctrine of salvation from original sin, redemption, and faith through a Church, must sound quite discordant if attempt be made to force a harmony with the nature of the Akan Deity, Onyame or Onyankopon, or Odomankoma.

First of all, the Akan does not imagine that man ever could have had a fall. His conception of the Nkrabea and Hyebea for each particular individual precludes any such possibility of one man's soft heart or one woman's indiscretion, making all the rest, even their countless generations, to suffer a fall. To the Akan each man holds his own message (*nkrabea*) or intelligence or *nous* in his own hands, and, moreover, each man is in direct touch with the Source, and only needs, on this earth, an examplar or intermedium who will take him nearer to the Source or make the Source better understood.

Secondly, there not having been a fall, there could not have been, to the Akan, any original sin. He is born the purest soul, with an Nkrabea ordained and endowed for him direct from and by the hands of Nyankopon. Possibly he may have suffered a previous incarnation and failed to realize to the full that Nkrabea, but he returns to this earth a reincarnated soul endowed with his original Nkrabea to continue doing good from where he left off, and not for the purpose of working out a graded series of punishments for his sins in previous incarnations. He returns, imperfect, certainly, or he would not need to return, but not imperfect because full of sins ; imperfect because his fullness in goodness is not complete. It is like a man who dips a bucket in a deep well. The weight of the bucket when lifted up from the well would tell whether it is full of water or not. If it is felt to be light and not full, down goes back the bucket for a second, and may be a third and a fourth dip, until the weight assures the man the bucket is full. So is the soul's coming forth and going back into the source. He is not lifted up and taken into service with the source until his bucket of *nkrabea* is completely filled with good—until the destiny of the soul is fully realized. And then it is a glad homegoing for the fully integrated soul. The return of a soul to earth is not therefore like a condemned criminal to be hanged, but more like a little child ready to learn more and to do better. A little child is an imperfect immature man. So is the incarnate Okara. Maturity comes with *hyebea* realized to the full.

Thirdly, because the Akan conceives God as He of the Greatest Brightness (that is to say, if we like it, Goodness in Essence), he does not hold to the view that even a child needs God to be pointed out for him (Maxim 227). As Rattray indicates, the Akan holds that each man is in direct touch with God. Therefore an established Church with dogmas would seem to be a useful means to a necessary end, but not itself the end. On the truest view, in an ideal society, a Church would not be a social need.[1]

At the particular point of time where life begins for the individual the only responsibility he appears to bear is the *nkrabea* with its corresponding *hyebea* which he has to realize in the course of his growth. The realization or actualization may take a whole lifetime, or several lifetimes, yet the process is not a salvaging of wreckage, but a building up or developing of powers and capacities which the *sunsum* (personality) sees in the *okara* (soul) to be available for his own growth. Every effort of the *sunsum* to make an entry of the *okara* possible constitutes an advance in the path of progress to make the *nkrabea* actual, and, which is here of great importance, the good or virtue so achieved in that effort is never wasted or thrown away but stored up, preserved and conserved as a merit in the *okara*.

In this sense we may speak of the conservation of moral effort or virtue as marking the first rule or canon of moral experience. It is the first because it concerns, in particular, the individual even before he becomes conscious of his community, or of a Nana, who serves as the exemplar for that effort. It is a rule or standard because of its general application to all human beings whatsoever. It is an experience because it is born of effort, a mental or conscious exercise to live the life of the *okara*, to be it, or become like it. It is conserved because, like the hewing out of nature by the Great Architect, it is in the line of the end of which the cause is in the beginning, or given, and its actuality is a permanent fact of being. It has to form part of the accounting that the *okara's honhom* has to make when reckoning time comes, when return to the Source is made.

The great drawback in other systems of salvation is the unaccountable wastage of energy and effort towards the good. It makes the hypothesis of growth in virtues an impossible predication of the good. For, unless every stage in the process is to count in the growth, the passage from seed to tree and its ripening

---

[1] Plato also appears to have come to a similar sad conclusion, namely, that a really good community should have no need for lawyers and doctors, for the good people would be law-abiding and healthy.

fruit would seem a magical process. Growth is not a matter of a day's sudden glorification. Nor is lack of growth or stunted growth a matter of a day's sudden depravity or misfunction. The lesson of Maxim 192 must have full value in this respect : " *You couldn't say of a man you have just met that he had grown thin.*"

And this, it seems, is just what the salvation marks in other systems impress on people. A man may live the most exemplary life for the best part of three generations, then, if at a critical climacteric, he " falls from grace " according to the dogma of his Church, he, thereupon, is damned from then on and perpetually, unless forgiven or another grace is conferred upon him. All the result of the previous energy and effort goes entirely to waste, nothing absolutely is conserved. This may sound beautiful in theory, and up to a point, very useful for discipline of children, but it is neither just nor natural, and our human experience shows that the conservation of energy and of goodness are permanent and visible values in reality. The first canon or principle of conservation of moral effort is therefore of vital importance to the appreciation of the Akan viewpoint. The canon briefly stated is as follows :—

First Canon

EVERY EFFORT IN GOODNESS IS CONSERVED AS A MERIT IN THE OKARA (SOUL) AND FACILITATES THE PROGRESSIVE FULFILMENT BY THE INDIVIDUAL OF HIS OKARA'S HYEBEA (DESTINY).

This, in effect, is to render sudden conversions and forgivenesses of no more value than merely steps in the achievement of a total whole. Forgiveness of sins when the sinner does not change heart or does not bring a positive contribution to the effortful whole, would not appear to have any permanent merit to the benefit of the recipient. As an act of grace to which the giver contributes everything and the recipient nothing, it cannot possibly have a meaning (in the Akan view) in relation to the value of moral effort. To be virtuous must be worthless if it has only a fleeting virtue.

CHAPTER II

THE ELIMINATION OF EVIL

1. THERE IS NO EVIL IN THE SOUL (''OKARA'')

THE term " to forgive " in the Akan language is " *fa firi*," *i.e.*, to credit with value or merit.[1] It is not, as it were, a mere giving of pardon, but includes a positive increase in the meritorious achievement of him who is forgiven. It is not a wiping off of an error, revealing a negative result as on a schoolboy's slate, such that there is a starting off again from scratch, but the actual ascription of some token of good act to the forgiven. If he, before being forgiven, stood in the scale of merits $O + G^1 + G^2 + G^3 + E$ (where O is equal to the starting point in life, the zero hour, G, is equal to a virtue of an achievement of goodness, and E its opposite),[2] then the person forgiven is credited with a merit or value which implies growth for him, namely, $G^1 + G^2 + G^3 + G^4$ and not merely that an evil in him, E, had been wiped off from the goodness of his soul.

There is never any evil stored up in the soul, for the soul is part of the Source, and maintains its pristine goodness of sacredness unimpaired. A deathbed confession thus brings the self-confessed sinner no nearer the attainment of glory than the murderer shot in cold blood. It means no more than that the way is open for him to achieve greater or a better glory unimpeded by any contaminations, but it can never mean that by that one confession he had been able to cheat his *okara* of the satisfaction and the necessity and the pleasure of enjoying a progressive growth in goodness, an uninterrupted actualization of a satisfyingly good life during a particular incarnation. A soul stunted in its growth by the deprivation of acts of growth in goodness does not suddenly blossom forth into a fully matured *honhom* by the single act of confession and the goodness or merit accruing therefrom. That soul returns to Nyame with its *honhom* very little filled with any consciousness of achievement, and the one act of goodness remains, at bottom, just a faint glimmer of the good, a little point of a star and not the great sun to which all souls aspire—a pure *honhom*, in glory for his achievement.

On the other hand, whilst the opportunity is available but is

---

[1] *Firi ade*, means to credit a thing, as in a shop. *Fa* means to take, an auxiliary verb ; *Fa firi* therefore means to take to credit, *i.e.*, confer credit.

[2] " E " would stand for what in the Fanti proverb is signified by *brada*, Old Nick or evil ; *Domankoma boo adze, nna brada woawo no, na n'enyi na ommfirii*, meaning " At the time God created the world Evil had been born, only he was lacking in craft," literally, " his eyes were not yet open."

not utilized by a Sunsum for the merit of his Okara, there is no moral progress, and the achievement of goodness in the Okara may remain at O plus $G^1 + G^2 + E$ without ever reaching its full development in $O + G^n$ at which time E is fully eliminated and the Okara is fully actualized in the *sunsum* with its *honhom*, which returns to Nyame, doing so to become God's, to its mystic reunion or identification with the Divine Godhead, the final communion.

2. ''GROWTH'' OF THE SOUL (OKARA)

This, for the progress towards the Good. But if there is no original fall, is there never a falling back from some state of goodness attained by the individual ? This it would be futile to deny in bare terms. In the experience of mankind, the phenomenon of retrogression is almost as common as that of growth ; in fact human nature or community is so constituted, namely, is essentially good, that there is a greater sensation at a great fall than there is at a great advance. Those who, as a rule, are in the line of growth create much less impression in the minds of their community by their gradual accretions of goodness than those who fall. Their growth is taken by those around them as a matter of course. One conviction in the Police Court makes you a " convict " for the rest of life. Two or three more make you a habitual criminal not only to the Courts but to all your neighbours. But the daily acts of goodness you perform in your house or place of business, though gradually increasing the magnitude of your moral worth in the eyes of your fellows and your quality in yourself, excite no particular comment in the Police Court or the Church. Englishmen, with their genius for understatement, express this by the colourless phrase a " good neighbour," a man " unknown to the Police." Actually there is more truth, more beauty, more goodness in the world than the percentage of criminals in the courts, than the percentage of divorcees in the social community, would lead one to believe. Sin itself is so disfavoured in the general community that a greater dislike and aversion are expressed against him who sins than particular likeness or appraisal for him who does good or grows in goodness, or multiplies in good going. There is certainly evil in our world and that evil is undesired and condemned, but in so far as the Okara is concerned, no evil stains or singes its goodness, but evil can arrest its growth to its full *hyebea* if the *sunsum* is not prepared for its entry.

An Okara is the intelligence or *nous* that comes out of the Nkrabea of the Sunsum and the Hyebea of God. It is a part of true being, or is in the path to share in true being, is in its nature

86

divine, and no contamination with sin or evil is possible for it. The evil soul or Okara is a chimera of our own imagination. God never made a decree for an evil soul. God never made an evil man. No truly divine being can have any truck with evil as part of man's *hyebea*. In classical terms, God never said to any man upon his birth, " Be evil thy ' good.' " The Okara, being divine, never seeks to enter into experience, into the *sunsum*, unless the preparation made by the *sunsum* is completely and divinely acceptable to it.

Evil, therefore, exists but only on the *sunsum* side ; the world of the *sunsum* not the world of *okara*. It consists in the neglect, the omission, or the furtherance through ignorance of the *sunsum*, to make itself acceptable for the habitation of its *okara*, or to perpetuate an error or evil. Sin also exists but only in this world. It consists in the deliberate commission by a *sunsum* of an act which knowledge of its own self or being shows to be repulsive to the entry of the Okara, or against the consciousness of the community's intermedium. It consists in giving opportunity to " Brada " to open its eyes, to grow in craft. To eat the food tabooed, of deliberate choice, is to sin. Anything that has the nature of voluntary contamination with polluted or wicked desires is a sinful commission, a toleration of " Brada " indulged in deliberately, knowing that it would protract or delay or render abortive the entry of the *okara* into the *sunsum*.

There is also a third kind of evil, namely, physical suffering, for the explanation of which Christian apologists would seem to have wrestled perpetually without much result, because they found it irreconcilable with the existence of an omnipotent deity.

3. WHY DOES EVIL EXIST?

If, Christian apologetists ask, God is good and Omnipotent why does physical evil exist in the world ? Why is there pain ? Is it suffered by Him ? And the answer usually given by the learned many is that God suffers moral and physical evil as a way to glorifying his own name, a good attained through suffering being more beautiful than the other, just like, they say, the apprehension of the beauty of dawn by one who had experienced a plenitude of darkness. In the words of St. Augustine, evil is the dark colour that throws up the light. " For a picture with dark colour, set in its proper place, is fair ; so is the universe of things, if one can behold it, even with sinners, though they, considered by themselves, are stained by their own ugliness." St. Augustine held also that evil had no positive character.

But this is to leave us no better than at the start. The dark colour in a picture, be it ever so dark, is as positive and real as the lighter shades. Even to be visible a " light " shade must have some colour, at least.

What, then, is the Akan solution for the fact of physical pain in man's animate experience ?

On the Akan view, we could only regard this as a difficulty if we lost sight of the fundamental basis of their outlook, namely, that Deity does not stand over against His own creation, but is involved in it. He is, if we may be frank, " of " it. If we postulate, as the Christians do, that the principle that makes for good " in this world," Nyame or God, stands over against the community, is external to it, and commands it with a will to be obeyed, irrespective of the will of " this world," and if we postulate again that the aforesaid principle is omnipotent, and is also responsible as creator of this world, then the existence of physical evil or pain which is thus, at the same time, taken to be independent of that principle, becomes an insoluble mystery. All that could be said of it is that it is, indeed, an evil, an illogical and an unjust condition. We could, on this view, explain its existence side by side with Omnipotence only on the comforting assumption that the standards or canons of morality, as we humans understand it, do not apply to " the principle that makes for good." And in holding that view we, at the same time, undermine the whole justification for good, divine or human. It is quite obviously untenable to have in one universe an Omnipotent God as well as a dominant or omnipotent evil which came into existence as issue of no one's creative activity. Of course, the familiar myth of an independent Satanic power at whose will evil exists, is so well accepted as a myth that we need have no recourse to it in this argument. The existence of any such Satan automatically limits the omnipotence of the Omnipotent if that Satan can create conditions beyond the powers of the first postulated omnipotence to control or extirpate.

4. THE MASTERY OF EVIL

It is quite otherwise if we deny that the principle is omnipotent but is itself a " Spirit striving in the world of experience with the inherent conditions of its own growth and mastering them " at the cost of all the physical pain and evil as well as the moral pain or disharmony that stain the pages of human effort.

That is to say, in Akan language, where the Nana, the principle that makes for good, is himself or itself participator in the life of the whole, and is not only head, but because it is head,[1] has to strive and struggle for the place of leader or *opanyin* as the individuals of the group do, then physical pain and evil are revealed as

[1] Before deification, in his capacity as *Opanyin* or head or Chief.

natural forces which the Nana, in common with others of the group, have to master, dominate, sublimate or eliminate.

At the higher remove, we may say that the Nana as the pattern or paradigm of Nyankopon serves as the source of the several revelations leading to the mastery of physical evil-conditions to hold down " Brada " from .opening its eyes, growing in craft. The being of Nyankopon, in the ideal the pursuit of which man hopes to be good, is revealed in its greatest perfection where all evil is progressively mastered. The revelation may be slow, delayed, thwarted and obstructed by man's own ignorance, or sheer unwillingness to see the light, where it shines most, but until that revelation is complete, evil will continue, not as apart from life, but as part of life, a condition which makes it all the more necessary to have a complete knowledge of Nyankopon, for it is only in knowing him fully that evil is eliminated from the *sunsum*, and the Okara becomes complete master of each man's *hyebea*.

In both ethics and religion we cannot afford to ignore or pretend to despise the existence of a natural order, the *sunsum* of each man, or of the world, as essentially the medium for transforming the given into the ideal, the Sunsum into the Okara, and eventually Nyankopon to Honhom or Spirit. Growth consists in Sunsum growing more " crafty " than Brada itself. The virtues conserved make for the greater growth.

CHAPTER III

MORAL PROGRESS

I. GROWTH OF GOOD MEN

IN summary view, our conclusion in the last chapter comes to this : Our mastery or dominance of the natural order, or of physical nature, of " Brada," registers for us our first victory for the spiritual. The traditional or the scientific knowledge, which the growing community acquires or possesses over the processes of nature, is therefore destined to be used by the community for the furtherance of its own good in order that men of the community should live well. With man's dominance of nature—reduction and gradual conquest of the resistant medium called physical evil—comes an enlarged opportunity for a greater achievement of good.

A community or family which has no knowledge of how to build a house, or even to make fire, enjoys a much narrower synthesis of real harmony with the environment than the community that lives in a town, has mastered fire, has developed agriculture, knows the causes and cures of diseases and can thereby provide a wider, richer, and more stimulating life for its members. If a community is so ignorant of the causes of the physical conditions which paralyse action, then however well intentioned its members may be, they would grossly be lacking in the opportunity to utilize the inherent blessings in a Nana who, under such conditions of hardship, would be quite incapable of bearing the full vigour of the pattern of a good life, for he would be an imperfect paradigm of the revelation Nyankopon condescends to yield for man, through him. The head of a primitive village community is a good man, but he is not so great in goodness as the head of a city community who has mastered a greater measure of resistance opposed to the good, greater by far than the village headman ever expects to encounter. The wider the horizon the greater the good achieved, in quality and quantity. Otherwise the term " great man " would have no positive value, but only relatively.

Physical evil is not therefore a good, nor, in itself, is it an independent evil, but is a resistance or given medium of the total community attainment, the index or measure of its contact with the revealing perfection, of how far that highest consciousness of what man may become, namely, Mind, in its most developed state, had effected an efficient " marriage " between Sunsum and

Okara. The evolving process is from $O + G^1 + \ldots G^n$, where O stands for the zero of community life and G for the good progressively attained. The community or family, not unlike the individual, has the world of experience as its Sunsum and the world of the ideal as its Okara, and G^n, or the state of Honhom or the Spirit, fully evolved, cannot be attained unless the progression has passed through all the stages, G^1 to the nth power. Conquest of the resisting medium constitutes therefore the growth or progress of the moral power.

Further, physical evil cannot be said to be an inevitable precondition of moral progress, but for that progress to reach the absolute of what is good it should be eliminated where it exists. In a paradise without physical evil there would still be conditions to control and maintain until the true ideal of Honhom is attained, but though physical evil would not be found in such a world, moral evil would still exist.

On both sides, then, namely, both moral and physical evil, as also sin, we see the conditions the dominance of which would render possible the actualization of Okara. By Sunsum eliminating these resistant media of its full incarnation, the Okara gains entry into the Sunsum to ripen into Honhom. What is aimed at is harmony of Okara and Sunsum, the organization of the intelligence for absorption in the Source, and until physical and moral evil are completely eliminated, perfect harmony of experience is not possible.

It is clear, then, that the cumulative experience of the community, its experiment or effort in goodness, its knowledge of the laws of life, its struggle against disease and ignorance, its effort to eliminate pain, nay, even its ordering of human relations by the laws of society, and, above all, the accumulated knowledge of the laws of physical nature—are all modes of traditional inheritance which make for a greater and a more constant achievement and a greater and more real correlation of total effort of virtuous men with the complete good.

This insistence upon knowledge and experience of the community as essential elements in the cumulative effort to dominate or eliminate evil may appear to others sheer intellectualism, but to anyone conscious of the underlying principles of Akan thought, that conclusion is inevitable. Evil, to the Akan, not only is a sort of existence to be mastered by craft, it is also as old as creation, if not older, and the greater a man's consciousness of his own genuine good, the more apparently grows the horizon of the evil he has to conquer. It would seem, indeed, as if it was the very birth of a being such as man's *okara* or soul which quickened evil into active resistance of the soul's progress. No. 683 of Rev.

Gaddiel R. Acquaah's collection of " Fante-Akan Proverbs " (1940) aptly exemplifies the Akan idea of the relation between the Creator (Odomankoma), the created (man) and Evil (personified) and of Evil's own consciousness. The maxim already quoted in a footnote is as follows : " *Domankoma boo adze, nna brada woawo no, na n'enyi na ommfirii,*" meaning " When Odomankoma (God) created the Thing (the World) Old Nick (Evil) had been born, only he was lacking in craft." That is to say evil grew to what it is to-day in craftiness and cunning and deception *after* and not before the creation. Evil, apparently, goes hand in hand with good, the greater the one the more extensive the other, until the complete victory, the total elimination of all the " craftiness " of *Brada*.

The second canon of moral experience may therefore be stated as issuing from the constant and continuous dependence of progress on the principle of tradition—the knowledge of how much resistance is handed down, in proportion as the gains of the past are handed on to form a basis for advancing operations of the future. In more precise terms we may state the canon thus :—

SECOND CANON

MORAL PROGRESS IS CONSTANT AND CONTINUOUS IN PROPORTION AS INDIVIDUAL GAINS OR MERITS OF THE PAST ARE HANDED ON AS TRADITION TO FORM THE BASIS OF RACIAL EXPERIENCE.

Hence, too, the necessity for reincarnation and its justice. For if the effort or virtue of the past generation was to be utilized only by an entirely new generation which had made no contribution to the growth of the tradition, whilst those who had, by dint of their own effort, built up the tradition, but had not completed the cycle of the *hyebea*, or had not become " saints," were condemned to eternal punishment, the whole moral structure would appear insanely and insecurely founded upon an inherent blot, a moral deception and a divine injustice.

And this, too, brings us to a contemplation of the third canon of moral experience, the justice and necessity for which will make a universal appeal, at least to all those lovers of good who, without knowing or asking the reason why, feel that goodness in itself is preferable to wickedness, even if the way of the wicked looks like leading to a pleasurable hedonistic existence, an existence which, however felicitous, is often empty of true contentment or genuine and abiding satisfaction.

92

2. THE SUPERMAN

Now, whilst modern science appears totally baffled by the place of heredity in the collective achievement of the race, it being largely inexplicable how great men and great geniuses could issue from the loins of simple country folk or peasant women, the third canon of moral experience, that the fruit of a developed character

PLATE V

KWATAKYE ATIKO (Behind-the-Head mark of Kwatakye). "Kwatakye was a war captain of one of the Ashanti Kings ; at the Odwira ceremony he is said to have cut his hair after this fashion." Kwatakye or Katakyie means simply, a brave person, valiant man ; bravery, valour.

brings added strength to the whole of community achievement, ensures the possibility of heredity and the utilization of acquired characters. Heredity facilitates the effort of the future both for the individual and for his total future community. This must bring hope and comfort to the solitary worker neglected or ignored in his lifetime by lack of recognition. Let him rest assured that, in a future incarnation, not he alone would benefit, but all around him would improve by his past bequest of good and his inheritance of present good. The virtues registered by him live undestroyed in his community, and in a subsequent incarnation he stands a better chance of evolving the supreme qualities of a superman. Here, we have the justification for self-sacrifice. It is much less a loss or sacrifice of self ; it is more like a fixed deposit for future benefits or incomes of good. A full " return " of virtue for any good invested in the community is thus always assured.

THIRD CANON

RACIAL PROGRESS FACILITATES THE DEVELOPMENT OF INNATE CHARACTERISTICS IN OUTSTANDING INDIVIDUALS WHO CONSCIOUSLY LIBERATE SUCH CHARACTERISTICS TO STRENGTHEN THE INHERITED TRADITION.

Hence the surest way to goodness and to God is education.

To make the achievement of individuals social, there must be progress in the race, and to make the achievement of the race progressive, there must be individual progress. In other words if, as Clement Wood points out,[1] the end towards which mankind is tending is the socialization of achievement, the liberation and strengthening of the social tradition, then, says Kant, " In education lies the great secret of the perfecting of human nature." The liberation of individual abilities is the liberation of the race.

" The man denied education is denied in advance any genuine chance of achieving eminence ; and the race is robbed correspondingly. The percentage of genius and talent, from various social classes in certain typical districts in France, Odin discovered to be as follows :—

Social Classes.	Genius.	Population.
Nobility	26 per cent.	1 per cent.
Official class	30 ,,	3 ,,
Professional class	23 ,,	6 ,,
Bourgeoisie	12 ,,	10 ,,
Manual labour	9 ,,	80 ,,

" From Odin's purely mathematical study of genius and eminence, Ward arrives at the conclusion that a well-organized system of universal education would increase the social effectiveness of genius at least hundredfold. Instead of two of the great and eminent to every 100,000 of population, we could have 200. Society's present organization callously and calmly kills off 198 out of every 200 potentially great men and women. A hostile environment throttles genius, as adequately as could a thug." [1]

[1] " The Outline of Man's Knowledge," pp. 336–337.

The superman is, in a sense, both born and made, but more made than born. Says Maxim 194 : " No one can by design give birth to *opanyin* (hero, or elder)." In other words, you cannot, as a parent, deliberately wish to give birth to a great man and expect to have your wish fulfilled as a matter of certainty. But in the mystery process of the power that makes the *e-su* wish to come on to this earth for *obra* or *abra-bo,* a mystery which, we found, could not be explained, there comes to be born to certain parents, in certain localities, children who excel even the parents in their combined moral or spiritual assets. Often, indeed, such children may stand head and shoulders above anything previously known in the particular community.

Here, then, we have a superman *born,* but not born as a superman by his parents, but because, and in virtue, of his own previous achievement in a previous incarnation. In that past epoch he had *made* himself, and in the present age into which he is born he appears to be a novation, a sort of being excelling all the prevailing standards attained in his environment. How his *nkrabea* or *hyebea* directed him to be born in that particular community will remain a mystery into which it is profitless to enquire. He may have lived his previous life in that same community, or he may have chosen or been assigned that community now for his present essay in life, believing that a new country, a new environment, lacking in some of the opportunities, and some, possibly, of the resistances of his previous life or community, may afford him just that beneficial advantage and accommodation for actualizing his soul for an accelerated progress towards the good. We can never know which is the whole truth, but experience teaches that the superman arises in the community, often because of his community's advantages, but quite often in spite of them. In fact, it was in the sense that he rises superior to great disadvantages of environment that superior nature shines through the superman, as if a god had revealed itself in him. It is otherwise difficult to explain how the human Jesus, in a ministry of only three years, could have established a tradition which, for 2,000 years, has spread and continues to spread over wide and divergent communities throughout man's variegated universe.

In the superman—who may be a great hero, a great warrior, a great statesman, a great religious leader, a great thinker, or great in some other sphere of life—we sense the consciousness of an evangelizing spirit or reformatory mission to save his community or even mankind in the name of the God, the Nananom or Nyame, or to set forth the particular ideal for which he stands superior to all others in a light which should shine as a portion of divinity itself. In him, the consciousness of something sublime comes near to experience. This sublimity means there is now something at work which is more pervasive or extensive than the accustomed horizon of the community. There is, so to speak, a demand to reach out to beyond the known or acknowledged ethos. He is a " super " because he rises superior to the accustomed resistances of his community. There is, in a word, need for self-transcendence, and the superman readily shows the way. If the good had, up to that point, been confined to the group alone, such as a tribe, or a clan, or a chosen race, the superman's greater and wider outlook suggests an extension or a widening of the basis of the moral experience, and, thereupon, the particular " group-morality " is transcended, and a passage made for the great army, the superman's community, to follow him to a greater recognition of a wider human comprehension. Great advances in progress are thus seen to come about through the *nova* of the superman's star which leaps into full effulgence in the apprehension of his age.

Where the community is highly conservative, this condition may not lead so easily or immediately to progress, and may well foster a reaction from a Bethlehem to a Golgotha. The superman may suffer the death of a martyr because he had lived beyond the horizon of his age. But where the conditions are favourable the group ideal passes from (1) the family to (2) the tribe or race, to (3) the clan or nation, and finally (4) to humanity as such, crossing the great barriers of nationality, even of race, of religion, of sect, of trade-guild, of class or of colour, to a recognition of the one true family of man, humanity itself, as the only complete and justifiable objective, the only " family " for the total good of God. The fourth canon therefore follows necessarily from the condition of society itself :—

Fourth Canon

THE CONSCIOUS LIBERATION OF OUTSTANDING CHARACTERISTICS WHICH DEMAND CORRESPONDING FIELDS FOR EXPANSION LEADS TO THE COMPREHENSION OF GREATER SOCIAL WHOLES AND THE LOGICAL RECOGNITION OF HUMANITY AS THE ALL-EMBRACING IDEAL FOR FULFILLING AND DEVELOPING RACIAL EXPERIENCE.

This canon may be further explained by the fact of so-called natural selection and the other fact, already noticed, of the conditions under which the superman influences community experience.

CHAPTER IV

HUMAN PROGRESS

I. THE SUPER-COMMUNITY

THE energy for natural selection if taken to operate only through one generation becomes a wasteful effort. If, however, reincarnation is posited as with the Akan, and, working with the first canon that a merit gained in the Okara is conserved, then the principle yields the most useful results, because, even where death of individuals or some greater catastrophe, such as famine or war or plague or fire, supervenes to eliminate from the present generation the best who should have survived for the good of the society, the uncertain residuum as to how far acquired characters can become hereditary, or be passed on to the next generation, no longer remains insoluble, nor distressing to contemplate. It can be seen at once that, in effect, there is no mystery as to heredity, because no good ever achieved, according to the first canon, is ever wasted. The death of an individual is therefore a matter of little consequence, unless he had, in his life, achieved nothing, having lived purely as the " Honourable Mr. Cipher " of his community. In which case his death is more than calamitous, it is a vacuum.

The third canon follows as a corollary of the first, namely, that the good conserved is reproduced or made use of in the subsequent incarnations. The fourth canon shows that the conservation of effort issues in the birth of the superman, and may be, even of the super-community.

Speaking empirically, it can be questioned whether, as a result or consequence of the operation of the third canon, the human breed has really improved in moral progress ; for instance, that the people who lived in the first twenty-five years of the seventeenth century were much less moral than those who lived in the first generation of the present century. But the uncertainty arises from a wrong perspective of what appears to happen. The argument assumes that the identical men who lived, say at Accra, in the first generation of the seventeenth century, are those who were reincarnated *there* in the first generation of the present century. But we have not the slightest evidence for that assumption. Movements of peoples and of races tend to dislocate whole groups of peoples such that within 200 years the race who lived in Accra may have changed completely from a Ga tribe to an Akwamu tribe, or *vice versa*. Not only so. The argument further assumes that those living in Accra in the twentieth century are all reincarnates ; whereas the contrary may quite well be the case, that quite a large proportion of the people might be first stage incarnates, namely, primitive souls coming to the earth for the first time, whilst a small proportion of the population may be in the sixth or seventh or G^n incarnation. Between them would be the second, third, fourth and fifth . . . to just before the nth power incarnates, all at different stages of moral development, and all, unfortunately or fortunately, compelled by the levelling laws of their community, to keep pace at a particular rate of progress, the rate being, in all such cases, measured by the pace of the slowest, unless of course, the superman supervenes and intervenes. It is open to see that, in such a society, men in the higher incarnate stages would find their progress retarded by the backward pulling of the lower incarnates, primitives or first incarnates who are just making their debut in life's court. Hence, the value of the superman is beyond computation, for he it is who clears the way both for the lower as well as the higher incarnates. He liberates energy and overcomes resistance of all sorts. The picture is much about the same on the world pattern, though perhaps not so obviously.

On the whole, however, there is that much in the history of mankind to indicate that the decline and fall of nations has been due to the entry into those nations of elements not originally dominant, and further, that the progress and development of hitherto unknown nations or races has been due to the entry into those nations of some other races or peoples whose own apparent progress seemed to stand far below that of the invaded race. The example of the races who entered the Roman Empire, believed to have caused its fall, and who, however, were subsequently able to raise or generate from the ashes of the fallen Rome, a newer and, on the whole, a higher type of advance, should serve as an illustration for the two aspects suggested. The Goths and Vandals and Germanic races who fell on Rome and destroyed the Empire were not as " civilized " as the Romans, but does not history record that modern Europe, and the modern European, accredited the most civilized of the advanced nations, arose from the inheritance which followed from the fall of the Roman Empire ? The story of the Moors in Europe, of the conquest by the Arabs of half the known world and their Mohammedan religion, the dominance of the ancient nations of the East by the newer nations of the West, all these indicate that, from both sides, progress has been made possible by the infusion of new blood, that retardation has come about also by the invasion of the old by a new fusion of blood. But man cannot, off his own bat, tell which admixture of races would make for good, and which evil. The apparently " lower " often bear qualities that the obviously " higher " lack, and the eventual supervention of leaps and advances in progress may come about by the interaction and communion of distinct and even disparate characters in the cauldron of race-brew.

2. THE GILT ON THE GOLDEN AGES

Recall, for a moment, the prevalent belief in " Golden Ages " of several races and nations. The general characteristics of golden ages are that the nation or people attained to the highest in moral, intellectual and artistic endeavour in some time past. Looked at closer, it has often turned out to be the truth that the attainments of the subsequent non-golden age really stood far superior to those of the so-called golden. The golden age of England, the Elizabethan age ; the golden age of France, part of the reigns of Louis XIV and XV ; the reign of Charles V in Germany ; of John I to Sebastian's reign in Portugal ; the reign of Peter the Great in Russia ; of Ferdinand and Isabella in Spain ; of Gustavus Vasa and Gustavus Adolphus in Sweden ; or, to come to the Gold Coast country, the golden age of Osai Tutu in Ashanti, of Ofori Panyin in Abuakwa, of Asebu in Fantiland, of Manche Tackie in the Ga State, of Akonno in the ancient Akwanu State, who would exchange the life of to-day for any of those gilded ages, with or without the heavy gilt that the historians and poets and portrait painters have put on them ?

What had happened was really the attainment of a certain harmony of thought and action in those gilded ages, but it was a harmony attained within a narrow and very limited compass, a compass which might well fail to respond to the scintillating magnetism of our own time. Were those who lived in those ages called upon to cope with the difficulties, complications, disciplines and expanded organizations by which the modern man is faced, they might well fail as the pre-industrial age of England failed. As soon as expansion had set in, the intensive and heightened life and harmony of the limited group or family, Augustan, Elizabethan or Osai Tutuan, completely broke down, unfitted to survive the strains and stresses of a world in which Raleigh's cloak would be condemned by the modern press as a primitive and quite inadequate excuse for affording passage for royalty over an insanitary area, and Okomfo Anokye's magical control of the Ashanti kingdom might be quite inadequate to cope with the demands of a British Chief Commissioner of Ashanti acting through cohorts of police and regimental soldiers. Soon after expansion had set in, new values entered and the high sense of satisfaction with the gilded age was replaced by a disgust for what soon seemed defective, inadequate and partial to satisfy both feeling and intellect, even of a refined artistic sense. A new resistance had then to be faced, old values had to be revalued or expanded ; the enormous killings or murders, on or off stage of the Shakespearean drama, had to be frowned upon in a more sensitive society ; " drunk as a lord " had to become more and more a term of reproach and less a social distinction. Even where, as in the very harmonious Greek community, slavery had been thought beneficent and natural, where, as in many States of Europe and Asia, the subjection of women had been deemed necessary for a purified society, where child labour and human slavery had been deemed indispensable for industrial progress, and where freedom of contract had subjected large masses of the population to exploitation and servitude of the worst type, the new and enlarged contacts or orientations made the earlier gilded society look very puny and maladjusted, compared to the vaster possibilities and liberties that the expanded vision opens out for all, or, at least, for a greater proportion of the community.

Throughout these changes, it would be rash to suggest that human nature, as such, had made no advance, or what is more pertinent to our point, that humanity as a whole had not made a far greater advance towards its ideal, compared to what even the Golden Ages of different nations offer. We cannot tell what has been the nature of the material with which human society, in any epoch, had to work, whether of prime incarnates or of developed or secondary ones. But whatever may have been the nature of that material, the necessity for expansion has never made it possible for the smaller and narrower circle of the golden age to stand in the way of a wider opportunity or a greater horizon. The clash of the narrower with the wider has almost always resulted in the survival of the wider, and although the latter had involved the throwing overboard, as it were, of values that had been accepted as permanent and excellent, the fashioned result of the melting-pot has been, on the whole, more valuable than destructive. The example of the melting-pot of modern America has shown that the barriers of tribe, of language, of race, even of nations, can be surmounted for the attainment of far greater ideals, far higher orders, than the earlier standards of the village, the narrow geographical state, or even the continental empire of a Charlemange or a Napoleon had seemed to assure.

This is a conclusion that the most arid bigot or die-hard Conservative would accept. No one can possibly deny that a richer meaning, a more enduring value, a more satisfying harmony, comes on the nature and being of man when the good he has to share is a good in which all men, or a greater proportion of his community, can share. The only trouble is that man's selfishness prevents him from sharing the plenty with the many, and the cry of our age is not that there is scarcity of production, but that there is inequality in distribution. There is plenty for all, but only a few have all.

3. UNITED STATUS OF MANKIND

We do not see the end as yet. We do not see that that absolute whole, embracing the total experience of mankind, is as yet a welcome proposition for the practical politician. As we shall show in a concluding chapter, just as the individual had to know himself and realize his Okara before sensing the need for a Nana to serve as his paradigm to the great ideal or Nyankopon, so too, nations, or to begin with, races and tribes, have first to know themselves as units of the great family of humanity, from which the ascent is to be made to the greater or final and supreme ideal, the Odomankoma or all-embracing unity, a unity which may be here expressed by the term Humanity.

But before the ascent can be made, there would have to be recognized for the nations, as was recognized for the families and tribes, a Nana who should serve as the pattern and paradigm—Mediator and Exemplar—of the Supreme Ideal. A Nana for Humanity may take the form of the head of an individual nation or of a group of nations, but total and inclusive, a league of states, or union of nationalities—a world in which racial or national status had ceased to count, superseded, as group morality in the tribe was superseded, by a recognition of all mankind as a community of one kind, not only in interest, but in status, a single family in race of one blood linked and held together in one contemporary ancestor—one anointed head, nay, one Pope-Philosopher-King—a Nana. Mankind will then regain its status among the animal-kind and the angelic-kind, a race in status revealed as one, and because sharing that revelation in one Nana, will exist together in him, perish together in him, and be immortal in him who links their kind to the eternal-kind.

This insight into the nature of man and God, made known to the Akan by the inspiration of the Nana, this revelation of the reality of a united status for all mankind, is at the centre of the contribution that the Akan doctrine makes to the thought of man and the reality of life. It assures us that happiness is possible for man, and not only happiness, but perfection ; and even peace, the peace of the domestic family loyal to the family head becoming the peace of a humanity loyal to the family head of that revealed family—the Nana of all men of one kind. In precise terms, it is impossible, because of man's own obstreperous intransigence, to say how the fifth canon of moral advance is to shape itself on this high level, but the possibilities for future advance seem to be indicated in the following formulation of this last canon :

FIFTH CANON

ABSOLUTE EXPERIENCE, OR REALIZATION OF
THE WHOLE, REMAINS UNATTAINABLE SO LONG
AS RACIAL EXPERIENCE EXCLUDES PART OF THE
WHOLE, AND THE MORAL MIGHT OF MANKIND
FALLS SHORT OF THE ABSOLUTE THING.

Man's moral hope is greater than his present achievement.
The comfort is that he knows he can achieve more. The tragedy
is that he is unwilling to share that more, or even the little now
achieved, with the whole so that the hope may become a fact and
a common possession of man. Man had started life with *e-su*
from what may be called the interminable origin or block of the
race, and life makes the continual effort to return to the interminable in apprehension or experience of the whole ; the *e-su* of
each experienced in the *honhom* of the whole. Life had started
on the individual or ontogenetic plane, but the search is for a
completion or fulfilment in him, in each individual on the social
or whole or racial plane, a phylogenetic plane, wherein the
Absolute would appear to live for all as one, a completed or
fulfilled achievement of the race in one *honhom*. Despite the
stubborn, obstinate and perverse will of man, ever refusing to
reverse the Latin adage in his favour and the favour of his race
(*spero meliora proboque, deteriora sequor*), there is, as we have
hinted above, a large credit on the balance sheet of progress
in the effort towards the goal. In spite of man himself, that is
to say. Life, as the insurgent overflowing of a spring, would
seem to carry man along in its current, despite the resistance
his selfish will offers against his own good. And, of this fact,
we have evidence from animal biology, as something common to
all organisms.

Progressiveness, says Professor J. A. Thomson, is the crowning
characteristic of life, even on the lower biological plane. " No
doubt," he states, " there have been eddies and stagnant pools,
but on the whole there has been a flow in the stream of life, and it
has been uphill ! As epoch has succeeded epoch for inconceivably
long ages, life has been slowly creeping—sometimes swiftly
leaping—upwards, towards greater fullness and freedom. The
whole process," he adds with supreme vision, " must be
envisaged in the light of its outcome ; organic evolution in the
light of man."

And yet it is ever in the realm of man who, as Thomson says,
often carelessly interferes with the loom of the threads of progress, that the flow of the stream is most downhill. He who, *i.e.*,
man, because most endowed with most mind, could have directed

the course of the flow forward, is the greatest impediment and obstruction in life's insurgence. He sets up meaningless systems and authorities, he idolizes senseless group distinctions, he invents powers and machines of destruction, and generates and accommodates large masses of physical and moral evil which, for long and many dark ages, halt his advance forward and upward. But, all in all, there has been some progress, and the hope for the attainment of the whole is more than an ideal hope, it is an evolutional certainty, the destiny of man.

SECTION FOUR

THE EIGHT AKAN POSTULATES

CHAPTER I

THE TRUTH OF THE POSTULATES

I. IDEAS OF THE "PRIMITIVES"

LET us pause briefly in this chapter to review the substance of what has gone before. The reader unaccustomed to Akan ideas has seen trooping before his eyes a list of concepts which, being mostly peculiar to the Akan, have had to be expressed in the vernacular. A few of these the reader would tick and catalogue as either useful or original. Others he may discard or pass by. Among the former are certain irreducible fundamental postulates upon the recognition of which the reader may come to classify the Akan-Ashanti of the Gold Coast as possessing a distinctive theory of life and being.

Not that it would matter much to the Akan whether such a recognition for his postulates were forthcoming or not. He would continue to believe in them and build his present or future on them, never mind what others thought. But it is painful, sometimes, to encounter learned men and civilized anthropologists who refuse to believe that the non-European, non-Moslem or non-Aryan, or, lately, non-Japanese, races are capable of any originality which is not merely " primitive."

Among that class of thinkers anything showing signs of maturity or high culture but found among people they consider primitive, especially if such people happen to live in Africa, south of the Sahara, is hastily or studiously ascribed to " borrowing." Their mode of argument is quite familiar. " I found among the X tribe that they have week-day names which are dedicated to seven celestial gods, so they must have borrowed the ideas from the A culture." The logician naturally recognizes that there is a hiatus in this argument, the minor premiss being missing, but learned anthropologists are probably not all extremely fond of logic.

I cite one instance to prove this lack of generous and catholic judgment among certain writers on Africa. I refer to certain passages in a famous book by Professor Lucien Levy-Bruhl. He called his book " The Soul of the Primitive." At pp. 195 and 196 of that book he was confronted with (1) the Akan *kra* (soul), whose lot is marked out for it by God when, says Levy-Bruhl, it receives its marching orders on being granted permission by God to return to earth, and (2) the opposite number of the pure or good *kra* (*krapa*)—" the inspirer of all good thoughts and one who helps to put them to practical use "—namely, the *gbeshi* (Ga language) or *okrabiri* (Akan language), *i.e.*, the black *kra*—a being or entity who leads man into all kinds of evil, and then pursues him day and night like a guilty conscience.

Having discovered these high ideas among the Akan and Ga races of the Gold Coast, one would expect Levy-Bruhl to say of them either that their postulates were not primitive, or that they were on the way to developing advanced concepts of life and being. But Levy-Bruhl did not say so, probably because of his starting premiss that all those who live in Africa south of the Sahara were " primitives," *i.e.*, people incapable of high or developed ideas, or perhaps because of unwillingness to appreciate that the so-called " soul " of the primitive possesses ideas about the soul which are not primitive.

Under the circumstances, Levy-Bruhl did quite the obvious thing, just as some civilized anthropologists do in similar circumstances. That is to say, he ascribed the presence of such ideas among the Akan-Ashanti and Ga races to " borrowing." The stock description for such way of thinking is : " If my theory does not suit the facts then so much the worse for the facts." But that even did not satisfy Levy-Bruhl. He said in so many words that the ideas were possibly borrowed from the Moslems ! " Possibly," to quote his own words, " it manifests Moslem influence " (p. 195), and also, " Possibly here, too, there is a trace of Moslem influence " (p. 196).

Of course, had the author of " The Soul of the Primitive " had an opportunity of knowing the Akan-Ashanti and Ga races better, he would have known that such an ascription of " Moslem influence " would be hotly contested by them as an insult to their native genius. If there is any tenet which the Akan-Ashanti most particularly despise it is the tenet of Islam, and if there is any race the Akan-Ashanti ever looked down upon, it is the West African race which professes Islam. Both Sir Francis Fuller and the " Encyclopædia Britannica " are agreed that whilst Christians in Akan-Ashanti are on the increase, Akan-Ashanti Moslems are practically non-existent. And yet the Moslems have been with the Akan-Ashanti for 800 years at least (since the tenth and eleventh centuries), and the Christians have been in Akan-Ashanti land only for 400 years (fifteenth century).

The reason for the Akan-Ashanti rejecting the tenet of Islam is what has already been pointed out, namely, the absence of the ancestral concept in the Moslem approach to God, whom they regard as a Sultan. Islam rejects " God the Father." Akan

religion says, " Either God is Father or He is not God at all."
There is even to-day no Akan city of any importance—from the
flourishing days of great Ghana and the later beginnings of
Timbuktu, to the modern twentieth century Gold Coast—in which
the Akan and the Moslem races among them ever live and mix
together in the same street or quarter. The Moslems usually live
apart in what they call the *Zongo*. The Akan and the tribal
representatives of Islam in the Gold Coast hardly intermarry, and
hardly have any ceremonies in common. The Moslems live in the
Akan country mostly as servants or workmen and as pedlars of
dubious charms and talismans and fortune tellers. Because of
their unsettled nomadic habits, going and coming to Akanland
from their country, and tending their cattle in the open fields,
their social status in the eyes of the Akan is only a little higher
than that of gipsies in, say, Great Britain. In the old days the
country of the Moslems near the Gold Coast was known as the
" Country of the Slaves " (*Nnonkom*), for it was from their terri-
tories that the Ashantis drew many slaves for the slave markets
of the south.[1]

Despite the long history of their contact, the number of Islamic
words (not to speak of ideas) in the Akan language must be very
few. How then could the Akan have *borrowed* this very fabric
of their doctrine of being from Islam, especially when it is known
that the Islamic qismat, what the Turks call *Kismet*, is even
older than Islam ? One should not, of course, discount the possibility that both Islam and the Akan may have borrowed from a
common source, or that even Islam borrowed from an older Akan
race, but no one seems to have the time or the patience to go into
these abstruse suppositions.

However that may be, it is essential that what is found among
the Akan to-day should be properly catalogued and indexed. In
a world where most people live on credit, which, in turn, is dependent on borrowing from other people's stock and capital, it is
sheer carelessness not to place one's own stock or capital in a gilt-
edged security. The eight Akan postulates, so far discovered, are
the stock and capital of the Akan system, and to prevent other
people from getting credit for them, their security should now be
gilt-edged.

These postulates, which are also the working tools of the Akan
practice of morals and religion, are all the more valuable because
whilst they may be considered exclusive to, and distinctive of,
Akan thought and as original with the race, they yield on several

---

[1] Rattray, " Religion and Art in Ashanti," p. 65. The Akan word for slave
is *odonko*, pl. *nnonko*, and *Nnonkom* means simply " In the place or country of
the Slaves."

points to an accommodation with other ideas in some other racial philosophies, and are readily reducible to terms already established in the accepted body of human knowledge.

Had it been otherwise, had these postulates of Akan morals and religion proved to be of such a disparate character that neither Jew nor Gentile could discover any of his familiar ideas reflected under these time-weathered thought-forms, it would have gone hard with the Akan to convince the world of thought that he was not talking of an entirely new and unknown universe concerning which the postulates are posited.

In other words, since whatever Jew, Gentile, Christian or non-Christian might say or do, they all postulate one known universe within which the whole of their thought forms are contained, the propositions of any other system about the same universe must, to be susceptible to reason or to an ordered system of thought, make no pronouncements about that universe with which other incontrovertible truths discovered by other systems cannot be reconciled.

2. ''WHAT IS TRUTH?''

The last statement is not intended to claim ultimate truth either for the Akan thought-forms or for those already established by the better known racial systems. Obviously, a few of the Akan truths may quite well expose some of the better known postulates as really partial expressions of the truth or to be even untrue or false. Equally some of the better known truths, or accepted truths, may, upon the Akan showing, so readjust themselves as to express the real truth better than any one of the Akan postulates might appear to do.

For, indeed, the pursuit of knowledge is nothing more than a discovery of truths. We may set out on a quest for beauty, at a beauty parade, and discover not one beauty but a whole bevy of beauties, each, in her own way, expressing an aspect of that essential harmony of form and substance that is called beautiful. But we did not create those beauties ; we only discovered them. No system of knowledge, however ingenious, however elaborate, civilized or refined, can be of any worth which pretends to create its own truths. The universe is a reality and those who deal with it must realize their dealings in verity and in truth. Upon this writing table, here, is a piece of British coin, change from the evening's shopping. A bare glance at it shows it to be round and thick and bright. These are aspects of truth about this coin. For our present purpose, its roundness and thickness and brightness might be all that we are interested in. But some one might use it as a paper-weight or as a lever to prize an oyster open. He would discover other aspects of truth about the coin : that it has weight, and an edge, and is relatively hard. ·These are also truths about the coin. Again, a chemist might disregard all these momentous discoveries and say that the essential fact about this coin is that, on analysis, it is found to contain so much percentage of pure silver and so much of alloy. The chemist has expressed a further aspect of truth about the coin. Another measurer of truth, not so precise in analysis as the chemist, may disregard the alloy content and describe the object as a coin made of a soft, white metalic element, very malleable and ductile and capable of high polish. In other words, that it is a silver coin. This also is a momentous truth about the coin. And so we may go on and on, down to the dear market woman whose one interest in the reality of this coin is that it is a genuine product of the British mint bearing the familiar mark " B.M." which is worth or is capable of buying not a trifle less than a florin, or twenty-four pence. She also has expressed a true aspect of the coin.

But of these different facets of truth which are we to regard as representing ultimate truth ? Or is there ultimate truth ? Which proposition about a coin or about anything can be held up as for all time standing head and shoulders above all others and rendering the other truths of no real account ? We might quite legitimately hold that the dear market woman made the most proximate approach to ultimate truth because she had her eye on the purpose or function of the coin, what it was made for, its capacity for buying, or for exchange. Here, she might quite surprisingly find herself in the honoured company of an Aristotle where the function of a thing is held to be all that is worth discovering as its truth. But to accept the dear market woman's proposition as all that is worth acceptance might be to disregard the fact that many a florin coin might never go into currency, but be retained in a scientific laboratory merely for the purpose of demonstrating its chemical and metallic composition to a long succession of students until, at last, it becomes a museum piece. A numismatist may also arrest the progress of the coin in currency and keep it as an example of the coinage of a particular British epoch, and the florin piece may in time come to have a value placed on it that might make the dear market women gasp with wonder. Are we to say that these other functions, because not designed but adapted, are not true functions of a British florin ?

Pursuit of this line of thought may lead us to quite an interminable search after *odomankoma* propositions. Unless we are prepared to enunciate a different or new definition of truth, the acceptance of the general one that the true is what is in conformity to fact or reality must compel our acceptance of the proposition that any statement about reality which is in conformity to fact is itself of some value in so far as it serves adequately the purpose for which the discovery was made. To return to our example of a bevy of beauties. If the beauty we are looking for is to serve a beauty chorus, the aspect of beauty that may appeal to us may quite well emphasize youth and harmony of form as more important than if maturity and height were our quest in the service of eugenics, or to maintain a Nazi race theory, or to satisfy the particular demands of the owner of a harem. All such aspects, like every aspect of reality, are worthy of examination so long as they are true aspects of the particular reality.

So, too, the Akan propositions or postulates about morality and religion are of some value because, whilst not deigning to repeat merely what Jew and Gentile, Christian and non-Christian have discovered about the coinage of morality and religion, they emphasize aspects which had appealed to the Akan as valuable and probably fundamental in man's approach to the problem of how to make men in any community live well. For that is all that matters in morals and religion, the right ideals to make men live well. Some may think the bogey of a gehenna or hell the right way ; some may think the fear of eternal punishment the right way ; some may think the heroism of the Greek ideal the right way ; some may think the ideal of the English gentleman the right way. The Akan offer is the example of the dignity of the *opanyin*, of the alderman or head of family who is to become a *nana*, as the right way to make men live well. One need not be an eclectic philosopher to be able to say each of these several ideas expresses an aspect of the truth about morality and religion, that each, in fact, has some value. As to which expresses the ultimate truth, or whether there is ultimate truth, this treatise has nothing to do. Put to it seriously, the Akan would probably claim if not ultimate, at least a pragmatic, value for his postulates. He would say that they are adequate for him because they enable him to understand life and to make him live well.

3. THE POSTULATES CLASSIFIED

What is the nature of these Akan postulates of morality and religion ? We can begin by listing the names as we found them :—

(1) The E-su, or φύσις ;
(2) The Nkara or Chosen Soul ;
(3) The Sunsum or Experiencing Soul ;
(4) The Nana or moral and religious exemplar ;
(5) The Nyame or suprasensible E-su of Being ;
(6) The Nyankopon or suprasensible Experiencing Soul of Being ;

(7) The Odomankoma, or the exampled Reality ;

(8) The Honhom or Mind, Spirit of Reality.

These are the main essentials of the Akan system or theory of morals and religion, and the whole of this treatise has served as an exegesis giving the exposition or systematic interpretation of the place of each in the whole system. In the present chapter we intend to provide the simple handles or definitions by which they may be recognized and distinguished or related to some of the essentials in other systems.

Note, further, that the eight postulates lend themselves to easy classification : First, those which have an ethnological value, concerning the race or family, quite self-sufficient for the family's ethical and religious completeness without special reference to a greater whole of the human family. These are the E-su, the Nkara, the Sunsum and the Nana, in their nature absolutely original constructions of Akan mind. They afford an easy understanding and articulation of the racial life—the Family, its members' Environment, and their contribution to its growth.

But among these, the Nana, middle term of the Akan existential logic, stretches forth a hand of fellowship, or, better, relationship, to the remaining postulates, the universal postulates of Onyame, Onyankopon and Odomankoma of whom the Nana is exemplar, and whose universality is also reflected by the Nana in the race. Through the Nana the Akan family participates in the greater family of the universal whole in one union. He is the example to the ethnic Akan of the universal man, or the divinity in man.

Nana, therefore, partakes of two natures, the ethnic and the universal, and stands in a class by itself. In the arrangement of chapters, the title will be treated separately, whilst E-su, Nkra and Sunsum will receive treatment under a single chapter. Likewise, the three universal postulates will each receive separate treatment, not because they are separate in their nature, but mainly for convenience.

But, again, Honhom, like Nana, stands in a class by itself. As the informing spirit of the whole, of the Absolute Thing, it is both universal and ethnic, what the schools describe as a concrete individual, a total and all-inclusive entity beyond which there is neither a thing nor nothing. Its natural place is at the beginning in point of time, but in the order of thought—man's thought—it is more convenient to consider it last, and it therefore receives treatment in the last pages here as both a roof and root to the entire edifice of the Akan doctrine regarding God.

CHAPTER II

THE ETHNIC POSTULATES

I. E - S U ($\phi\acute{v}\sigma\iota\varsigma$)

E-Su is the postulate of a prime genetic basis for the origin of the social subject, *i.e.*, man. It provides the physical basis of a man's life or being, without its fully developed personality. *E-su* has some form of consciousness but is without conscious self-direction, the attribute of reason. The latter quality is acquired in the act of " leave taking " whereby a soul, *okara*, or personality, in the full sense, comes to inhere in man's being.

The idea seems to work in with the evolutionary conception of man's humble origin, the state of a being endowed with the beginnings or rudiments of mind, but not in its full bloom, until with the emergence of the flower of consciousness, called rational self-direction, man's mind sets in a teleological mould to realize his purposed being.

Stating the same view in other language, what we find is that *e-su* represents the fundamental bio-physical nature of man. The individual, as *e-su*, having broken away from the unformed mass of the race, presents himself to Nyankopon for *nkrabea* or his purposed decree, thereby acquiring *hyebea*, the *e-su*'s soul or *okara*, namely, the distinctive capacities of a truly human being with a corresponding responsibility to realize those capacities.

In biology or organic science, protoplasm is taken to be the lowest form of life, but its nature is so simple it is hard to call it organic ; and, from the chemical standpoint, its composition is so complex it cannot safely be classed as an inorganic substance. Protoplasm contains, for that reason, both life and lifelessness, and may well be looked upon as the missing link between the organic and the inorganic.

E-su, like protoplasm, has life. It is conscious without having, at the same time, a fully developed mental life. Taking the original concept of *e-su* as meaning race, species, kind, sort, we are led to conclude that the Akan took it to be the primitive root of being.[1]

---

[1] The word " e-su," besides meaning " nature," " quality," or " character," is connected also with water (*nsu*), river (*asu*) and rain (*osu*). In a secondary sense *nsu* means also vow, oath, solemn promise. Other developed forms of -*su* are *susu* (measure), *nsusui* (thought), *suma* (hide, conceal), *sunsuma* (shadow), *sunsum* (looks, personality, ego), and, probably it is the root also of *esum* (darkness. literally, in or at the place of " su ") and *suman* (talisman, fetish, amulet, or " any protecting power "). *Suman* means literally " the world of ' su.' " If the Akim form *sumane* is taken, it may mean " ' su ' gone wrong," or " ' su ' by-passed." As meaning species or race, the connection of " e-su " with *abusua*

What, then, is the character of the consciousness we ascribe to
e-su ? The answer is that it cannot be more than could be found
in the organic protoplasm, namely, the irritability and motility
associated with life, as such. Life, in contrast with lifelessness,
has the power of spontaneous mass motion, need of acting as an
unstable channel for the ejection of particles of its environment
in the process of digestion and reproduction. From this need
arises the irritable feeling or desire towards something or away
from something. It is a need, we may say, for an environment in
which digestion and reproduction and, much later, sex, could be
stabilized, namely, a world of individual experience. This irritable
condition gives rise to the desire of the *e-su* to depart from the
race or species, to be followed by a leave taking and an eventual
decree of the mode in which this chip of the main block could work
out its own individuality, apart from its race.

This factor of a longing to depart from the race-locked consciousness may be described in the familiar psychological terms of
feeling and desire or interest. From this arise the rudiments of
mind, " and," says Clement Wood, " in the end, brain, intellect,
and what is called soul." [1]

E-su, we may note further, does not disappear when man
acquires a soul or becomes a person. It is carried over into the
individual world of experience where it is known under the term
sunsum, the counterpart of the spiritual, of the *okara*. It is the
bearer of conscious experience, the unconscious or subliminal self
remaining over as the *okara* or soul, which the primitive *e-su* has
to realize in its individual being as its apportioned part of the race.

In terms of ultimate being, it cannot be difficult now to determine *e-su*'s origin. We have compared it to the Greek idea of
phusis, the physical basis of life, and we have seen that it broke
away as a chip from a main block, that block being the race. The
race, we know, is interminable, and the whole idea intuitively
suggests *e-su*'s origin from the interminable, from Odomankoma.
We suggest that this knowledge comes by intuition, but we could
claim a more compelling justification for it than that, namely by
simple inference from the very definition of Odomankoma as the
boundless source of all being, Borebore.

Further, the whole system of the final ontological position that
the Akan theology may maintain would seem to confirm this
derivation and intuition as justified in the finished harmony.
E-su gets its *okara* or soul from Nyankopon. *E-su* is also the

(family) is apparent in *a-bu-su-wa*, *i.e.*, a bit or portion of " su " broken off,
abusua being reckoned a portion of the race. " Su " enters into many compounds, *e.g.*, *nisu* (tears, from *ani-* eye and -su) ; *bosu* (dew, from *ebo*, mist or
fog and -su) ; *suban* (conduct, from -su and *ban*, form, shape, fashion, frame).
[1] " The Outline of Man's Knowledge," pp. 3-4 and 261.

matter of experience, of being in the world of the living. It is the basis of the *sunsum* of man. Likewise, Nyankopon is the Sunsum of Odomankoma, the Experience of Ultimate Being. Therefore, in the most common-place language, we may say that *e-su*, when it does appear before Nyankopon, does not do so as a stranger. For Nyankopon is already an expression of Odomankoma, his Sunsum. Hence, the Nkrabea or Hyebea that Nyankopon awards or grants to the departing *e-su* is a reproduction of the *e-su*'s ideal archetype pre-existing in Nyankopon as the Sunsum of Odomankoma. It were as if *e-su* presented a ticket of leave to Nyankopon bearing a specific number corresponding to a photographic negative stored in or by Nyankopon. Nyankopon, on his part, would appear to print a real picture of the *e-su* from its indexed negative. This printed picture is the archetype or photograph which serves as the *ideal* personality which the *e-su*, in its worldly form as *sunsum*, has to realize, or bring into the finality of being.

Later on, the ideal being fully realized, from *e-su* to *sunsum*, and from *sunsum* to *okara*, this okara becomes a *honhom*, a fully developed spirit or mind, an individuality which becomes God's, an *e-su* that, having shed its irritable condition of life without mind, now returns to the Source a fully developed and proved *honhom* or mind, part of Odomankoma's Honhom, an *e-su* which, through individual experience, has earned participation in divine immortality. It has become God's, one in substance and being with Spirit, the Honhom of the Thing, of the immensely rich Being, Odomankoma the Absolute Thing.

The ethical and religious implications of the postulate of *e-su* are dealt with in the main portions of the text and we need not recall them here. It is enough to remind ourselves that this, the highest that man can and has it in him to become, Odomankoma, is Mind or Spirit in development, and of its richness there can be no end.

2. NKARA (THE CHOSEN SOUL)

The Greek conception of *nous*, mind, reason, that is to say, the capacity for appreciation, seems to correspond fully to the Akan postulate of Nkara, message or intelligence, which each living person carries with him. Nkara is not usually spoken of as a thing possessed by the lower animals. No Akan would speak of the fate or destiny of a beast. Fate is a distinguishing quality of man, the self-conscious being of experience, this side.

In the idea of Nkara is already embraced that of Okara, in fact they are as the subject and predicate of a proposition. They do not fall apart when one is a definition of the other.

There are two parts to Nkara or Okara : (1) The Nkrabea and (2) the Hyebea. These have been fully explained in the preceding sections as (1) the conscious act of leave taking which the *e-su* performs in the presence of Nyankopon who seals for the *e-su* a living personality ; and (2) the giving of the leave, according to the nature of the *e-su*'s individuality, not as if invented, but already stored up in Nyankopon, and of which the *e-su* is dimly aware by feeling, and which he wishes or desires to become or to have realized. That becomes his decree (*hyebea*).

The value of the postulate is the emphasis it lays on the freedom of the man's will and his consequential responsibility for his own use of this freedom. The only sense in which that freedom can be said to be determined or decreed is that it is limited or stamped by the original nature of the *phusis* or *e-su* of the individual. It may have been formed, as a protoplasm, by the intensity of its irritability and motility, again depending on its own share of primitive feeling, but in whatever form it may be said to have arisen, there can be no question of anyone else being responsible for its chemical or organic composition or structure. Having now become part of a world in which individuality is realized, he has to bear the *nkrabea* as his share in the limitation of his partnership in ultimate being. Hence it is called destiny, a man's appointed lot ; it is not, however, wooden or cast-iron, but something lively, full of feeling, desired and rational.

A man can be absolutely free only if he is the universal individual.[1] But man is otherwise free in the sense that his own nature had prescribed for him what his destiny was to be. The only limitations on this freedom are the consequences of sharing in community being. The harmony which the universal community demands for itself imposes the limitations for the sake of general and particular harmony. It is inaccurate therefore to speak of the Akan conception of freedom as grossly undetermined, and it is also inaccurate to speak of it as absolutely decreed, beyond the man's own powers. Each individual has an eye in which he sees the world of being reflected in himself, he only errs when he believes that his being is the eye of the world.

This, too, is another reason why individual immortality is, in itself, illogical, as out of harmony with the immortality of the one unity of being which is not several eyes but one unitary eye. The only immortality worth having, and possible to have, is solution of the self in being, that you may be one with the eye, and see all, for all will be in you. This is divine immortality, to be in the whole

---

[1] The successful dictator always has this feeling or belief, namely, that he is the universal individual, until he meets his first major failure. Then he goes mad.

All. It makes social sacrifice, or service for the whole, a personal equation or service, and in no sense a sacrifice of the self for others. On the contrary, it might appear to be a sacrifice of others for yourself, if, that is, you wish to company with the immortals.

3. SUNSUM (THE INDIVIDUAL)

Christians postulate the World, the Flesh and the Devil as the antithesis to God, Freedom and Immortality, and the Akan postulate of the Sunsum answers in some material respects to the general implication of the antithesis. If God, Freedom and Immortality can be attained, the victory must come through the conquest of those evils and weaknesses to which the human flesh is heir. So, it would seem, is the place of Sunsum in Akan theology. With this difference, Sunsum is not *opposed* to the ideal as an evil standing in the way of its easier or quicker realization. Sunsum is necessary for the ideal, is complementary of the whole, and is, in fact, the matter or the physical basis of the ultimate ideal of which Okara is the form and the spiritual or mental basis. Further, Sunsum is not necessarily an evil, nor merely worldly, nor unquickened flesh. As a conscious counterpart of Okara its function is to prepare for the Nkara to be made good, the message to be carried out.

The ethical and religious implication of this idea has been discussed at length in the sections preceding. Here, we have only to show its psychological motive. And even for that we have the fruitful hypothesis of Myers's liminal and subliminal consciousness, showing how the Akan attempt to solve the apparent duality of the psychological life has been paralleled by modern European thought.

The father of psycho-physics, G. T. Fechner, had made familiar for that thought the conception of a *limen* (threshold) of consciousness, separating subconscious or subliminal psychical process from supraliminal or conscious psychical process, and the further study of the subconscious or co-conscious operations eventually compelled orthodox psychology to accept the inference of an organized personality with the co-conscious operations as its expression.

The attractive idea gave rise to the recognition of double or multiple consciousness or personality, and the manifestations of the underlying powers in post-hypnotic suggestion and telepathy were responsible for a new crop of theories to explain the facts. Some held that the facts were instances of division of the normal personality, and as explicable by the principle of cerebral dissociation ; others, concentrating their attention on the more extreme instances, treated all such manifestations as instances of the possession and control of the organism of one person by the spirit or soul of *another*, generally a deceased person. In fact such unaccountable manifestations as exaltation of the powers of the senses, of the memory and of control over certain organic processes, had appeared so magical to many that the appeal to the dead spirit as responsible for these actions was leading science itself to the degenerate dogmas of primitive fetishism which some, at least, even in Africa, had discarded (see 14th ed. " Encyclopædia Britannica," art. " Subliminal Self ").

Then came F. W. H. Myers with his brilliant hypothesis summarized as a conception of the soul of man as capable of existing *independently* of the body in some super-terrestrial or extraterrene realm. As already stated elsewhere, he regarded our normal mental life as only a very partial expression of the capacities of the soul, so much, only, as can manifest itself through the human brain. He regarded the brain as still at a comparatively early stage of its evolution as an instrument through which the soul operates in the material world. So much of the life of the soul as fails to find expression in our conscious and organic life through its interactions with this very inadequate material mechanism remains beneath the threshold of consciousness and is said to constitute the subliminal self. It is held to be in touch with a realm of psychical forces from which it is able to draw supplies of energy which it infuses into the organism, normally in limited quantities, but, in exceptionally favourable circumstances, in great floods, which, for the time being, raise the mental operations and the powers of the mind over the body to an abnormally high level.

There are three points of interest in Myers's theory similar to the Akan's : (1) conception of a material world in which the soul operates from an extraterrene realm ; (2) a manifestation of the mind or soul (okara), in exceptionally favourable circumstances, being infused with energy in great floods ; and (3) failure of the mental life through absence of an adequate interaction of the material mechanism (sunsum) with the soul. These factors could not but lead to the Akan postulate of the Okara as standing over and other than the Sunsum, the one in the spiritual world ready to enter personality for heightened mental action, the other in the material world, charged with the duty of preparing for the entry of the Okara. And the Akan, quite properly it would seem, thought of the mystery that makes this possible as something worthy of worship. Hence *Asum'guare*.

I do not, of course, recommend to modern European thought to follow the Akan and worship this mystery that explains why

any man, at his choice, has it in him to become a god or remain a
beast. But it is obvious that genius, which is said to be the
infinite capacity for taking pains, may be shown in Akan terminology to express the attitude of the thinker who treats his
mind as a god and worships it. He devotes his days and nights
squeezing out infinite ounces of energy from his mental storehouse
and realizes that he could be its master only if he prepared for it
and made his whole being ready for such energies to be infused
into him in great floods.

To the Akan, then, Sunsum is a form of consciousness or
embodies one, but it is a very partial and inadequate expression
of the full capacities of the Okara who, or which, remains beneath
or above the gates of consciousness ever waiting for the door to be
opened for its entry. And he worships the Okara and prays for
its entry into consciousness in much the same way as the psalmist
sang : " Lift up your heads, O ye gates ; even lift them up, ye
everlasting doors : and the King of glory shall come in. Who is
this King of glory ? The Lord of hosts, He is the King of glory." [1]
The glory of the Okara in regard to the Sunsum may sound
different compared to the glory of the Ascension, but the principle
is the same. It is in that manifestation of entry into the threshold
that the mind attains its most supreme beauties and beatitudes.
The man of genius, or the outstanding individual, cannot bring
out his innate characteristics to the benefit of the social tradition
unless conditions are made favourable in him for the flood gates
to open for glory to come in.

Sunsum is not therefore by contrast worldly, fleshly or devilish,
but of the very nature of that means to an end without which the
end can never be or become. It is an essential element in the
system.

And the value of the postulate is the same whether taken in its
usual sense as applied to the human mind, or in a higher sense as
applied to Mind or Spirit. For in metaphysics, too, the conception
of Nyankopon as Sunsum of Odomankoma, and the further conception of Nyankopon as the Experience of Interminable Being,
imply that Odomankoma attains full development as Mind by
the full play which its expression in experience obtains. The
theory of Myers may be applied to that realm also in the sense
that Mind or Spirit of ultimate being is a realm of psychical force

[1] Psa. xxiv. 9–10. According to Irwin (" The Universal Bible Commentary "),
this psalm was sung in the Temple on the first day of the week, as if in unconscious prophecy of Christ's resurrection. From ancient times the psalm has been
applied to the ascension of Christ to heaven. The ancient gates of Zion are
poetically called on to raise their heads, in token of reverence to Him whose
entrance is an act of condescension. The symbolism, we suggest, is most apt,
for the entry of the *okara* into *sunsum* looks like condescension into the material
by the sacred.

from which universal progress is able to draw supplies of energy which it infuses into the organism of the world, normally in limited quantities, but, in exceptionally favourable circumstances, in great floods, which for the time being raise the Spirit of Being over its material conditions of development to an abnormally high level.

The spurts of civilization and the corresponding facets of decline and fall throughout the ages of man's experience, bear evidence to the manifestation of this principle. Man, in a small way, has only partially divined this fact, and he is unable or unwilling to apply the principle to the universal good because of an unaccountable underlying nature of racial selfishness.

Preferring to interpret race, not in terms of the whole, but in terms of any little convenient geographical unit of peoples, different portions of the race of man, at different times, have come to imagine that their race, and not the other race, was the eye or being of the universal. They even call their race the choice or elect of God, meaning not an exemplar, but the only choice. Little did it occur to them that a God who could have the whole, but was satisfied with the little bit, was either defective as a god, or not a god at all. No evil is evil enough to happen to any man who worships a defective god.

Untroubled by this elementary self-condemnation, they pursue their belief that they are the elect, and hold that the great unchosen rest have been given them as means to serve their own end. That, throughout the ages, the chosen of one epoch had, in turn, become the servitor of the chosen of subsequent epochs, appears not to trouble the self-centred apostles of the chosen. To the end, consciousness of the whole eludes them until inevitable racial death, baulked for want of room to expand its genius, levels down the so-called elect of God.

For, indeed, this impartial acquaintance with the true universal may, for a time, give some impartial harmony of beneficence to those indulging in it, but soon it either palls on the imagination of genius or defeats itself in the attempt to pervert the conscious liberation of outstanding characteristics (Fourth Canon) not for the good of the total racial experience (Fifth Canon) but for the limited empire or race of the particular bearers of the liberated characteristics—Egyptian, Assyrian, Hebrew, Hittite, Greek or Hellene, Roman, European or the Nordic/Aryan craze of our own times.

Ample room is left over for development of the whole of which men are not, as yet, fully conscious. Even where moral experience or progress is recognized as essentially a human aim and achievement, consciousness of the whole is frequently deliberately sidestepped for the benefit of the limited group. The struggle towards progress therefore remains not only interminable but often undetermined, for the Spirit or Okara of Odomankoma would not seek to enter until the gates or thresholds of a Zion fitted for his glory are lifted up. Meanwhile the *limen* to universal and permanent glory is closed to humanity and, knock as hard as we may, because we are not thoroughly prepared for it, it stays unopened, even for the few who are chosen.

CHAPTER III

THE NANA (or EXEMPLAR)

I. A "DISCOVERED" NOT "EXPECTED" MESSIAH

THE Messiah is a Hebrew conception of a personage expected to come as the divine agent to fulfil a promise or covenant of delivery and triumph, and the Akan Nana may, in a certain sense, be said to be a Messiah, the anointed of the Akan people, king and exemplar. But there is a tremendous difference between the conception of a Nana as anointed and the original and hopeful Hebrew idea. The Akan Nana is not an expected but a discovered or revealed Messiah. He may even be said to be produced, invented, fashioned or hewed out by his community. For the Akan there had arisen the need for a more concrete representation of the supreme moral maxim for the practical life, namely, what a fitting man should fittingly do in honour and without disgrace, a man being in this sense understood to mean a son of the dignified Akan.

By a gradual process of elimination the elected head of the community—of the family, the tribe, the clan or the State—generally called *opanyin*—who had survived the great trial and ordeal of headship, was, on his death, discovered as a revelation of the ideal good and was, thereupon, deified as the worshipful product of what a dignified son of the Akan should be. The discovery had, in fact, taken place at an earlier stage, when as a member of the general mass of the family, he had been selected the fittest person to rule and lead his community, head of the family, chief of the tribe, patriarch of the clan, or king of the State. In that process he had been anointed and had, in addition, been worshipped with acts of adoration and reverence as some one like a god, or one who was about to become a god. The revelation became complete, the discovery confirmed, when the Opanyin reached a stage fitting him for deification ; when, that is, overtaken by death, he still was an honoured man. He had proved himself a ruler well and truly anointed of his people, an Opanyin became a Nana.

The Akan sense of a Messiah is therefore best interpreted in the Maxim referred to : *Animguase mfata Okanni Ba,* " A thing of dishonour and a son of the Akan go ill together." [1] In other

---

[1] Curiously enough, this very pregnant Akan utterance is not found in Christaller's Twi collection of the proverbs or maxims, but is happily found in Acquaah's Fante-Akan Proverbs, No. 1105 : *Enyimguase mmfata Okanyi.*

words, their sense of one fit to be called God's anointed is a man of dignity, one without disgrace, in nature like a son of Akan.

It serves no useful purpose borrowing more than this from the original Hebrew idea of what the Greeks called Christos, referred to at one place in the canonical books as " a prophet like unto Moses," at another as " prince of the house of David," and at yet another as the "suffering servant." In Dan. (vii. 13) he is referred to as " one like unto a son of man."

Nothing in the available moral tradition shows that the Akan people, at any time, did expect a prophet, a divinely born " Osei " who was to be their or the universal ruler and deliverer, or a self-effacing and suffering servant, like the ideal man of the Sermon on the Mount. The Akan society, large or small, at all times regarded the possibility of discovering an ideal personage living in their community who should embody in his person the positive qualities of a citizen of the moral and civil estates, as a present fact of the " practical " life. It did not occur to that society to dissociate the religious from the moral or both these from the purely civil estate. Prosperity in life, the ability to live well, the actual living well—more of the activity and less of the poten-tiality—was at all times that practical goodness the exhibition of which the Akan appreciated. Doing good, to the Akan, was beneficence, that is to say, he would appear to say with Aristotle that goodness is not a δύναμις, a capacity or potentiality, but an ἐνέργεια, an activity, an actual life of well doing, here and now, in every aspect of life, religious, civil, and social ; in labour, in art and in the pursuit of knowledge.

2. THE VIRTUE OF DIGNITY

Stated in some detail, we may say that the fact of the Opanyin not being a priest, or a professed man of holiness, with innumer-able avoidances, and the rest of that sort of life, made no differ-ence to the evaluation of him as expressive of the practical moral ideal. What made him a man of importance, outstanding in the eyes of his fellow-men, was the fact that he had lived their life as an ordinary citizen and had not lost in dignity or honour and not suffered disgrace ("Animguase," " face descending to baseness," " debasement of the person "). As a son of the Akan, he was born with an *anim*, presence or countenance, born in dignity or as man of dignity, a positively good Akan, and his success in life con-sisted in *not* having fallen below the high degree at his birth, that is to say, in not having allowed his face, presence or countenance (*anim*) (to *gu*, fall, *ase*, down,-) to be lowered. To the noble

Akan son, fall from grace is a fall during one's own lifetime, and not an inherited burden. It is a fall within the conscious power of each particular moral subject to avoid. Not to have fallen away from divinity is counted to the moral subject a thing of supreme achievement. We recall some of the maxims cited in Section I, for instance 464 : "Nothing is more painful than disgrace," and 2451 : "Better death than disgrace." This absence of disgrace, this attainment and maintenance of dignity, makes the moral subject an excellent person. He had married and been given in marriage with honour ; he had bought or sold in open or private market with honour ; he had been member of the Asafo or company of fighting men with honour ; he had taken wine and dined with men with honour ; he had sowed and reaped with honour ; suffered famine or enjoyed plenty with honour ; brought up children with honour ; worshipped at the shrines with honour ; had suffered bereavement with honour ; and, above all, had joined with others, or acted by himself, to settle family and other disputes, bringing peace and increase to the family, with honour. He had done all these and come up on top without disgrace, without debasement to the dignity of a son of the Akan. This, they say, is surely an *Opanyin*,[1] one fit to rule the family, tribe, clan, or State, anointed head of the people, revelation of God in man, discovered by man. And if he passed that further test of patriarch, dying in harness, the *energia* of honour and dignity in him still at a high level without disgrace, then he is truly deifiable, a proved divinity, bearer of the supreme moral ideal, a Nana, the exemplar and paradigm of Nyankopon, what God in Himself is, or ought to be.

The Opanyin who becomes Nana is thus defined by Christaller : "an adult, a grown up person ; a gentleman, respectable man, a person of rank, senior, alderman, senator, elder, grandee ; a superior, chief, master (is also used of kings and of God) ; eldership, magistracy, office." And Maxim 194 puts the reason plain : "No one can by design give birth to *opanyin*." In other words, the Opanyin is made, discovered, and not born. His community makes him, as much as he makes his community, good. And Maxim 164 shows that once so made he is impervious to the temptations of the moral life. He would not lie for instance, or as the Maxim puts it, "No one turns an Opanyin into his witness." He would not lie to assist you in defeating the law if that is your intention in appealing to him as your witness in your lawsuit. He would come and speak, but he would give the whole truth away, and probably ruin your case, all for the sake of truth and honour.

[1] Probably from *pa*, good, and *nyin*, grow : "One whose goodness has grown."

And so the young and inexperienced of the community are exhorted to measure their conduct by his conduct. Says Maxim 564 : " A smart child dines with his elders " (literally, " If a child knows how to wash his hands, he dines with his *mpanyin* "). And Maxim 2610 shows that, even compared with the fetish, the standard set by the Opanyin is preferred : " The Opanyin's word is more potent than fetish."

3. THE GREEK AND THE AKAN PARALLELS

The true parallel with the Akan Nana would seem to be, on this showing, not the saint of what Hobhouse calls the spiritual religions whose particular goodness can best be displayed by his withdrawal from the natural and practical life and who is so conscious of the sinfulness of his own nature that his only hope is the divine grace to lift him from the natural sinful state which tinges and stains all that he does, " matched against the white radiance of infinite perfection." The Greek ideal would be a better parallel for the Akan because it did not involve a man losing the whole world for the sake of gaining his own soul. The Greek ideal, like the Akan, was one made for human nature. It did not consist in overcoming human nature, avoiding wine, for instance, or woman, or song. It was an ideal, says Hobhouse, for the active citizens of a free state, and not for men who could only hope to practise virtue by retiring from state affairs. Even when Plato and Aristotle put the philosopher's life above the states-man's, they did not forget that they were members of a self-governing community, owing their freedom and their culture to the security given by their citizenship ; nor did they forget that the pursuit of philosophy itself was an impulse in the interest of moral stability. " Hence the first duty of man, whether in the Republic or in the Ethics, is to be a good citizen. . . . The good citizen is one who can both rule and be ruled. . . . And thus the Greek ideal is cast rather in the mould of the hero or the states-man than in that of the saint. Justice is far more prominent than benevolence ; in place of the mortification of the flesh we have a reasonable temperance, a self-restraint which prevents the lower nature from usurping the place of the higher." [1]

Thus the answer the Athenian of the fifth century B.C. found for the question " In what does virtue consist ? ", that is to say, the Akan question of " By whose conduct should I judge my conduct ? " or the modern question of what is the moral standard, was very much similar to the answer which the Gold Coast Akan, yesterday and to-day, find. At any rate, the Grecian and the Gold Coast answers can, without obvious strain, be reduced to

[1] " Morals in Evolution," pp. 558–560.

similar terms in one proposition : The practical expansion of patriotic devotion to a personal ideal of dignity that sustains the common life. Instead of the unrealizable rule of self-repression, a place is given in the social whole for the operation of basic human nature to expand in a harmony of common development with those who agree to share the common life. Instead of a possible withdrawal from the common life as something supremely to be eschewed, making the animal nature of man itself a taboo of the most heinous kind, the possibilities within the common life for the perfection of many-sided capacities, physical, moral, intellectual and spiritual, are courageously faced in order to ensure beneficence, that members of the community may live well ; and by holding up the hero, the statesman or the Opanyin as anointable exemplar,[1] the ideal enables the fitter man, or the supremely good man, to rise above the prevailing standard, setting forth new values for further expansion, discovery of Messiahs, of Nanas upon Nanas, the good gained to-day conserved for the achievement of the future in an ever expanding social tradition.

Diedrich Westermann looked into the living soul of the African, yesterday and to-day, and said of him that " his religion helped him to maintain life, to overcome hardships and, in his own modest way and within the narrow circuit of his life, *to live well*." Religion, he said, provided the African with power in daily life and in adversities ; it filled him with confidence and courage where he needed them, and it helped him never to abandon hope. " It was for man a way of life and of comfort." [2]

Leonard Trelawney Hobhouse looked into the living soul of the Athenian across twenty-five centuries, and said of him that the great-souled Greek learnt to govern his own nature, casting the Greek religious and moral ideal in the mould of the hero or the statesman, seeking the best life in patriotic devotion to the State, " an association that comes into existence that men may live, but continues to exist *that men may live well*." And even much better than the generalization on Africa made it possible for Westermann to suggest, Hobhouse shows the Greek ideal to point to a type-man quite similar to the Akan type of a noble son of the community imbued with proper pride for honour and dignity. " He should have an adequate measure of self-respect, and a great-souled man who is in a sense the perfect type of this kind of character, being worthy of great things, should deem himself worthy of great things. He should know himself for what he is,

[1] Rattray, " Ashanti Law and Constitution," p. 405. The Akan ruler, says Rattray, is even to-day, " still intermediary between the *Samanfo* (ancestral spirits) and his subjects and performs the ceremonies of the *Adae* festivals. His person, just so long as he is on the stool, is sacred.
[2] " Africa and Christianity," pp. 93–94.

and do nothing to belittle or demean himself. In voice, in gait and in gesture, his dignity should be reflected. He should feel a proper pride in himself, and trust to that pride to keep him from anything degrading." [1]

Naturally, and not unlike all human approximations to the ideal divine life, both Westermann and Hobhouse found defects in both the Greek and Akan or African ideals. The African or Akan sort Westermann found " was not a religion of high blown moral aspirations . . . the sacrifices it demanded were hard and cruel, and often enough it left empty hearts of its most ardent adherents " ; just so, Hobhouse found the Greek or Athenian sort to be " lacking in some of the graces of those ethical systems which are associated with the spiritual religions," for the Greek definition of full citizenship left out the woman, the child and the slave with inferior rights. On occasion, said Hobhouse, the Greek ideal involved it in the necessity of extreme self-sacrifice, an extreme expectation probably as cruel as found in some African practice, even to the point of dying for friend or for country. But in both these cases, because the search was mainly for a life here and now, the two Berlin and London University professors are agreed that the Greek and Akan search had not been unsuccessful. In more fortunate circumstances it blossomed into the full flower of human excellence conceived on a pattern of what was truly divine.

And that, perhaps, is all that morality and religion can ensure for man, until he knows all, apprehends all, and identifies himself or his will with all, for, as the sage of Oxford laid down for all time, " it will be hard to find a proper sense in which different epochs can be morally compared or in which the morality of one time or person stands above that of others. For the *intensity* of a volitional identification with whatever seems best appears to contain and to exhaust the strict essence of goodness." [2] The Akan says (Maxim 2451), " Better death than disgrace " (literally, " Of disgrace and death, death is preferable "), and a higher moral ideal than this in any epoch or people it will be hard to find.

4. A NYASALAND DISCOVERY

The question now before us is this : In their search for a moral standard, and in their finding it in a Messiah, called Nana, discovered by the community as their nearest-to-God man, did the Akan approach the moral and religious problem from an angle and for a product which may find living room in the mansions of man's philosophy ? It would be presumptuous for the present

---

[1] Hobhouse, *op. cit.*, pp. 559–561.
[2] F. H. Bradley, " Appearance and Reality," p. 432.

writer to answer that question dogmatically, for he cannot be his own final critic, but the evidence of the Akan tradition, in its practice of both morality and religion, a practice whose value may be tested by the strength of the moral peace that prevailed in Akan communities, yields ground for saying that their search has not been in vain. Certain it is that, in so far as large portions of Africa are concerned, and taking town by town, family by family, community by community, and so on to the tribe and state, and even the Akan community as a whole, the Akan moral peace has been adaptable to the end of making man good.

From other available evidence we are probably right in holding that the Akan is not alone in holding up the Nana, the Opanyin or elder of the town or community, as the informing ideal of the moral peace. Probably the Akan moral peace, the peace for every little and great Akan community, town or state, is in fact, an African moral peace. Edwin W. Smith illustrates this from Nyasaland. He states that the question was put to an old man in Nyasaland : " When you say, ' A good town ' what is the sense of your words ? " and this was the answer : " A good town is where the headman and the older people are respected by all, and where they, in their turn, give thought to all, even the children. It is only a good town where the young have respect for their fathers and mothers and all their relations, and where no person makes an attempt to do damage to another. If there is even one person who puts others in a bad light, or does damage to them, then the town is bad." Edwin Smith adds : It is probable that all wise Africans are in agreement with this old man in Nyasaland.[1]

Extending the term " headman " used in the above quoted passage—a peculiar word which Western writers seem to think is a property of all types of African leaders, whether city prefects or mayors or Paramount Chiefs—we would say that the passage might have been written of the Akan " Nana " or " panyin." The wisdom of the Akan is quite in agreement with the utterance of the old man from Nyasaland.

And if the Akan Nana is of the right sort and served his age and community by living well and aiding them also to live well, cannot a greater community, equally disciplined, discover a greater Nana as their Messiah to serve his age and aid the greater,

[1] Rev. Edwin Smith, " African Beliefs and Christian Faith " (1936), p. 176. The same quotation appears in T. Cullen Young's more recent work, " African Ways and Wisdom " (1937). From the evidence, Cullen Young appears to have been the missionary to whom these grand principles of the African metaphysic of morals were first enunciated. He uses, however, " village " where Edwin Smith prefers " town," and states that " the occasion of enlightenment . . . was a day when there was desultory conversation at the men's ' talking place ' of a village in Northern Nyasaland."

or even the universal, community equally to live well? The discipline of the universal Nana would demand that if there is even one person, one race, one nation which " puts others in a bad light, or does damage to them," then the universal community is bad. It stands in need of a good, a better, Nana. It needs to discover a new type of ideal, a new Messianic exaltation even as high and as exacting as the unsophisticated *Summum Bonum* of that old man from Nyasaland.

SECTION FIVE

UNIVERSAL UTILITY OF THE POSTULATES

CHAPTER I

O-TE or UNDERSTANDING (ONYAME)

I. THE FIRST PERCEPTION OF BEING

THE Akan postulate of Onyame, the first of the universals, is the conception of a primary sensed reality embracing the totality of being. This characteristic nature of Onyame is forcibly brought out in the creation ditty cited at p. 64. There we learnt that he was Hearing (*'Te* or *Ote*).

In common parlance, *te* as a verb means " to hear," but it has a more general meaning which Christaller gives, viz. : " to perceive by the nerves of sensation, to feel ; to perceive within one's self ; to be affected by ; also to be felt or perceived by." In other words, " Te " in general is any kind of sensation, so that the activity has the meaning of perception, or what is known, or the process of knowing or perceiving, the power of apprehension, what in philosophical terms is called Understanding. The full effect of the notion may be expressed as the sensation of meaning impressed on us by the being of reality, that is to say, the reality that causes " hearing," perception or understanding, to be, or to be felt or known. It is in a total view, the union or harmony of all the sensations, or 'Te, which gives us a total meaning of being.

The impression is as of a percept. In substance, its nature is a feeling, the awareness that a certain situation has meaning for the percipient agent, according to the self-direction of the sense of perception, be it hearing, or any of the other senses. Onyame, we may say in brief, is the feeling of reality, the understanding that God is. God or Onyame is " Te," Understanding.

Now, as the ditty shows, it was Understanding who first conveyed the intelligence to the Great Ananse, *i.e.*, Nyankopon, who, in turn, conveyed it to Odomankoma, who thereupon created the Thing. But the ditty commences with a query :—

" Who gave the word to Hearing ? "

That is to say, How came Understanding to be ? Tradition nowhere in Akan thought provides the answer. But that is because it could deserve no answer. To attempt to answer that is like attempting to go behind the back of being to find out what

128

is there. And you cannot go on going behind the back of being interminably. Man's senses cannot take him any further than what primitive, primary, undifferentiated feeling does give him, the sensing or awareness or understanding that something is.

This is a matter that psychology has settled for all thought. In knowledge, the first thing is the sensation. There is, if we may say so in a loose sense, an element of thinking in the process of perception. But, as Lotze pointed out, and as G. Dawes Hicks, foremost British authority on epistemology, seems to support, it is only perception that can bring before us the fact of change. That is to say, to come to close quarters at all with what truly is knowledge, the first psychological fact to consider is perception.

And that, as we see, is how the Akan's God, or conception of Onyame, came to him, through perception or understanding. Who first gave the word? Who knows?, but man sensed that the Word was there; it was given, and he understood.

Naturally, that awareness was initiated by an activity, something in motion, the fact of change. Motion, invariably, implies some sort of life. At least, so the Akan must have thought. This first activity, the *primum mobile*, then, came to the Akan as an entity, an apprehended content or presentation, initiated by motion or change of place. And the Akan called the activity, charged as it was with what looked like life, or, on the whole, what was life, as Understanding : " Te," something with a hold at the root of things, *Hearing*, audience, sensing, informing.

There can be only one conclusion from this : It suggests a passage from the non-animate, or non-spontaneous life—a genetic Mosaic chaos—the purely material *phusis* of physical being, to the primitive basis of life, a spontaneous activity, of the nature of what has so often come to our notice under the term E-su. Hearing, or Perception, or Understanding, then, as the first activity we know of being, must mean a conception of Onyame as the E-su or the primitive physical life of Ultimate Reality. In the ultimate analysis it is the ἐνέργεια of being.

The character of E-su we already know, namely, a psycho-physical mass of being, groping to get away from an undivided whole, called race or nature, to begin an individual existence of its own. It is, if we may put it that way, prompted by a motive or desire to see itself as it really is, to reproduce itself according to the true picture or ideal of being.

Here, we must warn the reader that many of these terms are metaphorical. When we speak of the E-su desiring " to see itself " or " to reproduce itself," we are using terms which, if we had the power of an omniscient, might be better expressed with dots . . . or blanks .   . Man is so utterly limited, he cannot think of Ultimate Reality but in metaphors drawn from the ordinary concrete things of common experience.

It was not easy to determine in earlier chapters how the individual E-su originated. It was suggested that it must have come from an interminable Source, and thereafter it approached Nyankopon for leave taking (*Nkara*). But as regards Onyame, since he is proved to be the physical basis of Ultimate Reality, the solution seems to be at hand; that, beyond or behind Ultimate Reality, any other E-su of Onyame is indiscoverable. Indiscoverable, that is to say, except within it, involved in the very essence of the Thing. In so far as the Understanding of man is concerned it is *the* Ultimate Reality. It follows that since the individual's E-su is of a piece with the E-su of Onyame or of Ultimate Reality, that, too, must have been derived from Ultimate Reality. That is to say, a man's *E*-su is an entire and total part of being.

2. A PROBLEM IN THE FOURTH DIMENSION

The next problem calling for solution is also amenable to a simple inference. Namely, does Onyame, too, like an individual's E-su, seek to be itself, does It go in search of Its true being? Is there an ideal form for Its psychophysical being, towards which It strives? Naturally, there must be. There must be a desire or feeling on the part of Onyame to seek self-expression, otherwise what It is, could not have been felt by other minds. Its movement must have been spontaneous, and more so than that of man, for it is not a part, but a total, movement. Of the consequences of this we shall speak in a later paragraph.

Here, it is necessary to point out, further, that the physical fundament of being is also fully present to the Akan consciousness as we saw in the poser quoted at p. 47:

> He went far away,
> He went long ago,
> He went before any one came.
> Which of them is the eldest?

Onyame, Onyankopon, Odomankoma, the There, the Then and the There-Now, which of them is the eldest?

This, too, had better be left without any futile attempt to find a flat answer. To suggest that space is older than time, or that time is older than space, or that space-time is older than either time or space, is to waste both time and space. Onyame simply is, or he would not be ultimate in his being. Here, indeed, we may take a leaf out of literary and scientific thought, out of H. G. Wells, Einstein, P. D. Ouspensky and those of that ilk, and say that the Akan had long anticipated them in the concept of a possible or an actual fourth dimension. The Akan had perceived that time could not be separated from space, nor space from time, nor both from either without expressing quite a half-hearted apprehension of the totality of being. If God is in time everywhere, then God is never late anywhere. Length, breadth, depth together ; Space, Time and Eternity together, time is already present as is space. Between the three, there is none that is first in time. They exist together. For things to *be together* involves time, it takes time, and the togetherness persists in time.

And the Akan makes this categorical affirmation of the unity of being on the bare consciousness of feeling. He does not reason this out or analyse it. He feels simply that being is. " Who gave the word to Hearing ? " the Akan asks, and would not stop for an answer. He proceeds to act on the apprehended reality as something sufficient, or, at least, adequate for what he needs of life. Not only does he call Him or It Onyame ; he worships what he affirms. It is the supreme " it " of his religion. Further, because he apprehends it or him as of the nature of the E-su of which he, too, forms part, he is quite ready to look upon him as the parent or head of the stock of which he is a scion. The stem and stock is Onyame, the trunk of the tree of which man is a branch, sap of his sap, blood of his blood, his race, his E-su. He is explained, or taken to be explained, but in fact he remains the mystery, the suprasensible *source* of man's own being, even of the Nana. And man is quite satisfied with the whole as a unity, his artistic sense, or sense of the orderly, prompting him to be so satisfied. Like the harmony that comes with a felt satisfaction, the Akan must have sensed also that with this felt awareness there should be satisfaction. The satisfaction is that all is, and is well. Enquiry, such as it is, is satisfied.

Thus, at the very outset of his attempt to explain reality, and in two simple affirmations, that God or Onyame is Understanding and also is extended reality, the Akan is brought, at close range, to a dogmatic attitude which takes Ultimate Reality to be what is sensed to be. Now, it or he could not have been so apprehended if, as a sensed power, the power did not dwell in it or him. In brief, Onyame is and is a feeling. Also he is a unification of all feeling towards being, and in that unity there is a union, a harmony or fruition of the artistic, a pleasing and articulate placidity, gateway to the beautiful.

3. ORDER IN ULTIMATE REALITY

But that is not all. Apart from the postulate of Onyame as a feeling of extension, that is to say, of the nature of Understanding of Reality, there is also the additional conception of him as orderly. We get this view of Ultimate Reality from the song of creation cited at p. 90 :—

> Odomankoma ;
> He created the Thing.
> Infinite Creator ;
> He created the Thing.
> What did He create ?
> He created Order,
> He created Knowledge,
> He created Death,
> As its quintessence.

These modes of the Thing we then saw to correspond to (1) Onyame, the naturally given, (2) Onyankopon, experience of the given, and (3) Odomankoma, reconciliation of the given and the experienced, of being and non-being. The three give us what Hegel called *Sein, Wesen*, and *Begriff*, Being, Essence and Notion, unification, differentiation and organization.

The prime interest of the Akan in his first apprehension of being was to feel his way, as it were, in a dark room, in order to bring some order into the chaos that confronted him. And he had not long to wait to decide that what his senses impressed upon him of being were, in so far, understandable and orderly. Indeed, a sense of order goes with a sense of the artistic, the beautiful. And, like Kant, the gaze at the starry heavens could not but give the impression of some Order behind it all, of God. The Akan universe starts with a world of order, not chaos, an order merely felt to underlie the being of the Thing.

In summary form, we may state the result of the enquiry into the Akan postulate of Onyame as revealing the apprehension of Him as Understanding, Extension (Space) and Order. We shall see in the subsequent two divisions that these form the thesis of a triad in which, on the one hand, Experience, Time and Knowledge, correspond to Onyame's antithesis of Onyankopon, and, on the other, Reason, Reality and the Absolute correspond to the final Synthesis of Odomankoma.

The Akan are not, of course, the first to make use of this original Fichtean idea. Hegel's copious, almost *odomankoma*, use of it gave, in addition, several groups in the triad of which the following are few : (1) Body, Mind, and Soul ; (2) Sense Perception, Presentative Conception and Free Thought ; (3) Art, Religion and Philosophy ; (4) The Beautiful, the Good and the True ; (6) Affirmation, Negation and Union ; (6) Dogmatism, Scepticism and Mysticism ; (7) the Legal (Customary) System, Morality and the Ethical system ; (8) Mechanics, Physics and the Organic ; and (9) the Symbolic, the Classical and the Romantic. All of which would seem to have arisen from the simple nature of the given, namely, nature and desire (motility), and the application of mind to the same. In psychology the triad appears under the forms of Feeling, Willing and Thinking, or Affection, Conation and Cognition, which again rise to a higher level of being in Life, Consciousness and Self-Consciousness, and in the final analysis to Freedom, Immortality and God. On a more serious survey, this triad may be found to interpret, with as much approximation to the truth as possible, the essential nature and unity of reality, bared of all attempts to split unity into trinity, or theism into pantheism.

4. THE RIDDLE OF THE RISEN MAIDEN

Now, of these orders, or triads, it is possible to hold that, ultimately, one aspect is more important than the other to the end of maintaining that Onyame is, for instance, of less consequence than Odomankoma, or that Odomankoma is a greater reality than Nyankopon. But to the Akan mind, this is the kind of insoluble riddle on which men of wisdom waste little or no energy. In the long view, the Akan would probably say, it is the totality of the series that makes the event, and that without the series there could not have been the event, the reality. The series is what makes the story. The following riddle is popular with the people.

" There were once three young men ; they all loved one maiden. Now these three young men left Bontuku to go to Cape Coast, saying they were going to buy things. When they reached Cape Coast, one of them had a mirror. He picked the mirror up, and he plucked some magic leaves and put them on the mirror, and he looked in it. He beheld their lover dead, and that she lay in an open veranda-room. He said, ' Friends, our lover is dead.' One of them said, ' I shall cause us to reach Bontuku immediately that we may go and bury her.' The next one, too, said, ' If you can manage to make us reach there, I shall immediately cause her to awake.' Now, one went and plucked medicine, and put it on their knees, and they set out. At once they arrived there. Another, too, went and got medicine and put it in a brass bowl ; and he took his cow-tail (talisman) and dipped it in the medicine, and sprinkled the corpse with it. He said, ' Corpse, awake ; corpse, awake ! ' and it awoke. Now of these three people, which of them did the best ? " [1]

He who looked into a mirror and brought news of the state of their lover ? ; he who brought them home to their lover ? ; and

[1] Rattray, " Akan-Ashanti Folk-Tales," p. 263.

he who restored their lovers' life to them, who did the greatest thing ? The human mind naturally inclines to value life above all else, and he who reconciles death with life, and makes what looks like immortality possible, naturally becomes man's hero. But are we being just to the other two ? We might ascribe similar honours to Odomankoma who reconciles death with life, non-being with being, but probably if it came to sharing honours Odomankoma would be the first to suggest that whatever may be his share in the series, it is the series and not an event in it that counts.

5. ARTHUR MAYHEW'S DISCOVERIES

A significant and important element to note is the fact that the Akan concept of Onyame, as the indispensable basis of ultimate reality, springs out of the character and environment of the people. Peoples and races, as such, do not build systems of the universe without relation to their own outlook on that universe and the environment from which they see that universe. Whilst it is conceivable for races accustomed to sharp changes in the seasons, extreme summer and extreme winter, to consider the one reality as split into two opposing and conflicting elements of light and darkness, good and evil, the birth of spring and the death of winter, with often a *tertium quid* to reconcile the two, it is difficult to imagine a people accustomed to the perpetual African summer, with its underlying background of interminable growth of vegetation and prolific supply of life, with little hibernation for either man or beast throughout the year, it is difficult to conceive men in that type of environment postulating an explanation for the ultimate power behind it all as split into two or three incompatible ultimates with a *deus ex machina* hiding round the corner for a chance to reconcile the two.

At an earlier stage, perhaps, in their first impact with being, animism and polytheism may seem the handiest way of escape from the sense of universality of power, power manifest in all movement, but the awareness of movement, as a power made manifest in all things, must be a proximate step to the awareness of that power as itself an articulate motility, an irritable centre for action. Motion often means life, and life as one perpetual summer, sooner or later, supersedes the multifarious concepts of power and is apprehended as just the one power that counts. Life in physical reality.[1] Obviously, those who begin their interpretation with a manifold of powers would find it far easier to reduce the manifold to a few, and eventually to one all-embracing power. It is much less possible for those who commence with the

---

[1] Even lightning, or rain, being lively, they would say, has life, *i.e.*, is a being.

antagonism of light and darkness, life and death, to arrive at a thesis or synthesis that the antagonists are one. In other words, the one in many is more directly a corollary for the pluralists or polytheists than for those who begin with sharp dualism. Further, it is easier for those who reduce the given from chaos to few and then to one, to appreciate more quickly the unified beauty that underlies nature than for those who start with the duality of repellence, of Ormuzd and Ahriman. Or, probably, some would say that it is because the appreciation of the artistic or the beautiful is susceptible of earlier development in a tropical people than in a frigid type that the manifold-in-one comes naturally to the former.

Arthur Mayhew, a great Colonial educationist, provides some evidence of this particular relation of the artistic to the unity of action and thought in the African temperament. He arrived at this estimate of the African justification of life by adding to their " gift for self-expression and an emotional attitude to life " the African's " susceptibility and receptiveness," a combination which, he holds, must produce nothing less than a temperament which is artistic.[1]

Now, the artistic is what is beautiful, harmonious, self-adjusted, organic, uniform. And of this uniformity or consistency of sense impression in the African Mr. Mayhew speaks with enthusiasm. The African's religion, he says, " is essentially sacramental. Life is a unity. Spiritual and material are closely interwoven. He is not illogical, but his conclusions are based on faulty premises." [2]

We have no reason to suggest that Mr. Mayhew intended these sentences to be taken as mere phrases, written because they are beautiful and sonorous. He may have met the African in the school-room or on the bush path and found him building systems of thought based on major and minor premises full of undistri-buted middles, but arriving at correct Aristotelian conclusions by some secret power of divine intuition, logical in every respect. Of that we cannot speak. But he goes on to show, for instance, why he holds African life to be a unity, and not, probably, like that of some other races, split into several incompatible compartments. Many Westerners, for instance, distinguish the veridical claims of science and the " sentimental " claims of religion which they hold to be a matter of faith, not of blood, or logic, the very essence of life as an organic thing in which each part is dependent on each other.

[1] Arthur Mayhew, C.M.G., C.I.E., Joint Secretary, Advisory Committee on Education in the Colonies, " Education in the Colonial Empire " (1939), p. 82.
[2] Mayhew, *op. cit.*, p. 82.

Not so, according to Mr. Mayhew, is the African view. For the African " Religion and science are not distinguished. Power is what he aims at . . . Tribal life comes to be revered as continuous and necessary. ' Extra ecclesiam nulla salus.' There is a social rhythm, a 'pattern of communal life in which, as the tribal dance, every member plays his part as a religious function." [1]

6. THE SYMPHONY OF THE TRIBAL DANCE

So, however " faulty " the Akan premises may be, their conclusion, their perception of the nature of reality, must be, of a truth, African in nature, namely, according to Mr. Mayhew, " not illogical." That is to say, the Akan perception of reality must be a pattern in which, like the tribal dance, every member plays his part, a reality in which there is a harmonious recurrence of accent —rhythmic, elegant, concordant, harmonious, orchestral, unified, or howsoever the rhythmic may be taken to be. And the measured harmony of the tribal dance of reality must also be logical, not illogical. It must conform to the science or the laws of pure thought—ratiocinative, analytic, synthetic, correct, sound, valid, in a word, rational and therefore true.

So, from this approach of the tribal dance, we see a pattern which runs through the social rhythm, the communal life, on to religion and science, and, without any break in the gradation or continuity which Mr. Mayhew finds to be a necessary part thereof, to the ultimate basis of it all, God, as one of a piece with Ultimate Reality, all a beautiful harmony, sensed and felt together.

One result of this felt and unitary harmony is that in this effort to relate man to what Hegel calls the universal spirit, objective both to morality and religion, even the deified being, the Nana, though he would appear to be man's own discovery in part, and God's creation or revelation in the other part, is not left out. He is the step towards, a chain in the continuity and gradation. The Nana's position is like a passage from the Hegelian idea of being to that of becoming, from the indeterminate to the determinate, from what both is and is not, to what implies a definite something, or some one, a being.

7. A MOVEMENT IN THE FOURTH CANON

Let us make this plain. In Onyame a final, or at least, a higher Nana seems to be attained. Final, at least, in so far as the Understanding can apprehend and understand. For the Nana does not come into being after the apprehension of Onyame, but simultaneously. He is felt as a revelation of something higher.

[1] Mayhew, *op. cit.*, pp. 83–84.

To be aware of him is to be aware of Onyame. Through him a greater approach to the moral ideal was made. It was naturally wasteful of effort to be having a cascading scale of Nananom who rise into prominence like illuminated centres of consciousness and then fade out of view, replaced by still brighter concepts of Nananom in rapid or delayed succession. Instead of this, we

PLATE VI

NKOTIMSEFO PUAA (" Headmark of the Not-To-Answer-Back "). " Certain attendants on the Queen Mother who dressed their hair in this fashion. It is really a variation of the Swastika." The Akan type of hair permits of different styles of fixed hair styles and plaits, called *Puaa*. The term " Nkotimsefo Puaa " is made up of different words and syllables thus : Nko-tumi-nse-fo puaa : Literally " Cannot go-with power-to say-persons' plait," *i.e.*, " the hair plait of those who are unable to go and say." The young girl attendants, fan-bearers of the Queen Mother, wearing this hair plait have to do and obey, it is not for them to reply back or give a retort. They do not confer with the Queen. (See Plate VI (*b*), p. 158.)

pass from what every Nana is to what all Nananom become, or strive to become, the definite one, Onyame. Just as Hegel held that the history of the world was a scene of judgment where one people and one alone held for awhile the sceptre, and continued to dominate the scene as the unconscious instrument of the Universal Spirit, till another rose in its place, with a fuller measure of liberty—a greater revelation of the Spirit in development—so we may look upon the development of the ethical ideal as a scheme of evaluations where one Nana and one alone holds for awhile

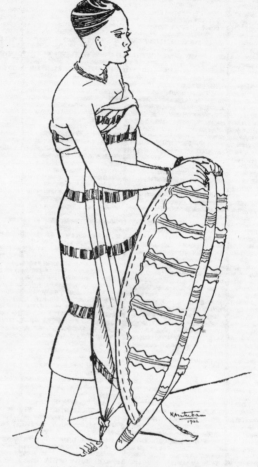

AN " NKOTIMSENI " GIRL
(By Kofi Antubam of Achimota)

PLATE VI (b)

An " Nkotimseni " girl, wearing the " Puaa," and holding (upside down) the screen, several of which secure the Queen Mother from the public gaze in an assembly or procession. (See Plate VI, p. 157.)

the highest or Messianic plane of exaltation, and continues to be the ideal of the family or community, the discovered exemplar or Messiah, till another Nana, embodying still higher qualities or embracing a greater or deeper expansion of the moral experience

—an enlarged family or a more complex and richer moral experience—rises in place of the former, a greater approximation and revelation leading to the goal enshrined in the Fourth Canon.

And thus far, and no further, we would go with the author of the Philosophy of History, lest we open ourselves to something similar to the familiar Hegelian charge of scheming to constitute and complete the scene of world history in the so-called three main periods of (1) the single despot, (2) the dominant order, and (3) the man as man—the pretended Oriental, Classical and Germanic periods. By these Hegel was taken to have suggested that with the advent and " perfection " of the European order, the history of the world had reached an end in the constitutional monarch or constitutional president or the totalitarian dictator. To follow that line of thought would mean ignoring the force of the Fourth Canon which gives the law of progress from the discovered Nana or Messiah to another still higher, greater, deeper and more exacting because more complex ; not leaving any part of life exclusive to Cæsar, but bringing all under the Nana's wing, until the totality of man's brood and activity is absorbed in absolute consciousness. That is to say, until man at last discovers the Nana of Ultimate Being, and not merely of a small family or communal whole such as many of the Akan States certainly are, or even, on a world scale, the Asiatic, Hellenic and Western cultures may show themselves to be. The Oriental, the Classical and the Germanic, or, to use modern post-Hegelian language, the Aryan/Nordic " scenes of judgment " leave quite large portions of the human race unaccounted for in the so-called universal history. The Fourth Canon as a law of progress takes no cognisance of such narrow stratifications of the moral or historical definition of race. There is only one moral race, the human race. It is also, we believe, true that there is only one historic social race, the race of man.

From the Fourth Canon we are led necessarily to the Fifth, namely, that so long as development leaves others as wallflowers or spectators outside the room, absolute experience or consciousness of the whole, remains interminable and unattainable for any particular racial experience because it falls short of the total moral experience. When, however, the total is at last attained, the whole realized, each man a god and all the universe godly, the need for an exemplar would seem to disappear, the concept of Nana of Ultimate Reality a mere predication of its substantive. For all being would have become one, and man become God's.

Thus, referring back to the comparison with established Western propositions on the similar problem, we are in a position to say that, all in all, the Akan postulate of Onyame has more in it than mere difference from Deism, the belief that Deity and the world are absolutely distinct one from another, the one being the external creator and ruler, the other the separate creation and the ruled. Onyame implies immanence of Deity and includes the idea of revelation of the divinity inherent in the object. But Onyame is also transcendant because the form it achieves in the end of the process is superior to the mere psycho-physical material of its beginning. But this is to take us beyond the bare idea of Onyame itself. The complementary characters of Onyame, namely, as E-su or the *phusis* of being and also as O-te or the Understanding by which it is apprehended, together with its inherent orderly nature, compel theory to exercise caution in equating Deism with Onyame in a full sense. All we need say is that the Akan's first universal postulate has the three qualities of E-su, O-te and Esen, or in English ideas the Root, the Understanding and Order.

CHAPTER II

SUNSUM or EXPERIENCE (ONYANKOPON)

I. AN APPEAL TO PROFESSOR WHITEHEAD

ONYANKOPON is the most vital and classical of the Akan postulates of divinity. Immanuel Kant would have described it as the Synthetic Unity of Experience. The English philosopher, Professor A. N. Whitehead, who had taken ultimate reality to be pure feeling, or the mode of experience proper to an unconscious mind, would probably describe the Onyankopon postulate as the principle of actuality and limitation through which or whom " the particular value of that shaped togetherness of things emerges." He had associated ultimate reality with the emotional intensity entertained in life, and the vital cause or ground of that intensity he ascribed to God as the principle of actuality.

We may pause here to look into this interesting theory of Whitehead's, for it has given balance and some correction to our own interpretation of the Akan view. In his theory, he has only two principles to explain everything. Feeling and that which actualizes it. The Akan have Onyame, which corresponds to the feeling entity in Whitehead's theory ; and further they have Onyankopon and finally Odomankoma. Probably Whitehead would include the last two together as the principle of limitation which, as it were, carves or hews the actual world out of the realm of infinite possibilities. This principle is described by him as the Subjective Aim of the universe. By Subjective Aim of a thing he means almost exactly the same qualities inhering in the postulate of an Okara or Odomankoma, namely, in Whitehead's language, that which determines what " prehensions " a thing will incorporate into itself in the continuous process of its own self-formation. Now since Onyankopon is, as we have seen, the greater actualization, or deeper meaning or the intent of Onyame, that is to say, since Onyankopon is the Okara of Onyame, that postulate would mean for Whitehead the Subjective Aim of Onyame. We can best know the real internal constitution of Onyame when we know what its Okara, its immanent end, is. For, if anything, an Okara, a Nkrabea, is nothing but the destiny, the end, of an E-su, or Sunsum, its teleological objective, or again, its Subjective Aim.

And this brings us to the original Aristotelian idea of $\tau\epsilon\lambda os$, or end, from which so many of the European " systems " seem to derive. But before leaving Whitehead's treatment of the classical idea, we may note this. That if, indeed, he holds that ultimate reality, or the " universe," is not a collection of individuals existing in separation, but an active process in which each event appropriates or " prehends " into itself all the other aspects of the universe which are relevant to it ; and if, indeed, he holds that the process which is the universe may be legitimately regarded as living, that is to say, not as a single organism which is alive, but living in the sense in which the process of the harmonious development of innumerable mutually prehending organisms may be said to be alive,[1] then for Whitehead to hold further that the principle of actuality and limitation is irrational and that God is the " Ultimate Irrationality "[2] would seem to mark the point of departure and difference between what, to Whitehead, appears rational and what, to the Akan, is irrational. For no ground is more patent than the ground and reason of rationality in the dynamic world which makes the universe a thing alive. Odomankoma must have hewn out the actual universe we know because it is and was intended to be an orderly and rational universe, the only one possible of its kind, a Leibnizian universe in a world of compossibles. At least, we know the world to be orderly and rational, and we see no reason to believe that its chooser did so irrationally.

The principle of choice, of limitation, must therefore be rational and not irrational. Nothing that is irrational can ever contain in itself a principle of " harmonious development of innumerable prehending organisms." The tendency of the irrational is to cancel itself out, to disorganize its innumerable constituents, but not certainly to develop them in harmony. As we shall see in the next section, Odomankoma is what he is because he makes for us a universe developing towards a rational end. That universe contains its rationality in its Subjective Aim.

And further, on Whitehead's own showing, there should have been no such qualification that the process in which each event appropriates or " prehends " into itself other aspects of the universe is limited to those aspects "which are relevant to it." Going solely by his own favourite quotation from Sir Francis Bacon on the mutual " sensitiveness " of bodies, the conception that bodies " perceive " or " take account of " each other should mean that "everything in the universe is sensitive to the presence of everything else." Dr. C. E. M. Joad, by whose summary of Whitehead's philosophy these paragraphs are guided, has confessed his inability to understand Whitehead. Probably, we ought to go behind both Joad and Miss Dorothy Emmet's ' Whitehead's Philosophy of Organism " to obtain a juster appre-

[1] C. E. M. Joad, " Guide to Philosophy," p. 583.
[2] Joad, *op. cit.*, p. 577.

ciation of what was in Whitehead's mind, when he spoke of God as the " Ultimate Irrationality." Perhaps so, but not for the task now in hand.

2. THE ARISTOTELIAN MATTER AND FORM EXAMINED

Which brings us back to Aristotle, whom they call the Master in philosophy. A most lucid and convincing account of the Aristotelian conception of matter and form, of nature or physical reality as given, and the ideal nature or end (" okara ") of that reality, is contained in the article on epistemology which the late Professor G. Dawes Hicks (teacher of the present writer in philosophy at the University of London) provides in the " Encyclopædia Britannica." That, together with Professor Dawes Hicks' lectures on Aristotle,[1] enables the writer to make the long and high jump of showing in what respect the Akan had been thinking in line with classical pronouncements on the subject.

Briefly, Aristotle conceived the world of reality as a connected and graduated scheme of being, extending from the pure indeterminateness of what he called first matter ($\pi\rho\dot{\omega}\tau\eta$ $\ddot{v}\lambda\eta$) up to completed actuality, the Deity. Each concrete individual in nature, each $\tau\dot{o}$ $\delta\dot{\epsilon}\tau\iota$, was to be conceived as a $\sigma\dot{v}\nu o\lambda o\nu$, a combination of matter ($\ddot{v}\lambda\eta$) and form ($\epsilon\dot{l}\delta os$ or $\mu o\rho\phi\dot{\eta}$). Matter was the substratum ($\tau\dot{o}$ $\dot{v}\pi o\kappa\epsilon\dot{\iota}\mu\epsilon\nu o\nu$) of all becoming, that which was to be determined ; form was that which determined, that which gave to matter qualities and properties, the intelligible essence of a thing, but in real existence they were never to be found in isolation. The whole realm of existence presented itself as a chain of consequences in which each transition was from the potential to the actual, from $\delta\dot{v}\nu a\mu\iota s$ to $\dot{\epsilon}\nu\dot{\epsilon}\rho\gamma\epsilon\iota a$.

And, with Aristotle, the two terms are strictly related to each other. Probably, says Dawes Hicks, the one notion that most comprehensively expresses the Aristotelian view is that of $\tau\dot{\epsilon}\lambda os$, end. The nature of a thing was equivalent to its end. Each thing was to be conceived as being, or as coming to be, in definite relations to its surroundings, and so ultimately to the whole of which it belonged.

In much the same way, Aristotle viewed the several forms of cognitive activity as falling into a kind of order or scale. The first, that which was the basis of the whole, was sense-perception ($a\dot{\iota}\sigma\theta\eta\sigma\iota s$) which had for its objects individual things ($\tau\dot{a}$ $\ddot{o}\nu\tau a$). Sense-perception was regarded by him as the faculty of receiving the forms of things apart from their matter, just as the figure of

---

[1] G. Dawes Hicks, an acknowledged authority on Kant and Epistemology, joint editor of the *Hibbert Journal*, never published a book.

a seal is taken on by the wax without the gold or other metal of which it is composed. But sense-perception was not merely a passive receptivity : it was an act of the mind, a discriminative act. It was, in a word, the awareness of a sensum (an αἰσθητόν) which was distinct from the act of sensing, and was a concomitant of an object (τὸ ὑποκείμενον).

Up to this point, then, we see some basic resemblance between the Aristotelian view and the Akan view of Onyame as a sensed objective basis of ultimate reality, an E-su. But, of course, the Akan view is not on all fours with the Aristotelian. For instance, the Aristotelian offers a complete solution or answer to the question, What is being, or reality ? What is knowing, or knowledge ? The Akan, at any rate in the treatment we discover for his conception in this treatise, does not seek an answer to all that. He is concerned with the practical question of asking what is man, and what is his place in the world. So that where Aristotle answers that each concrete individual in nature consists of matter and form, including all things, the Akan, in the postulate of an Okara, which is also of a teleological nature, only answers the question in so far as the human individuality is concerned. Only a human being has an Okara, or, at any rate, only an object that has a rational nature. So that for whatever may be the nature and end of things other than rational individuals this treatise is not much concerned. It is the case, of course, that whilst the Akan does not hold that things have *kara*, he holds also that they have a sort of inner nature analogous to the *okara*, that which is called *sesa*. Everything has *sesa*, a power or spirit, of the nature of the Melanesian *mana*. But that is neither an ethical nor a religious concept, and we are not concerned with other than these in this treatise. *Sesa* can even mean the spirit or ghost of a dead person, but Christaller points out that a *sesa* is an evil sort of spirit not like *osaman* ; the word often means the effect of mischief wrought by a spirit. In this sense, says Christaller, *osaman* could not be used. That is to say, when ghosts are thought of as evil they are called *sesa* ; ghosts as spirits (of the good) are *asamanfo*, not *sesa*. But we need not pursue this further in this book.

Further, Aristotle does not appear to say in so many words that matter (ὕλη) has what, for instance, Bacon would call a perception, whereas the Akan hold that E-su itself is an O-te, Understanding or Perception, and all that the term implies. But, even here, if we recall that Aristotle holds both form and matter to result in a combination which is the characteristic of each concrete individual (σύνολον), then it must be said of his conception of matter that it contains the germ of its own perception within itself, that is to say, whatever it becomes (ἐνέργεια) is its own potential (δύναμις).

In fact, by the interpretation of Professor Dawes Hicks, Aristotle held, further, that the sensum of perception was not only dependent upon the perceiver, but that it resulted from the meeting of a certain object and a certain percipient subject. If either the object or the percipient's body underwent change a different sensum was the outcome, and this was so for the fact that the object, through the stimulation of which the act of perception could issue, had a nature of its own, independent of its being perceived. A physical insensitive reality, without any potential of feeling, " an election to embrace that which is agreeable, and to exclude or expel that which is ingrate," could hardly be spoken of as being " stimulated " and, thereby, to give rise to a sensed or stimulated perception. Consequently we find Aristotle holding further that the functions of the so-called *sensus communis* were to apprehend the common sensibles and the incidental sensibles in things, as well as to enable us to become aware that we perceived, that is to say, to be aware of self in perceiving, and to enable us to discriminate and to compare the data afforded by the senses. In the final result, therefore, the Greek view is not greatly at variance with the Akan view as to the nature of reality.

3. UNDERSTANDING AND EXPERIENCE

Now, with the idea of perception, we reach what the Akan call O-te, Understanding. The perception of a thing is a total undifferentiated feeling. And that, say the Akan, is the nature of Onyame. And they appear to invite no argument on the conclusion. There is something very arbitrary and dogmatic in the form Understanding is taken to have. In words which Dawes Hicks used of the Aristotelian idea of perception, the Akan also seem to say, the idea of Understanding, of O-te, is " free from the antithesis of true and false ; the sense-particular must either be just apprehended or not at all." Onyame is, and feeling tells you so. Reality is either what it is felt to be or it is not. Its characteristics make it so. It is that, Onyame, or it is not its characteristics. The sum and substance of these characteristics are O-te, the kind of cognition given by E-su, the spatial, deep down, psycho-physical bedrock or reality.

Now, this notion of reality as the spatial E-su is easy enough to grasp for any simple mind. Space fills all space, and one cannot possibly be without feeling it. It is otherwise with time and the postulate that goes with it. To be, one must be in time, but the sense of being in time does not come to us with the instant assurance that primitive feeling gives. It requires an effort of thought, a comparison of this with that in order to " feel " the passing of time, to get the idea of duration. Classification, comparison and discrimination, these are essential adjuncts in the feeling of time. And, here, a wide door to the field of error is thrown open. Doubts assail the mind and certainty can only come through long experimenting with the various conditions. Hence Aristotle maintained that whilst all creatures endowed with αἴσθησις have a certain power of knowing, that is to say, of perceiving or sensing things, only those creatures that, in addition, possessed the power of memory (μνήμη), the power of (1) perceiving and (2) of reproducing presentations, and (3) of referring to what had been perceived in a past (time), were able to advance to generalized knowledge.

Now, memory was dependent upon imagination (φαντασία). It was the mechanically determined consequence of perception which was in operation, after the sensible object had gone, upon the relics or images (φαντάσματα) which remain in the sense-organs. Through the aid of memory there was generated in the mind that kind of knowledge to which Aristotle gave the name of Experience (ἐμπειρία), the essence of which was found in the grouping of resembling particulars under general heads.

Thus by a very penetrating projection of Greek genius into the essence of things, Aristotle arrived at the idea of experience or knowledge by means of abstract concepts like matter and form, an idea similar to what the Akan had postulated by the use of concrete personified entities like E-su or Sunsum and Okara or Honhom. For what it all comes to is this : that the Akan postulate of Onyankopon as constitutive of memory, namely, the ability to keep " the word " that O-te gave in order to convey the intelligence to Odomankoma ; and of time (" He went long ago ") ; and of experience (" Odomankoma created knowledge "), stands on all fours with the Aristotelian discovery that the advance to " generalised knowledge " was a special attribute of a being endowed with the capacity of conception, the capacity to compare, discriminate, relate, recall and synthetize. In a word, the capacity to do more than is implied in undifferentiated feeling. We can advance now from what is perceived with the senses in feeling to what is conceived with memory and imagination in the play of time.

4. THE DUAL NATURE OF ONYANKOPON

But there is still one important respect in which the Akan idea departs from the Aristotelian notion of ἐμπειρία. If, with all due apology for the outrage, we take the Aristotelian " Experience " to be some sort of deity in the manner of the Akan, then the comparison between that deity and the Akan Onyankopon falls short of one step in the relation. From a deity (Perception or Understanding) that just feels or perceives, we make, in one stride, a great leap to a deity who not only feels but compares, or in easier language, thinks ; that is to say, has the ability for conception. Now, the chasm between perception and conception is so vast that the Akan would seem to refrain from making the leap without first looking for a ground of linkage from the firm stand on this side of the chasm, and the uncertainty of the footing beyond. Hence in the postulate of Onyankopon the Akan sensed a double quality, or conceived the necessity for it. This further effort the Greek mind did not probably need. The Greek mind made the leap in one bound without any intermediate step. The Akan went about it gingerly, with the caution of one not quite sure that all was well. He, that is to say, conceived Nyankopon as not being absolutely bereft of all the primitive nature that had attached to Onyame. Onyankopon, too, is feeling. But feeling of a certain active mind, what, at a higher remove, is called conation, or will ; namely, an attitude of mind involving a tendency to take action.[1] And, again, the Akan conceived of Onyankopon as having the new and additional character of intuition or insight, the intellectual capacity that only an Okara other than Sunsum can possess. This double nature of Onyankopon comes to us under two modes : (1) the conception of him as the Okara of Onyame, and (2) the perception of him as the Sunsum of Odomankoma.

First, that is to say, we have given to us the substratum, E-su, which is sensed as Onyame. Next, we advance to an ideal content which appears to the Akan as the better self, the greater or better Onyame, the Onyan-ko-pon, the ideal which the E-su of Ultimate Reality affects. Then, at a still higher grade, this diety, Onyan-kopon, who had appeared as the ideal of E-su, turns out to be really at a stage below the highest notion of completed reality, and forms the Sunsum of that interminable Being, Odomankoma. That is to say, it is not as if we had three separate cardinals, 1, 2, 3, each standing by itself and a whole by itself, but as if we had

[1] According to the German psychologist, F. Brentano, no real distinction can be made between conation and feeling. He argues that the mental process from sorrow or dissatisfaction, through hope for a change and courage to act, up to the voluntary determination which issues in action, is a single homogeneous process. In answer to this, critics point out that the mere fact that the series is continuous is no ground for not distinguishing its parts ; if it were so, they add, it would be impossible to distinguish by separate names the various colours in the solar spectrum, or, indeed, perception from conception, or, we may add, Onyame from Onyankopon. But the Brentano view-point is useful. *Natura non facit per saltum.*

three grades or orders of a series, namely, the ordinals *first, second, third* shading into, and from, each other by imperceptible gradations. Better still, it is not as if we had three elements, earth, fire, and air, but rather as if we had three grades of chemicals, solid, liquid and gaseous, the content of each or all of which may form part of the composition of any element or of all the elements. We can think of stone, wood and animal as three distinct orders of being, but we do not think of matter, form and spirit except as interconnected and interwoven phases of one order, with emphasis on one aspect at a time, and some part of the one contained in some part of the other.

Now, it is obvious that, upon analysis, form would stand out as nearer to matter than spirit is, and again, form would stand out as nearer to spirit than matter is. Form is the articulation or intelligence or measuring rod of the two extremes : the heat, the equator, of the two poles. In form illumination begins and spreads as the vivifying base of the other two. The two are not completely comprehensible without it. Onyankopon was he, the Ananse Kokuroko, the messenger, mediator, intelligence, who carried the word of Hearing from Onyame to Odomankoma, whereupon the latter created the Thing. He it was also who mediated between Space and Reality. He is Time. He it was also who stood between Order and Death. He is Knowledge, Experience.

Recognition of this duality in Onyankopon may save critics a load of ink. The three postulates Onyame, Onyankopon and Odomankoma do not represent a severalty, a trinity of disparate powers each within a compartment and without interconnection, or, as Whitehead would say, without means of " prehension " with the others. It is a series continuous in every respect and merely distinguished for better comprehension by finite minds, minds, that is to say, who became aware of them by graduation, possibly as freshers at first, then as a class, something like dots . . . , and later at one great leap, as just one solid unit, a white patch (   ), a university that fills all, and takes all in even without the brackets. Remove the brackets and gaze into eternity. What you find is not *a* white patch, but white patch. But soon it begins to acquire proportion, to acquire body and shape ; and portions, sooner or later (much sooner than many are prepared to admit), begin to stand out, not now as freshers or sophomores, but as specialists in the same order and walking towards the same end, the realization or articulation of total experience, of the Absolute Thing.

But the unity of the whole is not thereby impaired by the divisions or sections that the human mind imposes for its own convenience. Probably Aristotle would say the same thing,

148

namely, that if even you do get down to it and make a separation into three orders, you will find that the " form " of one matter is the " matter " of another form. Onyankopon is as much the matter of Odomankoma as Onyame is the matter of Onyankopon. And the interminable progression is only halted by the need for a real halt somewhere, for we cannot go behind the back of the back of being interminably. In the postulate of Odomankoma, who died and yet lives, we have the reconciliation we need. Scepticism swallows dogmatism, and now we have a completed Synthesis, or, if you feel still dissatisfied, an unformed but definite world of Mysticism is there for your comprehension.

5. ONYANKOPON'S LIKENESS TO MAN

This solution, we repeat, has been brought about by the effect that the triad of the creation ditty :

" Who gave word,"

the quiddity of the space/time poser,

" He went far away,"

and the song of ordered creation,

" Odomankoma created the Thing,"

makes possible for Akan thought. From within this triad not only the explanation for reality, but of its different departments, ethics and religion, the human mind, nature of the created universe, the way we think about it, in a word, art, religion, and science, find their complete ground for final statement. Here we are concerned only with the way the whole impresses itself upon the active nature of man, in response to its effort to understand, whereupon he receives the impression or perception that the total or whole of reality is Understanding—Onyame. Then by further self-application the conception of the whole dawns upon the mind or, better, is apprehended as the means to greater knowledge and more certain action for the Sunsum or Experience—Onyankopon ; and, as we shall see in the last section, ultimate reality at last reveals itself to be the object of a higher form of feeling, an intuition or inner light or Being, whereupon we get pure Intellection or Insight, a transcendental awareness or understanding of Odomankoma. To worship this will be the highest form of religion for man. But the Akan would seem to have centred their religion upon Onyankopon, and the reasons for this we shall now state.

The Akan always had been and still is a practically minded man. The many-sided mysticism of the East would probably leave him quite appalled. He would prefer a straightforward absorption into a single unity. The imaginative phantasies of

Hindu Gods, with innumerable heads and milliard of hands and feet, would probably frighten him out of his wits. There is only one beauty of the human form that he knows and appreciates, the symbol that is of man, the supremely personal, fully integrated, and organic being. There is something very effective and solid about man. He is all there. And he wants to be there. Man, says Maxim 2418, is a creature of animal blood. The family life, the life in common, the here and now, the life of action, is his forte. Because of man the Sword is made, says Maxim 2413. The world he knows he takes to be an oyster and with his Sword he would open it. The world in which he lives. That is the practical thing with him. The world of action. The myriapod of Indian mysticism might be quite closed to him as a book unwritten. And he does not bother about it. He says in Maxim 2373 : " When a man puts on his knapsack, he sees to it that it is accessible." When it comes to having ideals, choose the most practicable, even pragmatic, something natural, and attuned to your nature. And so in choosing his diety, he plunged for the one he knew to be nearest to the nature of man, the personal God, the God like unto a man. And he loves this man-God because he knows him to be a thing of glory, of great beauty. Says Maxim 2404 : " The image of man is like the sun ; look on it, and it is peace."

This sunshine of peace, beauty and glory of man, has the added strength of certainty and solidity, substantialness, if we may use the longer word. It is *that* we find in experience, a substantial find. All that is sensed is made as one in Onyankopon, an impregnable combination. Immanuel Kant said the same thing from a very high metaphysical analysis. He said of experience that it was the organic combination of the data of sense with the individual unity of reality.

6. TIME AS CONDITIONING EXPERIENCE

Kant, indeed, stood much nearer to Aristotle than is generally appreciated. He did, indeed, use terms that were unusual and novel to the scholastic mind, but, in essence, he made no great departure from the logic of the Master. We may, without desiring to be tedious, state the Kantian view to bring emphasis to what has gone before. He brought out quite clearly the nature of the persisting or underlying fact of being and its necessity for experience. Without the idea of something persisting in the stream of appearances, it would be impossible to establish and to make intelligible that order of phenomena which we conceive under the name of " experience," said Kant. The principle of substance, according to him, belonged to the " analogies of experience," *i.e.*, to those principles on the basis of which alone it was possible to set a fixed, objective *time-relation* between phenomena and to conceive them as " nature " coherent in itself and ordered according to universal laws. Kant held that such an objectivation of time would be impossible without the category of substance. " The persistent is the substratum of the empirical notion of time itself, and it is on its basis alone that all temporal determination is possible." Time itself does not change, but all change occurs in it as the " constant corollary of all being of phenomena." However, the strictly " empty " time did not constitute any possible object of perception ; in order to think of time as constant, as " duration," we had to presuppose a persistent element within appearance itself and oppose it to all that was merely changeable.

Kant, consequently, held that the concept of something persistent was " the condition of the possibility of all synthetic unity of perceptions, *i.e.*, of Experience ; and in proportion to this persistent element, all being and all change in time can be viewed only as a modus of the existence of that which remains and persists."

This, at least, is how Ernst Cassirer, professor in the University of Hamburg, interprets the Kantian view. Its value lies in the further revelation that, from whatever angle the problem is approached, substance or *e-su* as the physical basis, would, with the help of the time-relation, lead to the perception of such differentiations which we call Experience in the whole. And this experience is a unity in itself, complete, in so far as all that man knows of reality can be made use of, in so far as sense-data lead us to know. It has the double nature of the given and the acquired, the duality of nature-hood and man-hood, of *e-su* or *sunsum* and *okara*. Its vitality lies in its lively drive towards a harmony of personality.

7. ONYANKOPON'S PERSONAL NAME

Like the Nana, Onyankopon is revealed to be the middle term of the Akan religious syllogism where he is confronted with the moral need for personal relation with a Godhead. Of the three postulates of divinity, Onyankopon alone bears for the Akan a personal name, Onyankopon Kwaame. He above all is knowable in experience and objectifies the ideals of morality and religion. If deity is to be worshipped at all it is the God Kwaame who should get the veneration. And this not because Onyame, on the one hand, and Odomankoma on the other, are not conceived as reverential or venerable, but because what is needed in religion is that which has the natural adaptability of experience, the trial and error that is really characteristic of life. Life, in a word, is one grand continuous effort, one grand desire to get things done, to answer the practical questions of how to live well ; that which generates the harmony and sustains it, that which makes of life one beneficent sharing out of responsibility to make men live well, affords the requisite answer to " Whither ? " And " Wherefor ? "

Therefore, the active deity, the one that most partakes of both aspects of reality, the sensible form and the intelligible form, the *sunsum* and the *okara*, is the one that actively objectifies the practical ideal. God so conceived, as Onyankopon, is the Nana of Ultimate Reality. He is known not to be the complete and mystic explanation of it all, but he is not known to be deficient in any quality that is ennobling in Godhead. Through him each man, each soul, obtains his intelligence, his *okara*, the message to realize a destiny ; to him the accounting is made by the *honhom* of each man's *okara*, till man attains full maturity of completed incarnation, whereby man becomes God's, is absorbed into the interminable Odomankoma, and shares in divine immortality. He is in working harmony with man, in co-operation with him for each *okara* to become a *honhom*, for each ideal to be realized, and as a present, practical, deity, the God Kwaame, he is the God who counts. His nature is *Amen*, and he answers to that appellation in all address to deity.

And all this was necessary for Nyankopon to be because man himself has the dual nature of Sunsum and Okara, man and not-man ; man- and better-than-man. In Onyankopon man finds this duality exemplified, and the conception makes the passage from the earthly to the heavenly not impossible or inconceivable. The God-man is as necessary to life as the man-God. In the conception of Onyankopon as both Sunsum and Okara, the primal Onyame and the final Odomankoma have a reconciliation that eases the way for the ascent of man from the terrene to the celestial. Onyankopon's value for life is *any* active value, a working value, the value for activity, of how best man should carry himself in conduct. Goodness implies value of something done. Onyankopon's doing is good. Onyankopon is good, is in fact the Supreme Good, the Akan God of Beneficence, practical content of the moral life. Why should he not be worshipped ?

CHAPTER III

OKARA OR INSIGHT (ODOMANKOMA)

I. ODOMANKOMA'S TRANSCENDENCE

ODOMANKOMA is the total intuition or insight of the nature and cause of the Thing. Of the three divine or universal postulates, Onyame appeared under examination as the perception or understanding of the psycho-physical basis of the Thing ; Onyankopon, the central or intermediate postulate, appeared as the conception, through memory and imagination, of the active principles underlying experience of the Thing. The notion of Odomankoma is similar to the perception of Onyame in this respect, that it, too, comes by a sort of feeling, an intuition with the character of immediacy, without discursive reasoning, or inference. The notion comes to us by sheer force of intellection, that is to say, by a complete and total insight or inner knowing of those essential qualities which the experience of being had at first brought to our knowledge by relation, comparison, and analysis under the guidance of imagination.

Take the case of a human child. Without using concepts, it feels the urge of a certain tender emotion towards the mother. That feeling is an awareness of a concrete thing—the mother upon whom the child can depend for everything that it needs—all the nice and orderly perceptions the provision of which make the child's life worth its while. Ratiocination is absent from this process of apprehension. It is immediate.

And so, too, is the concrete feeling or apprehension of Onyame, it is immediate, is a feeling, and ratiocination, properly speaking, is not needed for its completion.

Next, at a higher remove, the child having grown to adolescence and apprehending other children, other mothers and other persons who are not mothers, there arises in him, through imagination, an attitude of comparing one mother with another, one woman with his own mother, other persons with her, and one child with another. The adolescent by a series of inductions and inferences recognizes that although other mothers may mean mother to him in many things, yet the only real and near mother of his experience is the better one who constantly feeds and supplies his needs, the adorable, nay, even worshipful mother. Of course, he may not be quite certain that this judgment is without doubt, but since it gives satisfaction, and worth, he is satisfied with it. Here again the comparison with the Akan apprehension of Nyankopon —the most active of all gods—is close.

But, in the third place, the categories which had enabled the adolescent now grown to manhood to select his own mother as the one true mother—the tender emotion, the affection, the adoration, the desire—all these categories get transferred and applied to another type of woman—a beloved woman—a wife, the mother of one's children. *Is* there tender emotion of a concrete nature, and, if so, what is it ? Is it truly identified with the mother, or is it best to identify it with the wife only, or is there a true reality of a tender emotion which may be said to attach to womanhood or to all tender persons of desire, or to—whom ?

The answer to this must come by intellection of a high order—insight—a seeing into the thing itself (" I see the whole thing *now*, not, formerly, as in a glass dimly "), a full apprehension of the meaning of—not tender emotion merely but a greater thing—the reality—the core of tender emotion—love.

So, too, is the insight or apprehension of Odomankoma—a revelation of the inner meaning of the Thing—the dross, the incrustation, the veneer, everything drops off from the eyes of man that were blind, and, now enlightened and visionable, man stands in the presence of reality, face to face with it—the *God* in the Thing. This awareness is immediate, comes by intuition, and yields the instrinsic meaning of the thing—what *it* really *is*. Demonstration by mathematics or logic was not needed for its apprehension. It would be called second sight in other quarters. It is an awareness one knows to be true, and one holds to by " faith." Only those whose mind is illumined by the intellection or insight can apprehend and cognize or intuite it. It is the great I AM—Love, or Truth, or Beauty or Goodness in Essence, the ineffable unutterable Thing.

In this part of this treatise, utilities of the doctrine, our intention, already indicated, was to show the relation of the Akan postulates to other or similar ideas in other racial philosophies, or, at least, to show what place these Akan ideas might take in the accepted body of knowledge. This approach had involved the necessary examination and comparison of similar ideas in other studies to elucidate any possible resemblances. We had found that process profitable and we continue it here.

A French philosopher, Leplay, summed up the primitive community into three orders, the *famille*, or folk, the *travail* or their work, and the *lieu* of their place of work and life. These correspond, roughly, to the three factors that keep life in its tolerable balance : Organism, Function and Environment, and, following the biological treatment which J. A. Thomson made familiar to students of his work, we readily find in the three postulates of Onyame, Onyankopon and Odomankoma three co-ordinates analogous to the social orders of folk, work and place. Onyame comprises, as it were, the whole of the bulk that makes up reality ; Onyankopon is the activity principle of the reality, and Odomankoma is the entity which resolves both place and time into one total status within the environment in which Onyame and Onyankopon exist.

The first fact we notice about Odomankoma is therefore the fact of all-inclusiveness as well as the fact of transcendence. Here we need hardly point out that the term transcendence is used in the older scholastic sense and not in the modern Kantian epistemological sense. The *transcendentia* are concepts which are not confined to a specific type of being but are valid for all types. The scholastics distinguished several of these, such as *ens*, Being ; *res*, Thing ; *unum*, One ; *aliquid*, Something ; *verum*, Truth ; *bonum*, Good. Odomankoma is transcendental in the sense that, whilst not leaving out either the undifferentiated whole of being (Onyame), nor the compared or analysed concepts of that whole (Onyankopon), it comprehends the totality of being, the persistent or underlying whole, together with the *lieu* or place or total environment in which the whole is active. There is, as it were, in the nature of Odomankoma, persistence. There is still division of labour or function in the persistent whole, but the *reason* for the *unum*, for the possibility of harmonious persistence of the total activity, is now fully grasped, and the *organic nature* of the Thing is revealed as urged on by a purpose higher or other than the undifferentiated whole or our experience of parts of it.

But this reason is not identical with either the persistent basis or its experiential concepts. On the other hand, it explains and justifies them without exchanging place with them. Altogether, Odomankoma reveals the total of reality to have an end beyond its immediate self, and is apprehended as working towards the revelation and maintenance of a purpose which is the mind of the Thing. It exists in and works in that spirit or *honhom*.

2. FUNCTION AND PLACE OF MIND IN REALITY

This idea of " Mind " in reality is often illustrated by a railway train. Take ultimate Reality or the Thing to be the locomotive and the carriage and the progress or movement of the whole railway train. Then the spirit or mind of Odomankoma is that which minds or brings an organic completion to both the whole and the parts of the continuous activity. That minding or mind is not identical with either the coal or the engine or the wheels or the coaches or the fire. But without the mind to combine and bring all these into a connected and intelligent whole, to effect a synthesis, everything, that is, which constitutes the progress of a passenger train into an integral whole ; without all these the fancy thing we call a real streamlined train would soon over-reach itself and, with over-speeding, come to grief, or, with lack of movement, fail to service its function, meaning and usefulness. But with mind at work, the appeal that the whole activity and parts of the train should make to a visitor from Mars would suggest something like " purpose " ahead of or within or behind it all. He would say that there is plan in the movement and in the connected parts of the thing called " train," and that that purpose is controlled by—call it what you will—a mind. The controlled rate of speed, the rhythm of the movement, the halts, the warnings, the revolutions, the generation and regeneration of power, the growth and multiplication of that power, and its gradual or measured development (speaking, here, in mechanical terms), the main line, the branch lines, the central station and the sub-stations, the signals and the shuntings, all these cannot but suggest one thing, a controlled purposiveness, a mind. And the Martian visitor would come to the conclusion that mind was at work because there was no way of attributing these qualities to a mere machine. He sees at work an integrated whole, just as we see in Ultimate Reality, and that characteristic of unity in one organism, the Honhom or Mind, is what is called here Odoman-koma.

3. THE TRUE CONTRAST OF DEATH IN REALITY

The first vision of the Odomankoma comes to the Akan in the magnitude of that unutterable Maxim 964 : " *Deity, who created Death, and whom Death killed*." The Living Reality who is Dead and is yet the Living.

Man's first reaction to the juxtaposition of death with life is to contrast them like wealth with want, plenty with deprivation. Some even go further and think of death as the destructive opposite of life. But the true contrast of death is birth, not life, and this is not merely a splitting of hairs. The Akan call death *owu* , they call birth *awo* ; but life they call *nkwa*, an abstract concept with *ekwa*, new plantation, as a concrete ideal of the same concept. They often contrast it with *akwahosan*, health ; literally, *freedom of life*. To the Akan, therefore, death is less than a negation of life. It is not life's contradiction or negation but an instrument of the higher consummation, a planting or fruition of it. Unless, of course, we isolate death, as we often do in logical thought and in common language. So considered, with-out any relation to its *before* and its *after*, its east and west, to die would mean losing all, losing even the dawn of the next day, the continuous series of which death is an instrument, or more properly, of which it is a stage—like feeding the body, like reproduction—just as the katabolism and metabolism of the body are also instruments of an organic system—like sleep. Death is very much like sleep, in this sense. We can imagine a life of quite a normal nature to which sleep is not a necessity. So, too, is death. For an individual who lives for himself alone, death is a tragic fact, an abominable factor, much to be detested, not for its consequences, but in itself, a thing undesired for its own sake, a valueless thing. Such selfish persons must suffer the greatest mental anguish in cogitating upon their own inevitable annihilation from this earth through death. For such there is no need for philosophy, for them the postulate of mind is a wasted effort. Death is *their* reality.

It is otherwise with the race-conscious individual. To him death is nothing but a stage in the consciousness of the race, the experience of his kind. The primary fact with him is that within him is an inheritance, the blood of his race, and from him must go that heritable treasure to other descendants, the blood of his own body. For such, death, *owu*, is only an aspect of birth, *awo*, an instrument of the total destiny, the continuity of the kind, the permanence and persistence of the organic whole which is the greatest good of endeavour. It is of such that J. A. Thomson, speaking on the purely biological level, says that death may seem like a surplus of income over expenditure, for it means merely one of the primal conditions of organic growth ; for " there is no aloofness in the realm of organisms, nothing lives or dies of itself. . . . Animate nature," he continues, " is characteristically a system—a fabric that changes in pattern and yet endures. Though the individual threads of the web are always dying they are replaced without a discontinuity."

4. THE UNDYING COCOA SEED—A GOLD COAST EXAMPLE

The fact of the meaning and value of death for the race has so often been effectively illustrated by philosophers and divines, and, as often, effectively forgotten or its lesson lost on man's incommodious selfishness, that we have need to emphasize it again with a fact from Gold Coast life to bring it nearer home to the Gold Coast man. The illustration relates to the proposition that death and life in Odomankoma or in any other organism are not destructive opposites. The story is about Tetteh Quarshie, otherwise a carpenter or cooper by trade, whose descendants now live in Christiansborg. The story is not about his descendants. Returning from Fernando Po, then called " the Bights," Tetteh Quarshie brought with him a certain seed which he thought would suit the soil at Mampon, Akwapim, thirty miles from his home, and so he went and planted it there. That single seed died and came to life again in the many-leaved, many-branched tree called cocoa or cacao, bearing as many pods as there were branches, which pods also contained several seeds, similar to the single seed which had died and had given " birth " to the great tree. From these other seeds many plantings were made at Mampon and elsewhere, and, from the death and life of these others, the Gold Coast cocoa industry grew up to revolutionize life in the whole country, to supersede the long-established rubber, oil palm and coffee industries, and to raise the country in thirty-five years from an insignificant red spot on the British Imperial map to a vital asset in the life of the nations, to the Gold Coast, a land with the vast possibilities which a vision of Takoradi and Achimota conjures for an imaginative and hungry world.

Such is the history of a seed, its history over a cross section of its total life. For certain it is that the Fernando Po seed originated from another seed which had died and given birth to a cocoa tree, probably a Bahia seed, or a seed from some other South American country. And to trace the history of the South American seed would be to trace the history of the entire family of seed-bearing plants, from plants to shrubs, and down and back into the history and origin of life, to the protozoa or jelly-like organisms or whatsover is prior to this, which biologists may trace for us. Here, we have a total history of life in a total section of the world, and could we but detect a purpose or mind in the seed, we could say of it that, right from the beginning, each seed had considered itself a vehicle in the life of its race, a life from which it gave neither pleasure nor satisfaction to stand aloof, for living and dying for itself had nothing of value for it ; value only in living or dying for the race. In the latter form, it never really died, for it crossed the great Atlantic from West to East, and started a new life, a new race there, ever, as always, like all organisms, with the capacity to give origin to the new.

5. THE IMMORTALITY OF MAN

Such is the being of the fact which we men call death. But did Tetteh Quarshie's original seed die ? Death, in science and in ordinary language, means the permanent cessation of the vital functions of an organism. Here we are dealing with the essence of being, *qua* being, and we find it inadequate to stop where science would stop. In what sense did the vital function of Tetteh Quarshie's seed permanently cease when, in its further development, it gave rise to a new form of life, a new or continued series of vital function or functions, a traceable history from the Fernando Po father-plant to the latest seedling in Gold Coast soil ?

The realm of science lies in the world of experience, in Akan terminology, in the world of Onyankopon. There we see classifications, isolations, divisions, separations. Here, in the realm of Odomankoma, we see things, as it were, with the eye of the external, in their whole history, continuous, catholic, purposive, rational. Odomankoma both dies and lives because he has organic continuity. The characteristic nature of an organic being is the creative urge to excel its own limitations and unfold into greater and more articulate patterns ever fresh and (to us) novel or new lives. Tetteh Quarshie's single seed gave birth to several new seeds, scores, hundreds, thousands, millions of good fermented cocoa shipped, yearly, from the Gold Coast to the markets of the world.

It had first to pass through the stage of life where activity would seem to have ceased for it, it had to be a reality dead and also living. In dying, it created life. For the production of new life is nothing short of creation, rightly understanding by creation any vital activity directed towards an end evil or good. When we talk of the Nazis creating a new situation in Poland, there is no abuse of language. Evil as well as good is createable.

So it is, then, with every organic being, for it bears within itself the cause of its own continuity, the cause of its own death and birth, and has the ability to be as well as to become, to die as well as to continue to live.

The conclusion ought to be infinitely more true of Odomankoma, the interminable and immensely rich Being, the Creator of the Thing, of *Adee*, of the Platonic ἡ τοῦ ἀγαθοῦ ἰδέα, the Great Be as well as the Great Becoming. Odomankoma, as such, contains the ground of its own existence and is cause of an immortality which is not individual, but dividual, racial and total, a common sharing in continous reality of being, a divine immortality.

The solitary individual, selfishly conscious of the limitation of his own existence, enjoys his solitary existence apart from the race. But that existence is without moral value. The first certainty about it is its mortality, death in the grim sense understood by the hangman. That type of " dead " man is a lamp whose light is put out, a life made entirely sterile for all creative possibility. No kind of immortality is possible for him, except, perhaps, man's painful memory of his selfish sterile existence.

There would appear to be two kinds of immortality : (1) the vital immortality of such of the lower animals, like the protozoa, which, as the science of biology has proved, never die or seem to die, but continue to exist in æons of time, one vitality or life passing from parent to offspring in visible form by the simple process of splitting the parent's body into two directly descended offspring.

Due principally to the high differentiation and specialization of cells and their functions in the higher multicellular animals, such as men, death overtakes life and becomes part of it, apparently a necessary consequence. But only apparently. For neither senile decay, nor natural death is a necessary, inevitable consequence or attribute of life.

Natural death is, biologically, a relatively new thing on the plane of life, and death would not have appeared as a natural consequence of life but for the perfect integration which the highly developed animals fail to make in their lives, commensurate with the vital energy put forth by them, and of the mental development attained. The racing horse, for instance, lives an average of twenty years because of its high tension energy of exertion, and the high differentiation and specialization of its functions. Compared to its bulk, it ought to live as long, at least, as man, but it fails in that effort because the output of its mental calibre is not commensurate with the expenditure of its energy. Heroes, as a rule, die young, active, energetic heroes. Reptiles, and especially the tortoises, are known to live as long as 150 to 200 years. From all the evidence, the proper age for man himself would seem to be a true century, four generations, and not the Psalmist's three score years and ten, with an extra grace of ten for those too good or not really bad. It is no abuse to say of a centenarian that his life is reptilian. He is nature's immortal son. In mystic symbolism, in the art of the physician, the long-living reptile is the symbol of life. Its prototype.

In any case, death, as such, is a factor which made its appearance only after living organisms had advanced a long way on the path of complex evolutionary forms of life. There is no inherent or inevitable process in the individual cells of man to cause death. But parts of the body are dependent for the necessities of existence upon the body as a whole, and it is where any individual part of the organized body or aggregate of it fails to find the conditions necessary for its continued existence that death ensues.

Death, therefore, is not a natural thing. Basically, there is no reason why any man, any being, should die, barring accidents, and that death which overtakes us, as we say, in the natural course of life, is not evidence that life is *spent*, but evidence that something has gone wrong with some *part* of the integrated organism. This, we may say in passing, is probably why among unsophisticated and primitive peoples (not only primitive

Africans) the death of a brother or father or wife, of any person we know or hold dear, causes such amazement, an inexplicable occurrence for which a visible cause must be found, either witch-craft or poison or neglect or fatal disease. Death is not always a consequence of disease. Heart failure or the failure of some other part of the organism may accelerate or even cause imme-diate death.

The cause of this is not because life is spent. Deep down in the natural being of man there appears to be an instinct that man is not a dying animal, he was not made to die, and that he has that in him which ought to keep permanently his vital function working interminably. And this memory of an ancient, long forgotten immortal age, a life in a Garden of Eden, in which probably men lived for several scores or hundreds of years, is still part of the inherited mental blood of primitive, even of developed, man. Hence modern anthropologists, scouring the world for queer facts to illustrate how very queer primitive peoples are, think they make a very mighty discovery to say of them : " To savages death from natural causes is inexplicable. At all times, and in all lands, if he reflects upon death at all, he fails to understand it as a natural phenomenon."

But so, indeed, is the fact. Death is *not* only inexplicable. It is not *natural* as a phenomenon, if we understand these terms rightly. Science, at least, proves that death is neither natural nor necessary, and all we can say of the " savage " for trying or groping about to find a cause for every kind of death, barring accidents, is that he is probably a greater scientist than the " civilized " man who stands in great fear of death itself, and takes little account of its real cause, or lack of cause. Man, says the " savage," speaking with the voice of basic nature, ought not to die. Man would probably not have been a dying being if he had not wished to be like man, a picture of the gods. And the penalty we pay for wishing to be like gods is death. The godly, they say, die first. Man, an incomplete god, has to die to discover his completeness in the undying god.

Hence the Akan maxim that Deity created Death means, in one sense, that death is not coeval with life, but an after-factor, an after effect of complications which set in with the growth and complexity of life. There is no logical reason why the maxim could not have said that it was Death who created life, or even Deity. But the maxim is the other way round, in consonance and harmony, probably, with fact.

This, then, is the first form of immortality, vital immortality, that man was not made to die, and the simple beings, living the simplest lives, never die at all. For they have tasted not of the forbidden fruit. They have not complicated their lives by too much knowledge, too great a desire to be like unto the gods, a too high development of mind. That tree in the Garden of Eden was truly the Tree of Knowledge, and eating the fruit of it was death. It meant the beginning of man's knowledge of god Nyankopon—Experience, the factor of mind whose chief implements are imagination and *time*.

6. DIVINE IMMORTALITY

(2) Secondly, there is the other form of immortality, that which man makes for himself, or is set to make for himself, to reinstate the injured or damaged balance, after tasting the forbidden fruit. This is the immortality of existence, or better, the immortality of experience, racial immortality, what the Akan call the Obara—ethical existence. It is the immortality of self-conscious organisms, who, aware that death had become a certainty of their highly developed integration, set a special store upon the blood of the race and saw to it that the continuity of the race should become part of the permanent values of life. We must recognize this as a factor of great moral consequence if the race is to survive.

It is, possibly, of such value that the Akan mostly think when they speak of Deity as Creator of Death, whom Death killed. The value of this for the moral life is that it determines the condition for the continuity of the race. This is not an individual value but a racial, dividual, universal, divine value, and to share in it is to belong to a finer world, a world of hope, a hopeful certainty.

That hope is that the experience of man has meaning, has a future, namely, that there is a common continuous life to maintain for the good, the beneficence of the dying race. It is a new peace found by man after becoming conscious of vital death. It is man's covenant with nature, a treaty of peace in which the individual body is no more split to give birth to the new, but the vital function is passed on as the old body perishes. Thereby the old Adam is resuscitated, his life continued.

And the result is that the race is maintained. It has to be maintained at that rate until the mind of man becomes coeval with his life, until his energy is one with his differentiation and specialization, until he is so fully developed that the being of entire reality is realized in him and the experience of life participates *fully* in all existence, and man, the entire race, becomes God's.

Back to Methuselah becomes superfluous. It is either *forward*, or death. From the E-su man had broken away for an " experience " of life, and from the E-su man wishes to press on to identify his experience with the reality of all being, with Odomankoma, with the divine reality, the Absolute Thing. The passage, as we saw, is made through Onyankopon, the personal divinity who is the Sunsum of Odomankoma, and man's religious objective in the experience of life. And Onyankopon is also the Okara of Onyame, the ideal pattern of the E-su. The development is within a circle, a globular universality organic and shot through with a divinity which is supremely vital.

PLATE VII

NYAME DUA (" An altar to the Sky God "). Literally, God's Tree, *i.e.*, " the forked post to be found in most courtyards, on which is placed a pot or bowl containing a stone-axe and some offerings to Onyame (The Supreme Being). In many cases the vessel contains a stone-axe, water, certain herbs, and some offering to the spirits. People sprinkle themselves with the water to be guarded against evil spirits . . . the Onyame dua planted at the threshold of many Kings' houses is a sign that they stand under the protection of God " (Christaller, " Dictionary," p. 357).

Speaking of values in connection with immortality, we must be understood as referring to ultimate values, for these are not to be found in man's fitful attempt to find satisfactions in experience, but in an ultimate reality wherein there is no possibility of mistake, or error, and where the truth is known not by discursive reasoning but by a total insight into the true nature of reality itself, including all possible forms of experience.

This is a large subject, requiring treatment in a large way, but, for our present purpose, it is perhaps sufficient to say the experience of a dying God who is alive and real is the sufficient guarantee that, in Him, there can be no other value but the ultimate, for the return to E-su through Onyankopon is a return to the source where life began, and where, again, there can be no further death. The chasm or estrangement between the God of experience, Onyankopon, and Odomankoma, is bridged in the notion of the Ultimate Being whose spirit is the mind or articulate purpose of ultimate reality. We deal exhaustively with this in a later paragraph. Our present conclusion is that the notion of a living God who creates death, and also dies but lives, must presuppose a purposive control by that God, a control that is Mind. That mind is conscious of its need for life and struggles and strives to make it continuous, not only for the vital purpose of living, but also for the divine purpose of its value as the only sure guarantee for existence—continuity of the race.

7. EVIDENCE FROM EPISTEMOLOGY

Aristotle would appear to have arrived at a similar conclusion by his treatment of the Greek concept, *nous*. As before, our guide to Aristotle is Professor Dawes Hicks. The Stagyrite distinguished what we know in experience, empirical knowledge, from the higher forms of science (ἐπιστήμη) and practical skill (τέχνη).

Generalizations which are seen to rest on a reason or ground other than what, by comparing and relating two or more things, we know, were called by Aristotle knowledge by scientific insight. That type of knowledge had two aspects : (1) it must necessarily be universal, that is to say, as embracing a whole class in its scope, and (2) it is universal also in that it states the essence (εἶδος) which underlies the resemblances which we had discovered in experience to exist between several members of the class.

This knowledge of universals Aristotle ascribed to a power or faculty of the intellect or reason (νοῦς), and showed that the nature of *nous* was to be as receptive immediately of intelligible form as sense was receptive of sensible form.

In other words, just as in perception we know without any intermediation by a process of feeling, so in intellection we know without any intermediation by a process of intuition or insight. This feeling may be distinguished from the other by calling it " scientific " feeling, that is to say, an articulate and informed sort of feeling charged with intuition or intellection.

Reason, Aristotle seems to say, can " feel " the concepts of experience in much the same way as sense can " know " the precepts of sense particulars. Actually, therefore, there are two fundamental principles of knowing, namely, sense and reason, by one of which we feel percepts and by the other of which we know the intelligibles. The third form of knowledge, the concept of experience, is thus shown to be an intermediate, almost man-made mode of knowing, which comes about out of the desire or volition or conative activity of man to put what he perceives to use by the convenient mode of classifying and relating those percepts, aided by memory and imagination.

On this showing, concepts are not knowledge at all, in the true sense. The process is like the cataloguing of knowledge for the purpose of better acquaintance scientifically. The sense or sensed particulars are, as it were, filed away in the mind according to their classes or orders, a process not much different from classification in a dictionary, providing labels or tabs, or better, " definitions," for each of such sensed particulars.

This purely empirical process of knowing is of some value in that it enables us to distinguish what is good from what is not, what is better from what is merely good, and what is best from what is just better. In short, it enables us to compare values, but it does not give us the essence of what is truly good until, with the coming of that scientific insight, we intuite, amid the maze of concepts or definitions, what is the essence or true form of the many things held before us in comparison. Whereby we get Truth.

The higher or final process is deduction ; the assembling of particulars to find their common feature is induction. In the true sense induction only clarifies knowledge, is a preparation for knowledge, but adds nothing that was not known before. True knowledge, awareness of the truth, comes by absolute insight.

Now, having laid the foundation in knowledge, Aristotle made deductions as to the nature of the soul in connection with this concept of *nous*. Reason, he said, like other faculties of the soul, exhibited a contrast between the potential and the actual. Reason, according to him, was not constantly active in the human subject, and yet, in his own nature, it was nothing but activity.

Here, again, we find close similarity between the Aristotelian view and the Akan postulate of Okara. As we saw, the Okara stood outside the being of the *sunsum* and came into play only when a proper home was prepared for it. Aristotle stated that the limitation of the exercise of reason in man must be dependent on the fact that it was only realized under conditions connected with the life of the soul ; in man, *nous* existed potentially until called into exercise.

In this respect the Akan postulate of Okara is slightly different from the Aristotelian conception of *nous*. According to the

Akan, *nous* or *okara* is not *in* man but goes with him, accompanying him everywhere as his extra-terrene power and constant source of spiritual energy.

Further, Aristotle affirms that what calls *nous* into exercise is the presence of the intelligible (τὸ νοητόν) exhibited in sense and its concomitant faculties. This, too, is as near the Akan conception as can be expected. The Okara does not seek entry into the individual for the purpose of appropriating its activity or actualizing what is potentially there, unless the Sunsum or the human individual makes itself receptive for the purpose. Further, because in the apprehension of concepts *nous* or *okara* is not a participator, the possibility for error or for false inferences occupies a large ground.

In the apprehension of first principles this is not so ; *nous* or *okara* is present and the action is therefore free from the antithesis of true and false. " The first principles," interprets Dawes Hicks, " must either be just apprehended or not at all." It is the same with the sense-particulars : " The sense-particulars must either be just apprehended or not at all."

This has immense consequence for the problem of the origin and reality or unreality of error, of evil and even of sin. Namely, that there is neither error nor evil nor even sin in *okara* or *nous*, but only in its earthy counterpart the Sunsum or Experience. Conclusions on this aspect of the moral problem, arrived at in previous chapters, thus obtain their confirmation by the application of the Aristotelian theory.

8. GOD'S FINALITY AS MAN'S ANCESTOR

Thus far, we have now to state or account for Odomankoma's positive place in the religious and moral experience of the Akan. It is not an easy problem. But we comfort ourselves with the thought that, on a similar occasion, Socrates had to confess that giving final accounts was not simple. To the cry of Glaucon, imploring him not to hang back, as if he had come to an end, but that they would be content if he would only discuss the subject of the chief good in the style in which he discussed justice, temperance and the rest, Socrates replied :—

" Yes, my friend, and I likewise should be thoroughly content. But I distrust my own powers, and I feel afraid that my awkward zeal will subject me to ridicule. No, my good sirs : let us put aside, for the present at any rate, all inquiry into the real nature of the chief good. For, methinks, it is beyond the measure of this our enterprise to find the way to what is, after all, only my present opinion on the subject. But I am willing to talk to you about that which appears to be an offshoot of the chief good, and

bears the strongest resemblance to it, provided it is also agreeable to you ; but if it is not, I will let it alone " (" Republic,"
506 (d-e.)).

Glaucon and his friends were, fortunately, of an obliging and
agreeable sort, and so Socrates discussed with them not the chief
good but what he called the essential good.

We, in this chapter, are in a worse position than Socrates or
Plato. The virgin soil on which they worked had not, like the
Akan virgin soil, the disadvantage of centuries of disquisition
shipped on to it. The Akan soil is already much encumbered by
the thought or thoughts of Europe and the achievements of the
anthropologists.

The problem, to be well tackled, must be tackled from within.
How, common sense asks, how is the notion of Odomankoma as
both deceased and living to be made the object of religious experience ? How can man worship a dead God ? It is easy enough to
explain some of the difficulties away by the concepts of epistemology, but religion is a personal fact and a religious God must be
living and not both dead and living. He must have a personality
as vital as, if not more than, that of the persons whose worship
he is to receive.

The easiest way of getting round this problem, at least for an
English or modern European reader, is by appealing to him with
what is familiar. The most familiar is the Christian way, wherein
the mystery of the reconciliation between God and man is, says
Hegel, an open doctrine. Hegel's point was that the Christian
notion of God was a Trinity, and he was Trinity because He was
Spirit. Hegel held that the revelation of this truth was the
subject of the Christian Scriptures. In the immediate aspect,
the Son of God, said Hegel, was the finite world of nature and
man, which far from being at one with its Father was originally
in an attitude of estrangement. The history of Christ, he went on
to say, was the visible reconciliation between man and the eternal.
With the death of Christ this union, ceasing to be a mere fact,
became a vital idea—the Spirit of God which dwelt in the Christian community. This, at least, is how Wallace and Baillie present
the thought of Hegel to the modern reader.

Now, of course, we do not suggest that the Akan could accept
this empirical argument, dogmatic for the most part, as identical
with their own idea of how the death of Deity reconciles with his
suitability for the religious experience. First of all, the Deity
that dies in the Akan system is not the intermediate God, the
medium between man and nature, or God and man, but the
Supreme Deity himself.

On the other hand, the Christian treatment helps to take us

to the centre of the problem and to determine its limits for easier solution. It makes it possible for us to restate, with emphasis, what was said in a previous chapter, that, for the Akan, the central fact of life is not death, but birth, the means whereby the blood of an ancestor, the spark of the race, is generated for a descendant, bearer and vehicle of the spark. Further, the religious reason for the Akan search for God rests in the family assurance of continuity, its endurance, persistence and permanence. The first object of that religious spirit is the ancestor, not because he is dead, but because his blood continues to flow in the offspring. He had, that is to say, created them his enduring family. Whereupon he is worshipped as such ancestor, the greatest single factor or denominator in the pursuit of all being.

In this translation from father to ancestor, dying is incidental, for the ancestor would have been ancestor, whether he had died a centenarian, or a Methusalah, or had died not at all. Tracing as far back as the human mind is capable, Odomankoma reveals himself as Creator and Ultimate Ancestor. The revelation and the acknowledgment of it makes him the final spark, quite obviously and naturally, the supreme religious reason, the great solvent of the mystery and awe of how the original spark came to be and continues in being. Death, as such, may have been present from the beginning as a possible end for life ; on the other hand, it may not have been there at all but developed subsequently. In any case, it made no difference to the supreme reason for religion. God did not need to die before being worshipped. He would have been God all the same, *the* God, had He not died at all. That He made life manifest even after the so-called cessation of vital function only enlightened the reason for His worship, but did not create it. The Nana had been worshipped as *opanyin* before his translation. If, therefore, there is to be what Hegel calls a " reconciliation between man and the eternal " the union, according to the Akan system, does not become " vital " by the death, but in the recognition of relationship, the total and absolute insight into the nature of Odomankoma as the Ultimate Ancestor and the highest source of goodness and reverence.

On the level of experience, in Onyankopon, the supreme deity had appeared as a person, an ancestor very like man. But in this ultimate analysis the personality of God is transmuted in the awareness of Him as the Final Cause, the Supreme Creator who is father as well as father's father, the creator of the father and source of the Spark. In him, the family completes its genealogy, with every pedigree accounted for, backward as well as forward. When Odomankoma is head the entirely family is present, Ancestor-Father-Son, and so on continuously.

Here, we have, in its finality, the organic whole of the absolute religious reason, the unity of the spark and its sparklings, the goodness of the exampled reality is both cause and ground of the Nana's experienced example and inherited spark. This is an undying fact, with the divinity of eternity.

In a word, Akan religion, in its highest expression, is the worship of the race. This race has a universal possibility, being dividual and therefore divine, coeval with the very reason that makes it ultimate with reality and organic with the unity of the ultimate.

Obviously the Akan cannot justify his religion as perfect or complete until he includes the whole of that which could claim ancestry from Odomankoma as also of the unified perfection. Akan religion therefore strives for its fulfilment upon the discovery by man, by all men, that they are made of one blood, are of the race of God, the supreme Creator and final Ancestor. In the fact of creation, Odomankoma, the said supreme Ancestor, continuously persists, and of his creation there is no limitation to a chosen race or races, but embraces all. Maxim 1742 says : " The being of man has no boundaries." What that amounts to is in reality this : " The spirit of being (or life) has no limitations." We get the same result if we examine the position from the facts of scientific biology : J. A. Thomson concludes upon that examination : " The possibility is that ' Life ' and ' Mind ' are co-extensive." Which, on the Akan view, must afford further and illuminating justification—the spark and Odomankoma are as the life and blood of being. Odomankoma as the spark is eternal, " He went before any one came." His death was presage to foreshow the way of that future event when man would become God's, feeling ripen into knowledge, experience become insight, the spark one with its source, Onyame, Onyankopon and Odomankoma one and fulfilled in Honhom.

CHAPTER IV

HONHOM OR THE SPIRIT OF BEING

I. THE COMMUNITY OF HONHOM

OUR final account of the Akan system may be summed up thus : Ultimate Reality or the Thing is centred around a theocentric system the axis of which is spirit, the medial line between corresponding parts of ultimate being.

Axis is a very imperfect metaphor for the moving idea of spirit. At the centre of all reality, pervading and informing every part of existence, is an urge or vitality, called Honhom.

The term is one which we have encountered already in this work. In the sections on soul we met it as that which, when an Okara is fully realized, it becomes, and in the capacity of which it can return to its Source. Our encounter with Honhom in this chapter takes on the same form, except that now it is raised from the level of an individual's soul to that appropriate for the world soul. The Source to which the Honhom of ultimate being is traced is the cause of all being, of all existence and value, *Odomankoma Borebore*, the Interminable Creator. There is no need for any mystical flights for the adequate apprehension of Honhom. It is merely the efficient form of Odomankoma, the all-pervading and indwelling uncaused cause of ultimate being.

Or, to offer proof of the same in so many words, Honhom may be shown to be the complete actualization of the transcendent or suprasensible beings Onyame, Onyankopon and Odomankoma. It is the entelechy of ultimate reality. In more explicit terms : (1) The E-su of all being, the psychophysical reality has been shown to be Onyame ; the conative entelechy of Onyame is Onyankopon, that towards which E-su strives as its Okara ; Onyankopon is, therefore, on this level, the Honhom or " form " of Onyame, for Onyankopon contains that which Onyame's Okara becomes when its being is fully actualized. (2) But, again, on the other hand, Onyankopon is also, in relation to Odomankoma, a Sunsum or " matter " striving towards its ideal self, its Okara, and that Okara or form is Odomankoma. The Honhom of Onyankopon is therefore Odomankoma, the Okara of that which is the Okara of Onyame. (3) Obviously Odomankoma is the ultimate entelechy of all Akara, and is therefore the consummation of all souls and that to which all souls as Honhom return. As we are using Aristotelian terms, we may as well go all the way with the Stagyrite. If Odomankoma, even, is taken to be some form of matter, the last escape of solidity which the limited human mind can apprehend, then its form, the last of all forms, is Honhom, the highest beyond which there is no beyond, the most good, the purest beauty, and the absolute truth of all existence and value.

It follows as of necessity that neither E-su nor Sunsum, nor their developed form, Okara, could become Odomankoma's, or return to it as their source unless they had contained in themselves the capacity to effect such a return. In other words, Honhom is potentially discoverable in E-su, Sunsum and Okara. It is their entelechy. It is what they can and have to become or actualize. Honhom is therefore the source or cause as well as the centre of all reality, of E-su and Okara. In the language of the schools, Honhom is the spirit of ultimate being realizing the conditions of its own existence for its highest or most intelligible expression or actualization. It necessarily is common to all reality.

This conclusion ought not to startle any one. If all reality is Honhom then the character or nature of Honhom must be one that is possessed of every reality, is in every part of it, every part is in it, and it emerges to man's limited comprehension when it takes on some of the graduated concrete forms, called matter. Further, as the character which all reality strives to achieve, it has the value of an ideal individuality, namely, personality, that form of articulated universal self without which a being remains indeterminate. The personality of Honhom is as a supreme all-pervading impression of the total universe, articulate and insurgent, ever striving to emerge, ever striving to reach its end, ever striving to realize higher and higher goals in its interminable endeavour, but always and at all times identifiable with one dominating ineffable character: an informing energy and will and mind which some call Spirit, others Nous, a few Elan, and which the Akan call by that simple name, Honhom, Spirit of the Absolute Thing.

We may conveniently recall here the etymology of the word *honhom*, already referred to in a previous chapter. The word is derived from *ehon*, the marrow in the bones, or brain, the pith, the essence of mind. Hon-hom is a repetition of *ehon*, the *ehon* of the ehon (*ehon-mu hon*), the pith of the pith, the essence of the essence, the quintessence of the quintessence, the ineffable spiritual principle or soul of ultimate reality.

Quite clearly, if the Akan had to use a term like " natural selection " of this reality, they would not, at any stage, yield to the suggestion that it was blind or by chance. From the very beginning the actualizing of being is that in which must be detected intelligent and conscious or purposive selection. It is only " natural " because it is of nature and necessarily becomes what it becomes, and not because of practice or what is called adaptation. From the very beginning, if there was a beginning, from zero hour, the world as it will become and has been, was. If we, as men, could not see it until it emerged in some matter, that is no reason for saying the form, the Honhom, the Spirit was not there. *Ex nihilo nihil fit*, says the old Latin thinker. But it is only a phrase. We can only believe it to be truth if it corresponds to reality. To *us*, nothing cannot be unless there was something the matter with it, unless, that is, it had a form other than mere form, unless that something the matter with it was something that mattered, a because, a matter. But to Honhom, which cannot be wholly comprehensible to man who is of matter for the most part, what was not becomes, not because it was not, but because it existed in it, in Honhom.

Again, we must emphasize, this Honhom is common to and pervades all being unless that which claims to be in being is not part of the universe of being, which is absurd. We can therefore further define Honhom in terms of this further discovery of its nature : That it is the source of reality and the potential entelechy of all being, that which is and which all being becomes, an immensely rich being, multiform in function, uniform in nature, infinite and interminable, which was, and " went before any one came," the timeless, spaceless, all inclusive reality.

Or, in the words of Maxim 3680, it is as God, the end-cause of all being. *Nsem nyinaa ne Nyame*, literally, " All matter *is* God," or of God ; all that exists or becomes is God. It is not exclusive, but common, all universally, ultimately, and absolutely, for beyond it there is no matter, neither cause nor end. It is common.[1] All in common is Honhom, or of Honhom, the energy and power of being.

2. THE OMNIPOTENCE OF HONHOM

Now, to speak of Honhom as power raises the relevant question of its potency. What sort of potentiality has it ? Or, in the language of the schools, is Honhom omnipotent ?

This is one of those large questions in speculative literature which, from the Akan point of view, deserves small space. We saw the irreducible fundamental form of the first of transcendent beings, Onyame, to be psycho-physical. This E-su has a feeling of irritability, a form of force or energy which drives it or enables it to drive towards its ideal, Onyankopon, wherein it seeks

[1] In the salad days of the present writer in a first-floor flat in North-West London, with the idea for this book hardly thought of, and the mind wandering for a peg to hang on passing thoughts, the following lines, one summer evening,

expression. That such a force, such an energy is omnipotent may be deduced from the fact that it has, within it, the potential of understanding, enabling itself to be understood, through feeling or perception. Force is a great potential. But it is not itself creative, because we saw in the nature of Onyame that although it had some form of mind, it was not completely of the purposive character which, in later development, we saw mind to be. The mental in Onyame is a feeling mind, the sort of mind that Neo-Darwinian evolutionists seem to credit to animate nature, the Force that blindly leads to the preservation of the self through nourriture, giving the giraffe its long neck, but not through culture. This energy or Force in the hands of a self-conscious being, striving towards a higher ideal, the Okara of Odomankoma, and being itself an Okara, namely, Onyankopon, extends the field of activity or exercise of the feeling mind, enabling it not only to feel but to experience the sentience in the form of stored or analysed knowledge, through imagery and remembering.

---

came as it were, from nowhere, and stayed long enough to be jotted down : The title was " The ' All ' of God," or " The Philosophy of the Common " :—

i. Of God.

" The All of God is God.
God is not Christian,
Nor Moslem,
Nor King,
Nor Three,
Nor One,
Nor Many,
But all.
All is all all.
All is common.
All all is God.
God is common.

ii. Of Self.

Self is not all.
All is all.
Your self,
His self,
My self :
That is not all.
All is without self,
For all is common.
No self is, or can be
Unless there are selves.
No selves are in all,
For God is all,
Without relations,
But all-
Not All-Self,
But common."

" All things proceed from the necessity
That All evolves all,
All things,
Without exception."

173

There is, here, a form of spontaneous creation limited only by the fact that it builds its knowledge mainly from the analysis of unformed matter. In other words, its creative activity must, in every detail, be conditioned by its self-conscious limitation. But we have developed a further and higher form of omnipotence called by the simple name of Will, the inclination to choose between two or more presented objects of experience in a world of self-conscious beings—a social and cultural energy. The choice, naturally, is open to grave perils, for knowledge is not complete, what the mind commands being only that which it has been able to catalogue or store up in memory, like classification in science, or is able to imagine under the limitations conditioned by the nearness of sentience. Its omnipotence is therefore only potential. If it could know all, it would not make mistakes, nor commit errors, and then, of course, it would be more than what we call experience or Obra. It would be the exercise of genius, insight entirely supra-moral and supra-cultural.

Here, at this third stage, there is no consciousness of limitation, for the spirit not only creates but immediately knows what the conditions of the creation are and apprehends the end in the act of creation. It had been at first " What ? " Then it became " How ? " and now we have the certainty of " That." But there is still incompleteness of omnipotence, in the sense the schools understand it. But the boundaries are only those which compel the omnipotence to wait upon the limitation set up by E-su and Obra, by Onyame and Onyankopon, namely, the need for Force reaching out and for Will making choices. When these have been in action, then, the entire potential may emerge. This third creative activity is therefore more than will, and takes on the form of Cause, an efficient Will limited in potency only by its relation to the spontaneous or choice-making Will and sentient energy or Force.

Omnipotence, we may say in brief, belongs to Honhom of necessity, and the only limitation is that, in so far as the actualization is concerned, it is exercised in space and time, in the world of e-su and the world of obara, of Onyame and Onyankopon. In itself, as the Okara of Odomankoma, there is nothing Honhom cannot do. But it has to be done. Doing implies activity, and every activity takes time and requires place for action. Consequently any idea of omnipotence in a created world is a contradiction in terms. All true omnipotence in that world is a potential. There is no absolute limitation to the intellection of which insight is capable, there is no absolute limitation to a truth of which Odomankoma may know. But out of Honhom goes E-su for its actualization and until it returns as Honhom it limits the action of Honhom in its completed insight into all reality. Honhom, in other words, remains omnipotent until it begins to create, whereupon limitation confronts it, and until the created return to their Source their destinies completely actualized, omnipotence is in pledge, sold, as the Americans do say effectively, sometimes. The profit is that the potential omnipotence then becomes actual. As the Christains say, and say truly, the Word is then become Flesh, *i.e.*, every spirit is then become a true, a beautiful, a holy Honhom.

POSTSCRIPT [1]

I. ETHICS AND RELIGION

ETHICS is the science of conduct ; religion the æsthetics of it ; mysticism its logic. Behind them all is the fact of mind. It, too, has its own science, the science of psychology.

Within limits one could begin a work on Gold Coast ethics and religion with the fundamental fact, namely, mind, a stage in life's development, and say that given life and mind the major principles of ethics and religion could be deduced from demonstrable propositions to conclusions as unimpeachable as conclusions in geometry. Spinoza in fact attempted it ; and he achieved fair success. But the generality of mankind fairly rejected his proofs because of a common belief that he made God to look like anything, or like nothing, on earth—a horrid pantheistic Deity who is not to the taste of a mankind enamoured of personal Gods.[2]

Looked at fairly and squarely, man's reaction to any sort of *a priori* propositions put forth in proof of what is good in conduct and why, has always been like the youngster's first acquaintance with castor oil—rejection. On the other hand, if you try on the empirical method, starting with the joyful things people deem nice or pleasurable or simply marvellous ; and you gradually work out a scheme of values based upon those marvellous pleasantries, you are sure to win cart-loads of popular approval. " This," they would acclaim, " is ethics, the science of good conduct." To be consistent, they should have said " the science of pleasant conduct." Quite unpardonably they forget that what we wanted to know was not what was pleasant but what was good. And there is a world of difference between the two.

The trouble is that the popular idea of what is good is invariably quite abstract and volatile in nature. The substantial is stolen in parts and wasted away. The good, they like to hear, is the pleasurable, absence of pain ; the good is justice, absence of discontent ; the good is virtue, absence of vice ; the good is happiness, absence of worry ; the good is perfection, absence of distortion ; the good is what works, absence of illusion. And so on and so forth. From the Sophists to Socrates, from Plato to Plotinus, from the Scholastics to the Cartesians, and Bacon to

---

[1] This postscript was originally the " introduction " to the larger work, " Gold Coast Ethics and Religion," Parts I and II of which have now perished, and are beyond recovery. It is justly called a postscript because, like all genuine " Introductions," it was written after the text of the work had been completed.

[2] Professor A. Wolf, Spinoza's modern biographer and interpreter, strenuously maintains that Spinoza was not a pantheist in the common acceptation of that term.

Bradley, or Kant to Green or Hegel to Hitler, the inquiring mind has found some partial cause or ground of satisfaction with the great abstractions offered for his inspection and acceptance.

We have made no attempt in this treatise to examine the grounds for the acceptance or rejection of any of the great abstractions of the schools. One simple reason is that the Akan is a late and new discovery, in the world of thought. He was quite unknown and therefore quite unthought of until the anthropologists of our own times discovered that he postulates a soul called *Okara*, and a monotheistic God called *Nyame*, to whom he claims to be related through his ancestor, the *Nana*. Then people began to take notice of the Akan. One learned man of international repute was so impressed with the magnificent show Akan ideas were making that he left himself no alternative but to plump for a theory that the existence of such ideas in Akanland must be evidence of the presence of the ubiquitous Jew, father of ethical holiness, who had somehow penetrated western Africa and passed on his ideas to the Akan, or that, possibly, the Akan himself was a Jew, one, or a branch, of the lost tribes of Israel. The learned gentleman, Dr. Joseph J. Williams, S.J., wrote a classic book on the subject, " Hebrewisms of West Africa," to which we refer in the text.

2. THE SEX ''INTEREST''

A second reason for our refusal to examine the old theories in this treatise is that the vogue of Plato or Aristotle or Kant or Hegel is not the vogue of to-day. These great thinkers, whose theories of the Good, the Mean, the Categorical Imperative, the State as the Absolute, dominated European thought for upwards of twenty-five centuries, have, of late, been almost completely overshadowed by a certain revolutionary theory that twists the entire mental and vital gymnastic out of recognition.

Selecting one of the many biological functions of living organisms, that new theory sets up the sex vitality as the underlying cause of the glories of mind as well as its turpitudes—the achievement of genius as well as the ravings of the man of Bedlam. Working under the umbra of this basal crown called sex, the late Sigismund Freud, author of the theory, essays to explain almost everything in man's conduct—one's burning desire to write a work on ethics, or the politician's perfervid lust for power—as springing from the sex function or mis-function.

The theory is a nerve-racking profundity. It could never have been thought of in any Spartan age and must surely be a prelude to an age of decline or soft manners. How he got away with it will be the amazing story to be told, and retold with disgust, in the twenty-first century. Not certainly in this Freudian age.

Now, of course, sex is an interesting function. But so is the sense [1] of taste, or smell, or vision, as an object of thought. Especially so is vision. " Vision," one seems to hear the great genius of the next decade propound the new theory, " Vision of things visible and of things invisible is the basis of all man's experience. The things invisible are not really so ; there is a Censor, the censor of the Eye-lids, which takes normal vision out of focus because of certain taboos. But, once the appropriate moment arrives, the Censor ceases to operate, the eye-lids begin to work their way up and down, and then Vision *sees all*. This great reality, Vision, for so long neglected by the great thinker of old, and only now and again accidentally referred to by a few of the moderns, this window of the world without which we can really see nothing, opens out the most satisfactory explanation of man's chequered history, both of the individual man and woman—and of the race. At the very root of all our pains and all our pleasures, our hopes and fears, is the fact of Vision."

This, stated in burning language by a writer of genius, with appropriate italics and capitals, how, could smaller minds refute it ? *The Psychology of Vision. The Unopened Eye-lid. Child Visionaries. Negative Vision. The Camera of Your Soul. Facts Behind the Eye-lids. Rouged and Coloured Vision. Primitive Visions.* These and many more are likely titles of books in which the new psychology could be dressed up for the world of thought and the thoughtless. They would become best sellers, books to be bought in hundreds of thousands and talked of in the best circles. Vision pathologists would spring up in the wake of the theory, with Vision-Analytics. University libraries would be flooded with monographs on the psychology of vision from every possible abstruse and obtuse angle. A popular column would open in every great daily for the expert to tell of the secrets of vision to millions of untaught Visionaries. Vision reading clubs and chairs would become common and the whole world of the thoughtless and thoughtful would, for a time, be completely swamped with vision broadsides. All it requires at first is the fairly competent man to start the vogue in earnest with one or two books : " *Sight, a New Way to Vision*," or " *The Mystery of Vision*," and the deed is done.

Of course, it will be a mystery. Even so is sex, although we dare not suggest that this was probably how this sex invasion

---

[1] Nuttall's dictionary defines sense as " the faculty of perceiving what is external by means of impressions on an organ," such as nose, ear, tongue, the organs of smell, hearing, taste, etc.

of the world of spirit started. But to have to attend classes in experimental psychology in a European university only to be regaled with sex interpretations of the story of Adam and Eve, or of the form of man's and woman's attire, is worse than revolting ; it is boring.

What is wrong with the sex theory of life is its complete disregard of the fact that no organism is known whose nature hangs basically upon sex. That is to say, it is not the case that a creature without use of its sex would perish, or cease to be organic. The basic thing in every organism is its " constitutional " nature, that without which it breaks into pieces or fails to stand together. Vision, sex, taste, hearing, locomotion, growth, reproduction, eating, all these are organic activities, but they are not of the structural nature of the organism. They are *functions*. Everything, even the inorganic, has two ways of projecting its being upon the world : its nature and its function.[1] Without nature, function could not work, but without the working of a function the nature could be. Functions can be learnt, adapted, regrouped, selected and acquired. But the fundamental nature, apart from its unfolding or development, does not change at will, or at all.

To select one of the functions of an organic being, and hang upon it all its washing (dirty or otherwise) is merely to stultify the issue. Sex is no more the central fact of life than is vision or taste. This fact, at the outset of this work, compelled a going back into fundamentals with the urge to ignore any of the modern crazes.

3. THREE ORGANIC "INTERESTS"

Three things, every organism must have if it is to live : Mind, Life and Blood. But this, even, looks like some tautology. One thing every organic being must have if it is to live : Mind ; or if that is too high, Life ; or if that is too high, Blood. The very tissue of organic protoplasm is blood or whatever is the description of the vital fluid without which no being on earth can live. In most languages blood is a metaphor for offspring, because upon it hangs the racial life. Going by the facts of biology alone, the probability is that Life and Blood are co-extensive. And, if blood, then Mind.

Consequently, the ancients were wise who, concerned with the

[1] Thomson and Geddes, authorities on biology, suggest that instead of function we should speak of functionings. Further, what we here call nature they call Organism with the character O what we call the world they call the Environment with the character E. They represent the three in the following symbolism : $O \rightarrow f \rightarrow E$, and the reverse order. Living, they point out, implies an ever changing ratio $\frac{Ofe}{Efo}$.

ethics of the highest form of organism, namely, man, picked on the highest part of his constitution, namely, mind, and not on any morbid pot-pourri like his sex, for their study of the principles of his conduct. For over 2,000 years millions of followers believed that the starting-point of these great thinkers of old had been right and wise. If, therefore, because the mind is too high a development for general appreciation as a common and undifferentiated property of all men, the theories of the ancients, based upon mind, failed to satisfy all inquiry, that is no reason why, in seeking to improve upon the situation, we should disregard the other fundamental aspects of the organic being, *e.g.*, blood, and seize on one of its functions, namely, the abstraction of sex, for the total explanation we seek.

In the text the reader has found how the Akan met this problem of the starting-point for the study of man's community. Whether what the Akan did under the circumstances was wise, the reader can judge for himself.

4. THE ''INTEREST'' OF MAN

As regards the real question in ethics, apart from its mystical or metaphysical background, the question, namely, whether the good is pleasure or justice or happiness or perfection, the Akan has only one answer. If the good is pleasure, whose pleasure is good ? If happiness, whose happiness ? If perfection or justice, whose perfection and whose justice ? These abstractions are no better than the psychological abstraction we have just considered. They also are functions of society, or of men in society. None of them goes deep enough into the nature of society, nor answers all the questions. Take, for instance, justice. What element of social justice can be found in a daughter's refusal to show officers of the law the hiding place of her father ? There is a moral value in the conduct of the daughter, but we put a strain on language to call it justice. Indeed, pleasure, happiness, virtue, justice, perfection are all terms full of colour. Compared to the Akan answer there is more of warm humanity in the idea, for instance, that pleasure is the supreme end of life. Does not every man naturally seek his own pleasure ? So he does, apparently, but we are not, in ethics, talking of every man in abstraction, but of men-in-society. Unfortunately for the upholder of pleasure as the supreme end we all know for certain that that is not quite the case. Pleasure is never man's thought. for good. The warmth and colour in pleasure do not go far or deep enough. Mere colour is often skin deep, and, in ethics, we need more than pigment if our answer is to stand the softening changes and wild ravages of time.

Here, too, the only adequate answer to the question, " what is good ? " must be found in the nature and constitution of society itself, in the social organism. What is the general name of that without which society breaks into pieces or fails to stand together ? Could it be absence of pain ? The Spartan says no. Could it be absence of worry or discontent ? The hero, the patriot, and the statesman say no. Could it be absence of vice, distortion and illusion ? The idealist says no. All these, as it were, are functions or misfunctions of the objective thing we call society. So long as society has a determinable objective end, vice and illusion and distortion will not be welcome to it. But the absence of these negative qualities or the presence of their positive opposites is not the constitutional answer for the design of society.

What, then, is the Akan answer to the question, " What is Good ? " The answer, we confess, cannot but be merely nominal. Any other answer is bound to be an abstraction from the whole and not a full and complete definition of the real thing. To say, for instance, that God is good, or is truth, or is holy, is not a definition of God but only an abstraction from the whole which He is. The completest answer to the question what is God is that He *is* God. Quite obviously, as was anticipated, an answer without colour or warmth. But no more colourful description could be an ultimate definition of God. Equally the completest answer to the question, " in what does the social good consist," is that it can consist in nothing else but the good of the society. It is the practice, in society, of doing good, in other words, beneficence. This is the Akan answer.

The emphasis, here, is on the social nature of the good. Whatever the ethical aim is, it is an aim for society. Its good is what counts. This good is the only justification for the communion of society, that it should hang together without falling into pieces. It is something *to* the good of society.

And the knowledge of this notion has nothing to do with experience. The notion comes to man by some sort of feeling, that higher form of perception, *i.e.*, intellection, which is called insight or intuition, insight into the nature of society as such. Its certainty is not apodeictic, not given *a posteriori* by induction. Nor does it come by a demonstrative proof from sense particulars as come pain, pleasure and the like. Doing that never gets to any ultimate truth of the nature of the good.

The content of the good can be found by experience. In fact we cannot find it otherwise. By legislation, by religion, and by other social or moral drills, education, marriage, games, sports and various kinds of pleasurable, useful or strenuous activities, we do, somehow, determine the content of the good. But the nature of the good comes to us without need for trial and error, but *a priori*, by looking into the constitution of society itself. You may have to look long or in brief, but you have to look well, and looking well enough discloses only one possible answer, that as society is composed of rational self-conscious beings, its members can remain rational *and* self-conscious only in the consciousness of other selves, in the community of other rational beings. That is to say, man, by nature, is a social subject, and, for that reason, he can only attain his supreme good by remaining social and not otherwise. The good is therefore the practice of a rational being who has come to know his own worth as a person, a reasonable being, and not an unreasonable or irrationally constituted being. The test of the goodness of an act for such a being would follow equally from the nature of its definition : that the act must be reasonable, understanding by reason correspondence with a systematic whole, an organic adjustment of act to act, in other words, a harmonious community of action.

The harmonious or reasonable never falls apart but is ever permanently held together because constituted to stand together —an ethical community. Some have therefore defined the social good as a harmony of action. But that again is nominal, for harmony must mean good, that is, reasonable. It is best to retain the more general and creative definition that beneficence is the social good. There are creative as well as static harmonies. But beneficence, like love, is always creative.

All this, of course, may be disputed, has, in fact, in one form or another, been disputed throughout the centuries of ethical disquisition. My own justification for dragging it out for an autopsy is that the Akan system of life, with the family as the social centre, entirely presupposes it and necessarily requires it as the only satisfactory explanation. Whenever we contemplate Akan society as a plan for reasonable beings in being, a legal phrase meaning human beings who are not dead to the vital interest and who are members of a family, we cannot but arrive at the *a priori* vision of truth that the end of such beings is to make their society tolerable or lovable ; if possible, good. You may, if you wish, call the good, the pleasant, if that satisfies all your wants for real life, but that modification would remain your own, and the fact remains that the real objective is the good.

The Akan answer to the question " Why should I be good ? " is therefore that there is no abstract compulsion why you should. You can be or do anything else you like provided you do not lay claim to a share in the society of man and to belong to a human family. You have, that is to say, a choice between good and evil. Wherever men are gathered together there the good must be, or the gathered togetherness would be of no value and soon may fall apart in disharmony, and the family disappear. It would and could not bear fruit. It would be evil.

All this, of course, and the reasons therefor are fully dealt with in the text.

5. THE ''INTEREST'' OF DEITY

An ethical system must be judged on its own merits and not on general principles applicable to other systems which may not have the same foundation of facts for the superstructure often erected on them. Akan religion and morality are entailed in the fact and practice of Akan life, namely, one based on family (*abusua*).

The theory proves itself to be a complete philosophical system in that it affords a methodical explanation of an assemblage of facts adjusted into a regular whole. Its postulates of *e-su, sunsum* and *okara* are a near-perfect correspondence with the psychological co-ordinates of feeling, willing and thinking ; and its postulates of *Onyame, Onyankopon* and *Odomankoma* take it out of the hylotheism which, at first sight, seems to be suggested by the identification of the primal deity (Onyame) with E-su, the material or physical basis of reality ; and because the theory does not leave the personal and active deity (Onyankopon) to stand by himself, it refutes the charge of anthropomorphism against the system ; and finally the conception of the infinite Being, Odomankoma, as completing and affording an insight into the organic whole in which both Onyame and Onyankopon are understood and experienced, affords an integral picture of ultimate reality as having its ground in a pervasive spirit (*Honhom*) realizing its creative purpose in experience.

Between the three psychological co-ordinates *e-su, sunsum* and *okara*, and the three transcendental co-ordinates, Onyame, Onyankopon and Odomankoma, stands the Nana, the ideal father and ancestor whose function is to bring man to God and God to man.

God, therefore, is conceived to be creator, the ultimate ancestor. As such He is head of the great *Abusua*, Family, which, as we saw, is that for which the ethical good is good. Every human family is portion of the one Family which makes God a Head.

6. THE MEANING OF ''FAMILY''

A great hindrance to the student of comparative ethics and religion in any attempt to recognize features in the Akan system comparable to other systems is the peculiarity of the Akan family, *abusua*, which is a sub-division of a clan based on matrilineal descent. That may suggest, upon a first impression, that the ethical and social ideas of the Akan are entirely new, new, that is, compared to what great portions of the human race take to be a family. It seems the proper place here to emphasize that any such expectation to find an entirely new order of ideas in the Akan must be disappointed.

The system, as a whole, most certainly presents a new point of view. It would not otherwise be worth while expending energy on it to produce this work. When, however, it is realized that by *abusua* what is intended to emphasize is the fact of blood or direct ancestry, the hindrance begins to wear thin.

Taken part for part, the student of ethics is likely to find glimpses of resemblance between such parts in Akan ideas and other parts in other racial philosophies. The value of the Akan system consists in its capacity or adaptability for welding many useful concepts into a coherent system, based on the one original proposition that the ethical good is a family affair. That makes the Akan system organic. Everything in the system flows and follows naturally from that one simple proposition that the family of one blood is the ethical good.

The last proposition is not to be confused with one of the many clichés of the anthropologist who runs as he writes, namely, that the unit of primitive society is the family, and that in non-individualistic societies the individual does not count. We are not here concerned with the refutation of that great illusion. There can be no such community in primitive society, at least, not for ethics. Where morality is, there the individual must be. In the final reckoning, conduct or purposive behaviour implies an individual acting with consciousness of his own responsibility. To say that the family has a conscience as valid as that of the individual is a chimera, a palpable fallacy of *a dicto secundum quid ad dictum simpliciter*. The conscience of a group, in the special circumstances to which we may ascribe a conscience to *it*, can never be the·same as the conscience of the integral individual. And, in any case, that cliché about the family being the unit of society is not what is meant in the Akan system by saying the family is the ethical good. The implication of this is obvious : The anthropologist who goes on a *tour* of a month or eighteen months in Ashanti ought not to write a book about Ashanti.

7. IMMORTALITY IS DIVINE NOT INDIVIDUAL

In every religious system where a soul is postulated the question of its immortality irrepressibly crops up. That question is easily solved in the Akan system by the fact of the continuity of family based on blood and its consequence of several incarnations to realize one's particular destiny under the urge of the spirit (*honhom*). As the head of that family is the infinite Odomankoma, immortality becomes not a fancied hypothesis to explain a residuum we cannot understand, but a fact which takes its natural place in the organic whole, for no real part of a whole which is spirit ever perishes. The only difference is that each man's aliquot part in the immortal life is dividual and divine not individual and personal.

Here, again, the colour and warmth of the accustomed lust for personal immortality disappear, and in their place we are given the mystical identification of man with the divine, whereby the selfish ideal goes under. First thought of this loss may give you momentary pain, but on second thought, you may come to appreciate that it is much better to sacrifice the lust for egoistic hedonism as an end, and work for the social good, for it is the highest good, the *summum bonum*, the richest end for each man and all men.

8. THE AKAN TESTAMENT

Finally, I must pay my tribute to a great Teutonic name, the Rev. J. G. Christaller. My acknowledgments to living authors will be found on another page. Christaller, apart from his being an author, appears to me in the higher sense of that attribute, the *ancestor* of the thought that informs these pages with one lineal memory and imagination. In that sense, the spiritual sense, this book must be taken as having been written by him, or, not to be unnecessarily mysterious, with his spiritual co-operation.

He had come to the Gold Coast, because of his linguistic abilities, specially commissioned by the Basel Evangelical Missionary Society to study the Akan language and translate the Bible and other religious books into the principal Gold Coast language. He did his official work well, and his Twi Bible is a classic. But, in addition, he contributed that something " extra " to Gold Coast literature which takes him out of the run of ordinary translators. His " Dictionary of the Asante and Fante Language called Tshi (Twi) " and his collection of " Twi Mmebusem " (The Maxims), to the number of 3,680, show him to have been as great a missionary as he was philologist, anthropologist, scientist, philosopher, moralist and a man of genius.

Without these two books as my guide the present work could never even have been conceived in the present age, not to say written. His books form, as it were, the ancient testament which has treasured the Akan talent for the eventual epiphany of the Akan theory of life under a garb which the modern man can recognize. Anyone acquainted with Christaller's books will readily agree that, whilst the credit for originality belongs to the native Akan inheritance, but for Christaller's foresight in recording in permanent and highly intelligible form the scattered elements of the beliefs and hopes and fears of the Akan people at that particular juncture in the nineteenth century when European ideas in the form of a new learning, a new religion and a new economic life were sweeping the country, the Akan people of the Gold Coast of West Africa would to-day have failed to bring their indigenous contribution to the spiritual achievements of mankind.

That Christaller himself anticipated a work of this kind may be gathered from the preface to the Proverbs or Maxims written at Schorndorf in February, 1879. He suggested that " Regarding the objects mentioned in, or the doctrines expressed by the proverbs, part of them may be selected and systematically grouped together." He provided a scheme for the grouping and, under the fourth group, he included proverbs which point " to affections or states and dispositions of body or mind, as, pleasure and pain, happiness and misery, cheerfulness and dejection, rejoicing and lamentation, hope and fear, courage and cowardice, rashness and caution." In the last paragraph of the Preface he states :—

" May this Collection give a new stimulus to the diligent gathering of folk-lore and to the increasing cultivation of native literature. May those Africans who are enjoying the benefit of a Christian education, make the best of the privilege ; but let them not despise the sparks of truth entrusted to and preserved by their own people, and let them not forget that by entering into their way of thinking and by acknowledging what is good and expounding what is wrong they will gain the more access to the hearts and minds of their less favoured countrymen."

The intention of this prayer of Christaller's speaks for itself, but we would emphasize one significant phrase : " Let them not despise the sparks of truth entrusted to and preserved by their own people."

Such is our enduring testament, the Akan Testament. Who, in Christaller's opinion, entrusted these sparks of truth to the Akan people ? Does not his particular phrasing suggest that he had come to revere and look upon this old testament of the Akan as divinely inspired ? If so, then we would say of the Akan ethical system what George Bernard Shaw points out in the Preface to " Back to Methuselah " was said by Lorenz Oken concerning natural science : The system we have examined in this work is evidence " of the everlasting transmutations of the Holy Ghost in the world." In other words, the Spirit of God is abroad, even in the Akan of the Gold Coast.

To urge the recognition of this by the world outside as by the Akan within is the purpose which inspired my effort herein, the humble effort to let the spirit use my thought as its vehicle for expression.

J. B. D.

Accra,
May, 1940.

PLATE VIII

NYAME, BIRIBI WO SORO, MA NO MEKA ME NSA (" O God, there is something above, let it reach me "). " This pattern was stamped on paper and hung above the lintel of a door in the palace. The King of Ashanti used to touch this lintel, then his forehead, then his breast, repeating these words three times." It is sometimes stamped on sheep skin or leather.

TWI MAXIMS QUOTED

(With the original Akan Versions)

Note.—The maxims listed below are those cited in the text. They are taken from Rev. J. G. Christaller's " Twi Mmebusem Mpensa-Ahansia Mmoaano," published at Basel, 1879, entitled in English " A Collection of Three thousand and six hundred Tshi Proverbs in use among the Negroes of the Gold Coast speaking the Asante and Fante (*i.e.*, the Akan) language."

Christaller's collection was alphabetically arranged, and those quoted below are in the original serial numbering.

The translations are, as far as possible, idiomatic English, and not literal.

39. *Bakoma, wodi no won na gya ho, na wonni no obi ne na de ho.*
   " You may have absolutely liberty by your mother's hearth, but not at another's."

59. *Obayifo ba wu a, eye no yaw.*
   " Even the witch is in sorrow when her child dies."

60. *Obayifo oreko e ! Obayifo oreko e ! na wonye obayifo a, wuntwa wo ani.*
   " If some one called out : ' Witch, witch ! ' and you were not a witch, you would not turn round to look."

61. *Obayifo kum wadi-wamma-me, na onkum wama-mena-esua.*
   " The witch kills ' He-gave-me-not-at-all,' not ' He-gave-me-but-little.' "

83. *Obenya-adee kara nkyiri biribi.*
   " The soul of the man who would make good taboos nothing."

139. *Obi mfa ade-koko nsisi bayifo.*
   " No one can vie with the witch in red things."

164. *Obi mfa opanyin nhye adanse.*
   " No one turns an opanyin into his witness."

194. *Obi nhyee da nwoo panyin pen.*
   " No one by design ever gave birth to opanyin."

195. *Obi nhye kontromfi na onni son (son aba).*
   " The chimpanzee needs no coercion to eat the tamarind fruit."

209. *Obi nko asaman nsan mmeka abibisem.*
   " One does not return from Asaman (Hades) to talk of things African (*i.e.*, worldly things)."

211. *Obi nkofwe sikakese anim mmua nna.*
   " One does not go to see the Golden Stool and perish with hunger."

227. *Obi nkyere abofra Onyame.*
   " God needs no pointing out to a child."

246. *Obi mmu dua nnyaw so ba.*
   " You could not fell a trunk and leave its branches."

268. *Obi nnim bi ase a, onkyere n'ase se odonko.*
   " One should not say another is a slave not knowing his origin."

301. *Obi nnyaw asuten nkonom otare.*
   " No sensible man would leave a stream to drink from a pool."

396. *Obi nye yiye nnya bone.*
   " The pursuit of beneficence brings no evil."

409. *Obi se " bo wo bra yiye " a, onyaw wo e.*
   " If some one tells you to lead a good life, that is no abuse."

444. *Ebia wobedi sono na biribi nhia wo ; na wudi apata a, na dompe ahia wo.   (Owusu Akyem.)*
" Said Owusu Akyem : ' You may not be stuck for anything eating an elephant, but you may be stuck in the throat eating a fish.' "

445. *Obiako di 'wo a, etoa ne yam.'*
" If one alone eats the honey, it plagues his stomach."

449. *Obako nam hu apennuasa.*
" The odd man abroad meets the thirty thousand (*i.e.*, a multitude of evils)."

445. *Obiakofo na okum sono, na amansan nhina di.*
" It takes one man to kill an elephant. but the universe consumes it."

464. *Biribiara nye yaw se aniwu.*
" Nothing is more painful than disgrace."

474. *Wo biribi ne twea a, ankara worema no aduane fam' ?*
" Were the hound your relation would you feed him on the ground ? "

484. *Wobo bra-pa a, wote mu dew.*
" If you live a good life, you enjoy its sweetness."

488. *" Mabo no na oreba," wokyi.*
" ' I assaulted him and he pursues me,' is prohibited (tabooed)."

492. *Wobo annwo a, wo were mfi.*
" If you are discontent, you never forget."

503. *Aboa biara nni soro a odi kube.*
" There is not a beast of the air for which the fan palm is food."

505. *Aboa dompo nni asumguarede nti na onam asu ho bo akoto.*
" Because he has nothing with him to prepare for his soul the bush-dog goes a-hunting for crabs on the river bank."

509. *Aboa oketew na obuu be se : Odesani mee a, obo dam.*
" The lizard says : ' If ever man attains complete satisfaction he would go crazy.' "

535. *Aboa prako nim se ote nti na onennam mfikyiri.*
" Knowing what it likes best, the pig lives at the back-yard."

547. *Obodamfo m'fere a, ne mma fere.*
" If the lunatic has no shame his children have."

564. *Abofra hu ne nsa hohoro a, one mpanyinfo didi.*
" A child may dine with his elders if his hands are nice (*i.e.*, clean)."

568. *Abofra kotow panyin nkyen.*
" At the feet of the elder, the young bends the knee."

575. *Abofra se : obeso gya mu ; ma onso mu, na ehye no a, obedan akyene.*
" If a child insists upon handling live-coal, let him : he will throw it away when it burns him."

581. *Abofra nte ne na ne n'agya asem a, odi aduan a nkyene nnim'.*
" A child disobedient to his father and mother eats unsalted food."

587. *Abofra ye nea wonye a, ohu nea wonhu.*
" A child who does a forbidden thing sees a forbidding sight."

590. *Abofra yem a, nankasa na owo.*
" The young girl heavy with child becomes her own midwife."

594. *Bogya ne asem.*
" Blood is the thing."

595. *Bogya, wompopa.*
" Blood is indelible."

616. *Obosom a oye nnam na odi aboade.*
" Only the capable *bosom* (priest) gets the votive offering."

618. *Obosom anim, woko no mperensa.*
" One appears thrice at the *bosom's* presence."

619. *Obosom so, 'yenko no mperensa.*
" One does not go thrice to a *bosom*."

624. *Obosomfo ka ne nkonim, na onka ne nkogu.*
" The *bosom* tells of his victories, never his failures."

626. *Bosonopo ne Ayesu ntam', wugoru ho a, oboba si wo.*
" Between the sea-god Po, and the river-god Aye, play habitually, and the grinding stone will crush you."

659. *Abufuw te se ohoho, ontra obiakofo fi.*
" Anger is like a stranger, it does not stay in one house."

683. *Abusua nhina ye abusua, na yefwefwe mmetema so de.*
" We seek those of the stalk, but all are members of the family."

684. *Abusua te se nfwiren ; egugu akuw-akuw.*
" A family is like flowers, it throws off in clusters."

783. *Ade a ohene pe na woye ma no.*
" What the king orders is what is done."

785. *Ade a enye no na woye no yiye.*
" What ought to be made good is what is of evil report."

832. *Odefoo a oso ne boto, wokyi.*
" To leave your benefactor to bear the load is prohibited (tabooed)."

836. *Odehye, wodi no apataa, na wonni no sono.*
" Freedom is enjoyed in the manner of eating fish, not of an elephant."

866. *Wudi bi ade a, na wofere no.*
" You owe a responsibility to the man who gives you privilege " (*noblesse oblige*).

887. *Wodi panyin anom' asem, na wonni nè tirim de.*
" We act on an elder's language, not on his thoughts."

893. *Wudi sono akyi a, wontoa.*
" There are no entanglements to follow the elephant's lead."

899. *Wudi wo koma akyi a, woyera.*
" Follow your heart and you perish."

900. *Wodi wo ni a, di wo ho ni.*
" When people hold you in respect, hold yourself in respect, too."

964. *Odomankoma boo owuo na owuo kum no.*
" Odomankoma created death and death killed Him."

966. *Odomankoma na oma owuo di akane.*
" It was none but Odomankoma who made Death eat posion."

967. *Odomankoma kowui no, ode n' akyi gyaw agyina.*
" Odomankoma having died, he left his affairs in the hands of the Counsellor."

968. *Odomankoma owuo suro tutu a, anka obefa onipa ?*
" Would Odomankoma (universal) Death venture to take man if He could be scared by Discord ? "

975. *Odonko nya ade a, obo dam.*
" A slave who becomes rich goes mad."

1118. *Wo ferefo fere a, woafere.*
" If your peer is scorned you are scorned."

1196. *Wofwefwe asem mu a, wuhu fwefwe.*
" He who looks into matter comprehends it."

1225. *Guaman so wommara.*
" One doesn't cheat, openly."

1305. *Ohene bekum wo a, ennim ahamatwe.*
" If the king orders your execution, drawing lots will not help you."

1309. *Ohene nufu dooso a, amansan na enum.*
" If the king's breast is full of milk, it belongs to all the world."

1373. *Ohiani mpaw dabere.*
    " The poor relation never lacks a bed."

1400. *Ohoho a obae se 'wanto bi' a, nkurofo a obetoo won ka se : yeanhu bi a obae.*
    " The stranger who came says he did not see anybody in the town,
    and the people he met also say ' We did not see anyone come.' "

1403. *Ohoho akyi mpa asem.*
    " There is always some trouble after the stranger departs."

1404. *Ohoho ama wonya sikaa, oma woanya kaw.*
    " The stranger in your threshold brings you some money—and some
    debt."

1405. *Ohoho nni nko ye omanni-fonee.*
    " ' Let the stranger enjoy it and go' means, often, the citizen
    starving."

1406. *Ohoho ani akese-akese, nanso enhu man mu asem.*
    " A stranger has large eyes, but they see nothing in the town."

1408. *Ohoho nsoa funu ti.*
    " A stranger should not carry the coffin's head."

1410. *Ohoho te se abofra.*
    " The stranger—he is like a child."

1411. *Ohoho te se sunsuansu.*
    " A stranger is like passing water in the drain."

1412. (a) *Ohoho nto mmara.* (b) *Ohoho na oto mmara.*
    (a) " A stranger does not break the law." (b) " It is a stranger who
    breaks the law."

1420. *Ohonam mu nni nhanoa.*
    " The spirit of man is without boundaries."

1471. *Woanhye woho a, wonhye wo.*
    " Unless you control yourself, nobody would."

1517. " *Ankama, kotua ka !* "—" *Fa ka bera ?* " *wokyi.*
    " ' Old chap, go and pay my debt' is prohibited."

1528. *Okasa esu aduasa wo ho, efanim mmiako-mmiako.*
    " Man's one speech has thirty varieties, but they are slight."

1530. *Okasamee ye okarabiri.*
    " Garrulity is an affliction of soul."

1554. *Okisi-aku, wogye no Aku ; Akrante-aku, wogye no Aku ; Abotokura-*
    aku, wogye no Aku, nanso won nhinaa san kosom Akrante-aku."
    " We salute Kisi-aku as Aku ; we salute Karante-aku as Aku ; we
    salute Botokura-aku as Aku ; but despite this they all willingly
    acknowledge Karante-aku as Master." (*Note : Kisi* is the rat ;
    akrante is hedgehog, and *abotokura* is a forest kind of mouse.)

1567. *Woko obi kurom na woanko wo kurom' bi a, wobu wo aboa.*
    " He treats you like a beast who would not return your visit to his
    town."

1611. *Akoa na odi fo.*
    " The slave naturally is always guilty."

1612. *Akoa di guan a ne ho guan no.*
    " A slave who eats sheep, weeps."

1620. *Akoa nim som a, ofa ne tiri ade di.*
    " If a slave behaves himself, his purchase-price is discharged."

1624. *Akoa nyansa wo ne wura tiri mu.*
    " A slave's wisdom is in his master's head."

1626. *Akoa ampow a, na efi ne wura.*
    " If a slave is ill behaved it is due to his master."

1628. *Akoa te se kyekyere : wode nsu kakra gu no so a, na ahono.*
    " A slave is like *farina*, a little liquid and it is solvent."

1653. *Akoko nom nsu a, ode kyere Onyankopon.*
" When the fowl drinks water it shows it to God."

1695. *Akomboafo ye na.*
" Aids to the *bosom*-cults are not numerous."

1699. *Akomfo aduasa fwe oyarefo a, wodi atoro.*
" If thirty *bosom* priests look after one sick man they tell lies."

1700. *Wo nkommo ye den a, wofwere debisafo.*
" If your divining fees are high you go without clients."

1710. *Wo akonnua to wo so a, wosan ana ?*
" There is no denying the nana's verity."

1716. *Kontromfi kyea senea akyeafo kyea, nso ne to koo.*
" The chimpanzee could strut quite like a dandy but for his red buttocks."

1730. *Kore-kyerekyere ne kore-dada ne kore-a-na-obi-aba, hena ne panyin ?*
" He went far away,
" He went long ago,
" He went before anyone came,
" Which of them is the eldest ? "

1773. *Okramane atirimsem da ne bo, na enna ne tirim.*
" A hound's motive springs not from his head but from his heart."

1780. *Nkrante nko babi nnyaw ne nnam.*
" Where the matchet goes, there it sharpens."

1840. *Kurow gu, na menne abobow.*
" Even a city gate may be destroyed how much more the domestic gate."

1841. *Kuro so a, omanni-bere ye ona.*
" It is hard to meet an excellent man in a big and straggling town."

1860. *Nkuro dooso a, woyi bi aye.*
" Of several towns one must be above the others."

1985. *Woamma wo yonko antwa akron a, wo nso wuntwa du.*
" They will not credit you with ten, if you will not credit your neighbour with nine."

1987. *Amma-annwo-kurow biara nyee kese da.*
" A seditious town never prospers."

1996. *Oman rebebo a, efi afi mu.*
" The ruin of the city comes from the homes."

1999. *Oman Akuapem, wokonya ade a, wose : obusufo ! nso woannya a, wose : okarabiri !*
" These Akuapem people : if you are prosperous, they call you lucky devil, and if destitute, they say blighted soul."

2011. *Omanni, wokum no sum mu.*
" One kills a citizen only in the dark."

2012. *Omanni yera a, wode omanni aben na efwefwe omanni.*
" When a citizen is missing, the search party looks for him with the citizen's band."

2023. *Me a meda ayannya minhu Nyankopon, na wo a wubutuw ho !*
" I face upwards and can't see Nyankopon, but what of you sprawling downwards."

2070. *Na Abina se : onware ponko, na anka afunum !*
" Aunt Abina declines marriage with the horse, how much more the donkey."

2154. *Nea wadidi amee se : nea odidi anadwo ye obayifo.*
" The one who has had enough to eat states ' he who eats in the night is a witch.' "

2155. *Nea wadidi amee se : nea oresi pe ye ayen.*
" The one who has had enough to eat states : He who is sitting up late (without sleep) is a wizard."

2208. *Nea wo ani agye sen nea woawo wo.*
" Where you have had joy excels where you have been born."

2242. *Nea oso na omene ne yonko.*
" It is the greater (fish) that swallows its neighbour."

2285. *Nne-mma se : tete asoee, wonsoe ho bio ! na den nti na wontu tete 'muka abiesa no biako na enka abien ?*
" The modern man says : It does not pay to halt at an ancient refuge. But why don't they remove one leg of the tripod and leave still two ? "

2291. *Wo ani bere wo yonko ade a, woye bi, na wunwia.*
" When you admire something belonging to another, get your own, do not steal it."

2310. *Anigyebea sen awobea.*
" Joy-land (is sweeter) than birth-land."

2364. *Onipa a ompe se ne yonko ye yiye no, onye yiye.*
" He who does not wish his neighbour good, never makes good."

2370. *Onipa-bone biako te man mu a, ne nkoa ne nnipa nhina.*
" One sinner in our midst makes slaves of us all."

2723. *Onipa de ne kotoku se a, ode se nea ne nsa beso.*
" When a man puts on his knapsack, he sees to it that it is accessible."

2380. *Onipa firi soro na obesi a, obesi nnipa kuro so.*
" If even a man alights on earth from heaven, he alights in a habitation of men."

2385. *Onipa gye nkanare-a, osen dade.*
" A rusty person is worse than rusty iron."

2397. *Onipa-mu mfa n' anuonyam nsie ne to.*
" A gentleman should not hide his dignity in his pants."

2399. *Onipa na oma onipa ye yiye.*
" The beneficence of man depends upon man."

2403. *Onipa ne asem : mefre sika a, sika nnye so ; mefre ntama a, ntama nnye so ; onipa ne asem."*
" It is man who counts : I call upon gold, it answers not ; I call upon drapery, it answers not. It is man who counts."

2404. *Onipa anim te se ewi anim ; wuhu a, na wo bo adwo.*
" The image of man is like the sun ; look on it, and it is peace."

2413. *Onipa nti na wobo afoa.*
" Because of man the sword is made."

2418. *Onipa ye abogyaboa.*
" Man is a warm-blooded animal."

2420. *Onipa ye wo yiye a, mfa bone nye no.*
" To him who is good to you do no evil."

2423. *Onipa nye abe na ne ho ahyia ne ho.*
" Man is not a palm-nut that he should be self-centred."

2434. *Nnipa nyinaa soa Nyankopon a, obiakofo nnuru mu afu.*
" When all the world makes God its burden, none becomes humpbacked."

2436. *Nnipa nyinaa ye Onyame mma ; obi nye asase ba.*
" All men are the offspring of God, no one is the offspring of Earth."

2437. *Nnipa nyinaa ye ti biako, nanso won ti nse.*
" All men have one head, but heads differ."

2449. *Aniwa wu a, etuatua tiri no ara.*
" When your eyes bring you shame, they stick out in your head."

2451. *Aniwu ne wu, na efanim wu.*
" Better death, than disgrace."

2453. *Ano-bone ye okrabiri.*
" A foul mouth is an affliction of soul."

2455. *Ano-kurokuro twa neho adafi.*
" A chattering mouth is its own traitor (betrays itself)."

2475. *Nokware mu nni abra.*
" There never is fraud in truth."

2477. *Nokware nye ahe na woatwa mu nkontompo !*
" Truth isn't much to lie in it."

2482. *Anoma-bone na osee ne berebuw.*
" Only a nasty bird would ruin her own nest."

2501. *Onua-panyin ye owura.*
" Of two brothers, the senior must be master."

2538. *Onyame nkrabea nni kwatibea.*
" There is no by-pass to God's destiny."

2542. *Onyame ne panyin.*
" God is chief."

2543. *Onyame pe se ogye yen yiye nti, na ode Mankata besii agye yen.*
" Because Nyankopon wished to save us (ogye yen) he landed Macarthy at ' save us ' (agye yen)."   *See p. 76.*

2544. *Onyankopon ba de Mpatuw-nwu.*
" The name of God's son is ' Feign-not-death.' "

2545. *Onyankopon hye wo nsa kora-ma na oteasefo ka gu a, ohyia wo so bio.*
" Let living man empty your goblet of wine, God would fill it up. (If God gives you a goblet of wine and a living man kicks it down, God makes it up to the brim for you.)"

2546. *Onyankopon nkum wo na odasani kum wo a, wunwu da.*
" Unless you die of Onyankopon, let living man kill you, and you will not perish."

2547. *Onyankopon amma asonomfoa katakyi biribi a, omaa no ahodannan.*
" If the plucky sparrow got nothing else from God, it got dash."

2548. *Onyankopon mpe asemmone nti na okye din mmiako-'miako.*
" To save fraud, God gave each person a name."

2561. *Wunyin a, na wunhu ; na woye bone de a, wuhu.*
" You may not see yourself growing up, but you certainly know when you are sinning."

2578. *Wopa wo ho tam wo abonten so na wode be fura ofie a, enye fe.*
" If you are disrobed in the public square there is no grandeur enrobing at home."

2580. *" Pae mu se ! " ye fere, nso eye ahodwo.*
" Own up the truth openly, may be embarrassing, but it brings content."

2599. *Opanyin nni biribi a, owo batwow.*
" If the elder has no other power, he has the elbow, at least."

2606. *Opanyin kye a, edwo.*
" When the sharing is done by the elder peace ensues."

2609. *Opanyin anim asem ye oka-na.*
" It is an awkward thing, sometimes, to approach an elder."

2610. *Opanyin ano sen suman.*
" The word of the elder is more potent than fetish."

2618. *Opanyin nto bo-hyew nto abofra nsam'.*
" An elder does not put a hot stone in a child's hand."

2622. *Mpanyimfo na ebu be se : Gya me nan, na wonse se : Gya me ti.*
    " The ancient saying was this : ' Leave my feet alone ' and not
       ' Leave my head alone.' "

2623. *Mpanyimfo se : maye se wo pen.*
    " I was once like you," is a proverb.

2624. *Se mpanyimfo pe wo atoto awe a, wunhuruw ntra ogya.*
    " If the elders are seeking to make it hot for you, keep away from
       their fire-place."

2625. *Mpanyimfo ye wo guannuan, na se wuguan a, akyiri no woserew wo.*
    " If the elders cause you to be terrified and you run away, later they
       laugh at you."

2631. *Wo mpasua si wo nnuarem' a, wunnyae nkodi nea eye.*
    " If your place in a troop march takes you to a tight corner, you
       cannot desert it for an easier place."

2636. *Mpata ko a, ansa-na abodwo aba.*
    " You gain satisfaction before content. . . ."

2649. *Mepe obi makra Saben a, na biribi nte se Agyaben nankasa nam.*
    " I was on the lookout for some one to take a message to Saben (the
       expert), but now Agyaben (master mind) is here, can anything be
       better ? "

2652. *Wope obi ti atwa a, na wotwa wo de.*
    " If you want to cut some one's head, they cut yours first."

2656. *Wope aka asem akyere Onyankopon a, ka kyere mframa.*
    " If you would tell God, tell the wind."

2659. *Wope kurow bi muatra a, wututu mu nnunsin, na wonhye mu*
       mpam.
    " If you do not wish to be troubled in a town, uproot the stumps,
       planting no thorns."

2759. *Osaman-pa hyira ne ba.*
    " The good spirit favours (or blesses) his child."

2765. *Asaman nni biribi a, ewo nhyehye-wo-akyi.*
    " If the ghost is poor in possession he at least has pride of de-
       scendants."

2777. *Osansa se : ade a Onyame aye nhyinaa ye.*
    " Says the Hawk : All God did is good."

2782. *Sasabonsam ko ayi a, osoe obayifo fi.*
    " When the Sasabonsam travels to a funeral, he lodges in the wizard's
       house." (Sasabonsam is the ' Great Devil,' *i.e.*, Spirit of the
       Devils.)

2783. *Sasabonsam te-ase, wose oye obayifo, na menne se osi odum atifii na*
       odum nso sow mmoatia.
    " Living a normal life the Sasabonsam was called wizard, how much
       more now that he is perched on top of the odum tree and the tree
       is also bearing a crop of gnomes."

2787. *Asase terew, ne Onyame ne panyin.*
    " The earth is wide but God is chief."

2825. *Wuse wobesom Nyankopon a, som no preko, na mfa biribi mmata ho.*
    " If you would serve God, be thorough, attaching no conditions."

2832. *Ese tenten ne se kwatia didi biako (pe).*
    " The tall and the short teeth have but one grind between them."

2833. *Wo se nye a, nea wotaforo akyiri ara nen.*
    " If your gums are not tasty, you can't help licking them."

2844. *Osee asem te se kontonkurowi : eda amansan nyinaa konmu.*
    " Osee's command is like the sun's aureola : it encircles all men
       (*amansan*)." (*Osei*, the king.)

2855. *Asem a Onyame adi asie no, oteasefo nnan no.*
  " The order God has settled living man cannot subvert."
2857. *Asem a esen hene wo ho.*
  " There is a reality greater than the King."
2942. *Sika pereguan da kurom' a, ewo amansan.*
  " If there is Pereguan (£8) in the town, it belongs to the community."
2984. *Aso si abien, na ente asem abien.*
  " The head has two ears, but it does not hear in two's."
2992. *Woansoa no tuntum so a, wosoa no fufu (dwen) so.*
  " If the younger (black haired) would not carry, the older (grey haired) carry."
2996. *Som woho nye akoa.*
  " Serve yourself, that is no subjection."
2999. *Wosom wo fukwan so a, obi nhu wo hia.*
  " Faith in your own tillage never exposes your poverty."
3005. *Wosoma obanimdefo, na wonsoma nammontenten.*
  " The best bearers of message (ambassadors) are the wise, not those with long shanks."
3010. *Asomdwee ne oman-nyina.*
  " Peace ensures the public-good. (Where there is peace, there is stability.)"
3060. *Osu to fwe wo na owia fi hye wo a, na wuhu abrabo yaw.*
  " If you are soaked by rain and then scorched by sun you see the way of this world."
3061. *Osu to gu po mu. (Yenim se epo so, nanso nsu to gum'.)*
  " That the sea is all water is well known, but rain still pours into it."
3099. *Wusua asempa a, wunya anuonyam.*
  " He sees glory who fathoms the infallible."
3200. *Wote kuro-bone mu a, wo ani na ewu.*
  " If you live in a wicked town the shame is yours."
3240. *Tete asoee, wonsoe ho bio.*
  " It does not pay to halt at the ancient place of refuge (at an ancient refuge)."
3248. *Ti a edi kan ne panyin.*
  " The head that tops the list, leads."
3254. *Ti-densow mmo aguabum.*
  " The odd character never fits in."
3268. *Wutiatia obi de so fwefwe wo de a, wunhu.*
  " Trampling on another's right to seek your own ends in disappointment."
3275. *Wo tirim ye den a, wunnya otubrafo.*
  " New settlers always shun the tyrant."
3281. *" Eto baabi a, ' edum,' eto baabi a, ehyew " nye amanmui-pa.*
  " *Justice* to-day and *injustice* to-morrow, that is not good government. (On one occasion it quenches, on another occasion it flares up, that is not good government.)"
3285. *Eto sikyi o, eto mfuate o, yenya okomfo kum no.*
  " Whichever side the die falls, we get a priest to hang."
3355. *Tra nea midui !*
  " ' Reach full beyond my paces,' says the elder."
3395. *Otuo yera nifa mu na ekofi adonten mu a, na enkoo babi e.*
  " When a combatant misses his way from the right wing to the centre he has not strayed."

3465. *Wowoo Tafoni ba no, na onkura ta.*
" The native of Tafo was not holding Ta at his birth."

3485. *Owu ne wo ase hye wo adwumaye a, owu de na woko kan.*
" Summoned by death and by your mother-in-law, attend to death first."

3493. *Owu nye pia na woadi mu ahyemfiri.*
" Death is not a sleeping room for frequent visits."

3501. *Owura ne akoa ntam nni twe-ma-mentwe.*
" Master and slave can't engage in ' pull and let me pull.' "

3503. *Wo wura tan wo a, na ofre wo akoa dehye.*
" Your master calls you Mr. Free Slave, if he hates you."

3518. *Ewi nwo ba na onkose owansan.*
" The offspring of an antelope cannot possibly resemble a deer's offspring."

3523. *Awia mu nni aduoson anum.*
" There are not seventy-five degrees in sunshine."

3560. *Woye obi yiye na wanye wo bi a, na obu wo aboa.*
" He treats you like a beast who does not reciprocate your goodness."

3576. *Woye yiye a, wode gyaw wo mma ; woye bone nso a, wode gyaw wo mma.*
" Do good, and it lives in your descendants ; do evil, and it lives in them likewise."

3577. *Woye yiye a, ewo ne mfaso.*
" Every good you do, has its profit."

3591. *" Enye biribi," na eye biribiara ne no.*
" It does not matter, just means it does matter."

3629. *Enye tekerema na eboo nantwi nti na wanhu kasa.*
" The cow never learnt to speak, and not because she has no otngue."

3680. *Nsem nyinaa ne Nyame.*
" God is the justification (End-Cause) of all things."

3952. *Eye wo abodwo a, wonka se, enye biribi.*
" You will not say ' Oh it does not matter,' were you tranquil."

NOTES AND GLOSSARY OF AKAN WORDS

A—demonstrative pronoun, which, who, that.

ABA—another form of AMA, *q.v.*

ABENA—response of the Tuesday born (Mars).

ABERAW—response of the Thursday born (Jupiter, Thor, Jove).

ABO—it shines, *bo*, to shine, to spread out.

ABOMMUBUWAFRE—called upon in case of distress—a strong name of God, Nyankopon.

ABOSOM—pl. of obosom, fetish, god.

ABRABO—manner of living ; conduct ; experience.

ABUAKWA—one of the Akyem (Akim) States of the Akan race, capital, Kibi or Kyebi.

ABUSUA—family, one's mother's relations.

ADE—same as Adee.

ADEE—poetic form of " Ade," the Thing created. Normally, *ade* means a thing.

ADI—outside ; as verb, past part., has eaten, from *di*, to eat.

ADOMAKWADE—all sorts of things, medley of things.

ADU—common name in Akan, said to be variant of Anu, an ancient Akan name, much honoured. Other forms are Edu, Adu-akwa, Aduama ; Aduana ; Aduamenya ; Adu-amantem ; Adu-berawiri ; Adukoram ; Adu-ma-nnuro ; Aduobe ; Adu-warae ; Adufo ; Adutwum.

ADUAN—food.

ADZE—Fante for Ade, *q.v.* the Thing.

AFI—response of the Friday born (Venus).

AFUA—name of a woman born on Friday : Asase Afua, Goddess Earth of Friday.

AGYEMAN—name of a person, means probably saviour of a nation, from *gye*, to save, *oman*, nation.

AHONHOM—pl. of honhom, *q.v.*

AKAN—One of the principal races in West Africa, inhabiting the Gold Coast, the Ivory Coast, some parts of French West Africa, up to the old kingdom of Ghana (near present Timbuktu), and speaking the Twi (Twui) language. The word is often pronounced Akane, and it is said to mean " foremost, genuine " ; from *kan*, first. The best known representatives of the race are the Ashanti, Fanti, Akim, Akwapim, Assin and several of the present (Twi-speaking) races of the Gold Coast and Ivory Coast. The original form of the name, Akane or Akana, led to its corruption by the early Arabs of the Sudan into Ghana and by early Europeans who visited the Coast of West Africa into Guinea. The Akan people were driven from their ancient home in Ghana, on the bend of the Niger, by the Almoravides (Molaththemum or Muffled Moslems) in A.D. 1076. There was a tradition in Ghana (*vide* Flora Shaw, Lady Lugard : " A Tropical Dependency "), that the people of Ghana had originally come to the West Sudan from a country beyond or near the Taurus mountains (Taurudu). The current theory that the Ghana or Akane in Taurus was the same as the old Babylonian race known as Akkad, Agade or Akana, who lived on the Tigris and Euphrates, is strongly supported by the evidence of common features in the language of the ancient race and of the modern, as also in their customs. Archæology and anthropology have as yet revealed little, but Sir Henry Rawlinson and other

Assyrologists bear testimony to the similarity between the language of Sumer and Akkad and certain African languages, an ancient group which is not Semitic. The Akan people of the Gold Coast have not been written up as well as they could be, but there is everything in favour of the hypothesis that they are an ancient race ; that their institutions and customs are of ancient origin, *e.g.*, the seven-day week, and that their sojourn in the Gold Coast, which is less than 900 years, is much shorter than their traceable sojourn as a people in the ancient and modern worlds.

AKATABAA or AKATABAN—authority, force ; dictate by strength, from *kata*, to cover, and *abaa*, stick, or *aban*, fortress.

AKIM—Akyem, a generic name for many of the Akan tribes, *e.g.*, Akyem Abuakwa, Akyem Kotoku, Akyem Swedru, Asante-Akyem. It is written on English maps, etc., as Akim.

AKOA—slave ; subject of a king ; any male person ; *f.* afanaa.

AKOKO—fowl.

AKU—response of the Wednesday born (Mercury).

AKROPONG—name of a town, " big town."

AKWA—name of a person, or it may mean " for nothing."

AKWAHOSAN—self-dependent life, care-free life, freedom of life and health, feeling of good life, contentment.

AMA—female form of KWAAME, person born on Saturday.

AMANE—trial, trouble, affliction, misery, misfortune, calamity.

AMANIAMPON—great neighbour.

AMAOMEE—appellation of Onyame, God, " Giver of Repletion."

AMEN—the form of address for Kwaame or Kwame, he who is born on Saturday, or worshipped on that day. Probably from Amen or Amon, the Egyptian god of Siwa, in Libya, at the edge of the Sahara, whose day is Saturday, and who is called Saturn by the Romans, Cronus by the Greeks, Anu by the Babylonians, oldest of the Gods. Among the Anglo Saxons also Saturday is the day of Saterne.

AMOSU—appellation of Onyame, God, " Giver of Rain."

AMOWIA—appellation of Onyame, God, " Giver of Sun."

AMPON—suffix for great, as in Amaniampon, *q.v.*

ANANSE—ubiquitous hero of Akan folk-tales. The collection of folk-tales is named after him—Ananse-sem, fables of Ananse. Christaller says Ananse is " a mythic personage, generally called Agya Ananse (' Father Ananse '), to whom great skill and ingenuity is attributed (but who is usually caught in his own snare), a personification of the spider. His wife is Konnore, his son Ntikuma." It is now generally established that the identification of Ananse, the mythic personage, with *ananse*, the spider, is an ætiological mistake, arising from a confusion of names. Research has shown that the Akan name Akane has close resemblance to the Babylonian name Akkad or Akana or Agade, and there is evidence also that the Akan language is similar to the language spoken by the people of Sumer and Akkad. That being so, it is not a mere coincidence that the name of the Babylonian " mythic personage " of folk-tales is also called Oannes or Iannes, or Eunanes, a name which modern scholars have not been able to decipher accurately from the ancient cuneiform tables of Babylonia. Oannes was a mythical personage who taught mankind wisdom. He was identified with the God EA or YIYA, a name meaning wisdom in the language of Sumer and Akkad. The Akan word for wisdom is *nyansa*, itself quite close to Oannes. In most Babylonian stories, especially those of the creation and of the spread of knowledge or the arts of social life, the hero most often is Oannes, and it is not impossible that if, indeed, the Akan and the Akkad are connected, the Akan should have transferred that same name to the hero also of their own tales of creation, wisdom and social life. The name for God the Supreme Being himself, in folk-tales is Ananse Kokuroko, the Gigantic or Mighty Ananse. It has not been suggested anywhere that there is an equivalent " great spider " to correspond to the Great Ananse. The point and substance is that Ananse of the folk-tales was, conceptually and originally, a person, not a spider, and his origin is linked to that of Oannes.

ANIMGUASE—disgrace ; literally, " face descending to baseness "; indignity, dishonour.

ANOPA—morning.

ANUONYAM—glory.

ANYAME—*pl.* of Onyame, gods.

ANYIMNYAM—Fanti for anuonyam.

ANYINAM—lightning.

ANYINNYAM—glimpse, sparkles.

ARA—continuously, grammatical inflexion.

ASAMANFO—the spirit ancestors, the spirit of the dead ; ghosts, *pl.* of osaman.

ASARE—name of a person.

ASASE—earth.

ASESE-BEN—horn used for repeating set pieces of proverbs or sayings ; *se-se*, to keep on saying, and *aben*, horn.

ASI—verb *si*, to place, past tense, has placed, *asi*.

ASIAMA—name of a person.

ASON—seven : the names of the digits are : *biako, abien, abiesa, anan, anum, asia, ason, awotwe, akron.* Ten is *edu.* Each of these undergoes inflexion in certain sentences and phrases, thus—*mmiako-mmiako*, one by one ; *mienu, mmiensa, nan, num, nsia, nson, nnwotwe, nkron.*

ASUM'GUARE—washing or bathing in the river, the custom of " soul " washing.

ASUO—*asu* (Ashanti or Akyem, *asuo*), river.

ATAA—*Ga* Father, old one, venerable, equivalent sometimes to *opanyin*, *q.v.*

ATE—marble, the hard nut with the cover.

ATOAPOMA—" He fires and it is loaded already "—The Everready shooter, an appellation of the Saturday born.

ATWARE—*twa*, to cross, cut across ; *atware*, past. part. has crossed.

AWO—birth.

AWO or ADWO—response of the Monday born (Moon).

AWUSI—response of the Sunday born (Sun).

AWURADE—lord, master ; (*awirade*).

BA—*oba*, child.

BAABIARA—anywhere.

BABI—somewhere.

BEBREE—many, copious, several.

BEHU—*hu*, to see, *behu*, future tense, shall see.

BENA—Bona—husk.

BENADA—Tuesday.

BEREW—palm leaves.

BIAKO—one.

BO—to create.

BOADEE—same as Obooadee, or Oboade.
BOAFO—helper.
BODUA—appellation of the Sunday born—Tail of the Beast.
BO KWAN—to make or clear a road.
BON—crowing of a cock.
BONE—bad, evil.
BOREBORE—the Architect, Inventor, Odomankoma, the Infinite Being.
  From *bore*, to dig, *bo*, to create, or make, *-re*, being a repetitive or
  intensifying form.
BREKYIRIHUNADE—appellation of God Nyankopon. He who knows
  what is happening behind him. (Brekyi'hun'ade.)
BRADA—Fante for Brade, the deceiver, the enticer, personified.
BREKYIRI—return, go and come back.
BURU—probably the same as Biru, Birim, name of a river.

DAPAA—empty day, a calendar marking day, the day preceding Daponna,
  or Festival Day, *i.e.*, an open day, day of rest.
DAPAADA—day of " Dapaa."
DEEBEN—*ade ben*, what ?   (A pure Ashanti or Akim form.)
DI—to consume, to eat.
DO—love, grow warm, etc.
DOMA—*dom ma ?* army full ? The term is found at the ends of certain
  words to denote plenitude ; *e.g.*, moadoma, the world of animals.
  (*Aboa*, animal, pl. *mmoa*.)
DOMANKOMA—Fante for Odomankoma.
DUA—tree.
DUPON—mighty tree.
DWOWDA—Monday.
DZI—Ga for *ye*, to be.

EDOM—army, host, company.
EDOMWA—small army, little host.
EHE—Ga, *-e*, he ; *he*, self ; the skin, the flesh, himself.
EKRA—Fanti for Okra, soul.
EKWA—new farm, new cultivation.
EMA—full of.
ENA—mother.
ESEN—Court crier, herald.
ESU—character, nature, species, kind, sort, property, quality.
EWIE—the firmament, the sky, the horizon.
EWIM—in the firmament, in the sky.
EYE—it is good.

FANTE—the proper name of what is known in English as Fanti or Fantee,
  a branch of the Akan. They speak a dialect of the Akan language
  slightly more finer than Twi, but not so pure, in that it admits of
  " z " and similar sounds which pure Akan does not. The Fante live
  in the coastal areas of the Gold Coast mostly.
FARAO—Pharaoh.
FIDA—Friday.
FIRI—forgive.

GA—the name of a tribe or race in the Gold Coast speaking the Ga language. Believed to be a branch of the original Twi or Twui race.
  They live in south-east Gold Coast and are a branch of the Ga-

Adangme group. Their capital city is Accra, capital town of British Gold Coast.

GBESHI—Ga : bad soul (" died " and " left " soul).

GYA—fire.

HENA—who.

HIMA—see *nhima*.

HO—self, the personal identity, the flesh, *cf.* Ga, *he*, *q.v.*

HONHOM—spirit of the highest form. (Not ghost, or soul, or personality) that which a soul possesses, allied to God.

HUNU—*hu*, to see ; Akyem form.

HYEBEA—destiny, decree of life, manner of life as ordained by nature or God : (*hye*, to order, make law).

KAW—debt.

KAWU—touch and die (*ka-na-wu*).

KO—from *koro*, alone, *biako*, one, *q.v.*

KOFI—name of person born on Friday, *f.* Afua.

KOKUROKO—that which is great, term used of God in folk-tales, called Ananse Kokuroko, the Gigantic Ananse.

KOMM—quietly, peaceably.

KOSE—*ko se*, go and tell (him).

KOTOO—*ko to*, go and meet ; *ko too*, went and met.

KOTOKU—one of the Akim states of the Akan group, capital, Oda.

KRA—same as Okara or Okra, the o- being prenominal.

KRAPA—good soul.

KUAKU—difficult to place this word (in Rattray) in the Akan language.

KWABENA—name of person born on Tuesday, *f.* Abena.

KWABRAFO—nickname of the bear, the honey-badger or ratel. It is probably from *okwaberan*, a strong person or strong slave. An able-bodied man.

KWADWO—name of person born on Monday, *f.* Adwoa.

KWAKU—name of person born on Wednesday, *f.* Akua.

KWAAME or KWAME—name of person born on Saturday, *f.* Ama.

KWASI—name of person born on Sunday, *f.* Akosua.

KWASIDA—Sunday.

KWIFORO—name of an Akan country or State, Twiforo.

KYEREMA—the drummer of the Ntumpan drums, the poet-historian.

MA—so that, to let (to express purpose) ; for.

ME—third person singular of I, me. Also first person singular, I.

MEE—to be satisfied (with food) ; to be full of.

MEHYE—*me hye*, I fill, cause.

MEMENDA—Saturday.

MERE—manner or aura of a person, from *bere*, probably, time.

MMERE—times ; *pl.* of *bere*, time.

MFANTSI—full form of Fante in certain phrases and sentences.

MFATA—negative of *fata*, becomes, fits. *Mfata*, does not become, or does not suit, ill-becomes.

MO—Ga personal suffix, for person doing or acting, agent, *e.g.*, *gbo-mo*, person, probably dying-man, for *gbo* in Ga, means to die, *gbele*, means death.

MMOADOMA—the family of animals, the entire species of animals.

MOGYA—blood, family through the mother.

MU—post-position for in or at ; inside, among.
MMUBU—sorrowful, mournful, lamentation.
MMURU—from Buru, *q.v.*

NA—but, only, and.
NAA—Ga, female form of Nana.
NANA—grandfather, grandmother. The Ga form is Nee or Nene. The word is probably derived from *ena*, mother, *ena ena*, mother's mother. It is used as a form of address for kings and men of note. It is also a form of address for God, *Nyankopon*, *q.v.* It often means the ancestor, the originator, creator.
NANANOM—*pl.* of Nana, *q.v.* The Fante form is Nanaam.
NNAMERENSON—seven eras, seven periods ; all days throughout.
NANIM—n-anim, *i.e.*, *ono anim*, his face, his presence.
NE—his.
NEA—that which, he who.
NEHO—*ne ho*, his flesh, himself, round about him.
NENE—Ga-Adangme for Nana or Nee, Nii.
N'ENYI—Fante for *n'ani*, his eye.
NHANOA—boundaries, limits, bounds, edges, the outer edge of a farm, or cultivated ground.
NHIMA—early in the morning.
NII—*Nee*, Ga for Nana.
NKRA—message, intelligence, *nous*, the essence of *okara*, soul, or its cause or condition. In ordinary language, *kra*, means to send a message, of which *nkra* is the substantive.
NKRABEA—destiny, fate, decree of life, kismet.
NKWA—life.
NNA—*pl.* of *da*, day.
NNEEMA—things, plural of *ade*.
NNI—negative of *wo*, to have : *nni*, has not.
NNIPADUA—human body, human frame.
NO—the, him.
NSO—but, although, nevertheless, also.
NSON—*ason*, seven.
NSU—water.
NTONI—appellation of the Wednesday born—The Champion, the Vicarious Hero.
NTORO—stirps, the male family or connection, family traced through the male, as distinct from *abusua*, family traced through the female.
NTSE—clean, smart (*Ga*).
NTUMPAN—the double drums called by Rattray the Talking Drums. They stand on legs like what are called kettle drums. Ntumpan is the plural form, the singular being Atumpan.
NYA—to get.
NYAM—same as onyam, brightens.
NYAMA—to beckon, to move to and fro.
NYAMANEKOSE—tell your troubles to a hearer.
NYAMBI—an East African name for God.
NYAMEDAN—God's room, temple.
NYAMEDUA—God's Tree, a branch or stem of a tree with three-pronged branches, like a tripod set upside down, on which pots are placed, containing sacred water and other articles of sacrifice. It is usually placed at the entrance to a house.
NYANKO—Fante for *nyonko*, friend, neighbour, acquaintance.

NYANKOPON—God, the Supreme Being, called Kwaame or Kwame and addressed as Nana. (Literally, the Nyame who alone is Great.)

NYANKOMLI—a Ga name for God (M. J. Field).

NYINAA—all.

NYINAM—lightens.

NYOMO—Ga ; rain, properly *nunmo.*

NYON—Ga word for some elemental power, such as night or light, as in *nyonten*, middle of the night, *nyontsele*, moon ; *Nyonmo*, the " Nyon " person, *i.e.*, God.

NYONKO—neighbour, friend, companion.

NYONMO—the Ga name for God.

NZAMBI—an East African name for God.

OBOADE—same as Obooadee.

OBOOADEE—Oboo adee, " poetic " form of Boade, the Creator. Literally, He who created the Thing, an appellation of Odomankoma, God, also of Onyame or Onyankopon.

OBOPON—big game.

OBOSOM—god, fetish ; an elemental spirit or genius.

OBRA—the ethical life, conduct, behaviour ; moral life.

OBRAFO—the State executioner and also State minstrel.

ODAA—He who deserves this or that appellation. As, for example, Odaa Aku, *i.e.*, He who, when he salutes you, you answer " Aku." From *da* or *dan*, to fall on, depend upon.

ODOM—grace, also name of a tree : may also be abbreviation of *odo mu*, in love, or he has delved deep, sunk deep.

ODOMANKOMA—the Infinite, Interminable, Absolute Being. As God, Odomankoma is generally associated with creation as distinct from Onyame, associated with life as such, and from Onyankopon associated with religion. The appellation of Odomankoma is Borebore, the Architect, etc.

OGYAM—appellation of the Tuesday born—the Compassionate.

OGYE—he saves.

OHONAM—flesh of man, the human spirit.

OHEMPON—great king, emperor, king of kings.

OHYE—he fills, he prepares, he fixes.

OKANNIBA—son of the Akan, an Akan citizen, from Akan and -*ni*, personal suffix, singular, and -*ba*, *oba*, child, issue, product of.

OKARA—(Okra), the soul, the inner ego or self.

OKO—*o-ko*, *i.e.*, *ono ko*, he goes.

OKORO—from *biako*, one.

OKOTO—appellation of the Monday born—Suppliant.

OKRABIRI—bad soul, blighted soul or person.

OKU or AKU—response of the Wednesday born.

OKUNIN—Celebrated person, response of the Wednesday born. It probably is derived from *Okum anin :* he who slaughters the valiant men.

OKWAN—way, road, street.

OMMFIRII—had not sprouted, had not come out, had not opened, had not gained experience (Fanti).

OKYIN—appellation of the Friday born—Wanderer.

ONUONYAMFO—a dignified person, a worthy or worshipful person.

ONYA—he gets ; *o*, he ; -*nya*, get.

ONYAM—glory, dignity, majesty, grace.

ONYAM—a form of Onyame, God.

ONYANKOPON—the Great Supreme Being, the Great Onyame. He-who-alone is the Great Shining One. Often pronounced Nyankopon.

ONYAME—God, the Supreme Being, the Shining One. In relation to Nyankopon, Nyame or Onyame is held by some to be the female, or the originator, the *primum mobile*.

ONYANKOME—an Effutu (Winneba) name for God (Christaller).

ONYANKOMPON—Onyankoropon, Onyankorompon, Onyankoropono, Onyankoronpono—all accepted variants of the one name Onyankopon, *q.v.*

ONYE—Fante, he is.

OPANYIN—(or Opanin), elder, senior, superior, chief, respectable person. It often is a form of address, roughly equivalent to the English or French Monsieur, Mister.

OPONTENTEN—the long table.

OSEE—hurrah, hooting together, or acclaiming together.

OSEI—name of a king, name of a person generally. He who destroys.

OSORO—heaven, upwards, skywards.

OTE—understanding, *te*, to hear, to feel, to sense.

OTEANANKADURO—He who knows the antidote for poison of the python, or serpent. An appellation of the Saturday born.

OTUMFO—from *tumi*, power, and personal suffix *-fo ;* he of power, his majesty.

OWIA—the sun.

OWU—death.

OWUO—death (Akim form).

OWURA—master, mister.

OYIA—a shortened form of *oyiara*.

OYIARA—this very same (person, or thing).

PA—good.

PEEWA—innumerable.

PII—much, plenty.

PIESIE—the first born, a patriarch.

PON—suffix ; great, mighty, big.

PREKO—appellation of the Thursday born—Eager for war.

SEE—same as *osee, q.v.*

SESA or SASA—dangerous spirit, a spirit that haunts, spirit of a lower animal, not man. (*Sa*, to pursue, to fix (the eye) upon.) (*N'ani sa me*, he is prejudiced against me, dislikes me.)

SO—upon, on, over . . . *ma so*, to raise up.

SOADURO—Swedru, one of the Akim states of the Akan group, capital, Busumi.

SUMAN—amulet, talisman, properly called " fetish."

SUNSUM—personality, ego, looks, individuality, the opposite of *okra*, soul, the latter being inner, the former, outer or worldly.

SWEDRU—See Soaduro.

TAKORA—an appellation of Tano, the great river God. " Ta kora," Tano the god who keeps or preserves.

TE—to hear. Used as a substantive to stand for Hearing, or the sense of hearing. That which is heard. In a general sense *Te* means the understanding, or the senses generally ; (Ote).

TEBENA—the covering or husk of a hard seed.

TENG—(*ten*), middle of, among (*Ga*).

TETE—ancient.

TETEKWAFRAMOA—an appellation of God Nyankopon : " He endures for ever." Christaller suggests as its derivation : " ntetekoraframoa," " does-not-tear, preserve, mix, helper," but it is not easy to make sense of that. Whatever its origin, it now is just a name with a conventional meaning.

TETREBONSU—see Totrobonsu, same as Totorobonsu, an appellation of God, Nyankopon. (Also Toturobonsu.)

TIE—listen.

TO—fall, *totoro*, reduplicatives of *to*.

TOKU—name or appellation of a person.

TOTROBONSU—copious waters.

TUA—begin, infest, besiege.

TUMI—power ; verb, to be able.

TWE—to draw, pull.

TWEADUAMPONG—another form of Twiaduampong, *q.v.*

TWERI—to lean upon.

TWI—the language of the Akan people, spoken in the Gold Coast. It is best pronounced as Twui. It is often written Tshi. It is now the literary form of the language, there being other dialects. For example, Ashanti says, " *me see*," for " I say " ; and Twi says *me se ;* Akyem says *yen* for we, whereas in Twi there is a difference between *yen* (we) and *won* (they).

TWIADUAMPON—appellation of God Nyankopon.

TWIEDUAMPON—another form of Twiaduampon *q.v.*

TWIFORO—same as KWIFORO.

WAAWO—Fanti, *won awo*, they had given birth (to him) ; *wo*, to give birth to.

WAFRE—*wo afre*, you call.

WAMA—*wo ama*, you have allowed it, or let it.

WASE—*wo ase*, in the phrase " *ye da wo ase*," we thank you, *i.e.*, we fall prostrate to thee, or we prostrate ourselves beneath you, *wo* being you, *ase*, meaning beneath, below one's feet.

WO—upon, in (with *O* as in broad).

WO—you (with *O* as in chose).

WOMPON—*wo mpon*, you do not fall off.

WONTUA—*won ntua*—they do not pay.

WOTO—*won to*, they buy, one buys.

WUHU—*wo hu*, you see (him).

WUKUDA—Wednesday.

YAO—name of person born on Thursday, *f.* Yaa. Yao is sometimes written Yaw.

YAODA—Thursday.

YE—to do, to be.

YEDA—*yen da*, we render (thanks).

YEI—response to acclamation " Osee ! " Ordinary response when one is called ; means, " yea " or " yes."

YEN—we.

YENTIE—let them listen ; listen all ; let us all listen.

YEREKYERE—*yen re-kyere wo ;* we are showing you.

YI—this.

YIYEYE—well-doing ; doing good ; performance of duties, prosperity, beneficence.

YIYEYO—See YIYEYE.